AF835088

Private International Law in Poland

Private International Law in Poland

Ewa Kamarad
Anna Wysocka-Bar

This book was originally published as a monograph in the International Encyclopaedia of Laws/Private International Law.

Founding Editor: Roger Blanpain
General Editor: Frank Hendrickx
Volume Editor: Bea Verschraegen

Wolters Kluwer

Published by:
Kluwer Law International B.V.
PO Box 316
2400 AH Alphen aan den Rijn
The Netherlands
E-mail: international-sales@wolterskluwer.com
Website: lrus.wolterskluwer.com

Sold and distributed by:
Wolters Kluwer Legal & Regulatory U.S.
7201 McKinney Circle
Frederick, MD 21704
United States of America
Email: customer.service@wolterskluwer.com

ISBN 978-94-035-3020-8

e-Book: ISBN 978-94-035-2965-3
web-PDF: ISBN 978-94-035-2970-7

The Authors

Ewa Kamarad[*] is a Senior Lecturer at Jagiellonian University (Poland). She has studied European studies (Bachelor and Master) and law (Master) at Jagiellonian University and Københavns Universitet (Erasmus +). She obtained Doctorate in the field of Private International Law (PIL). She has carried her research in PIL at the Max Planck Institutes in Hamburg and in Luxembourg, and research in public international law at the Max Planck Institute in Heidelberg and European University Institute in Florence. Ewa has published on PIL, especially international family law, public international law and European Union (EU) law, including a monograph on entering into marriage (*Zawarcie małżeństwa jako zagadnienie prawa rodzinnego, prawa prywatnego międzynarodowego i prawa konsularnego*, Wydawnictwo Uniwersytetu Jagiellońskiego, Kraków 2019). She has given guest lectures on PIL and the EU law at Universidad de Lisboa, Univerzita Karlova and Kobe University. She is an editor of PWPM – Review of International, European and Comparative Law (*Problemy Współczesnego Prawa Międzynarodowego, Europejskiego i Porównawczego*).

Anna Wysocka-Bar[**] is a Senior Lecturer at Jagiellonian University (Poland). She has studied law at Jagiellonian University (Master and Doctorate), Université Montpellier I (Erasmus +) and Ottawa University (LLM). Anna is the Coordinator of an EU co-funded Jean Monnet Module on European PIL (EPIL@JU). She has carried her research in PIL at the Max Planck Institute in Hamburg, Swiss Institute of Comparative Law in Lausanne, Peace Palace Library, Heidelberg University and Erasmus University Rotterdam. Anna has published on PIL, especially international succession law, including a monograph on party autonomy (*Wybór prawa w międzynarodowym prawie spadkowym*, LexisNexis, Warszawa 2013). Anna is a member of the European Association of Private International Law (EAPIL) and a co-editor of the EAPIL Blog. She has given guest lectures on judicial cooperation in civil matters at Università degli Studi

* Photo of Ewa by Iwona Kowalska (2020).
** Photo of Anna by Adriana Mazur (2020).

di Milan, Università degli Studi di Ferrara, Minzu University of China, University of Istanbul and Università Cattolica del Sacro Cuore Milano. She was invited by Università degli Studi di Parma as a visiting professor in 2021. Anna is a licensed attorney-at-law and a licensed tax advisor.

Since 2017 Ewa and Anna have been teaching together an intensive course on PIL in the EU at the Radboud Summer School in Nijmegen.

Table of Contents

List of Abbreviations

BEL	Bill of Exchange Law of 1936
CC	Civil Code of 1964
CISG	Convention on Contracts for the International Sale of Goods
CJEU	Court of Justice of the European Union
CL	Cheque Law of 1936
CPC	Civil Procedure Code of 1964
Dz. U.	Journal of Laws of the Republic of Poland
EAPO	European Account Preservation Order
EC	European Community
EEC	European Economic Community
EEO	European Enforcement Order for Uncontested Claims
EFTA	European Free Trade Association
EJN	European Judicial Network
EPS	Europejski Przegląd Sądowy
ESCP	European Small Claims Procedure
EU	European Union
FGC	Family and Guardianship Code of 1964
HCCH	Hague Conference on Private International Law
IPrax	Praxis des Internationalen Privat – und Verfahrensrechts
KPP	Kwartalnik Prawa Prywatnego
NPN	Nowy Przegląd Notarialny
OJ	Official Journal of the European Communities/European Union
PIL	Private International Law
PILA	Private International Law Act of 2011
PILA 1965	Private International Law Act of 1965
PILA 1926	Private International Law Act of 1926
PPPM	Problemy Prawa Prywatnego Międzynarodowego
PWPM	Problemy Prawa Międzynarodowego, Europejskiego i Porównawczego

List of Abbreviations

RabelsZ	Rabels Zeitschrift für ausländisches und internationales Privatrecht
StAZ	Das Standesamt – Zeitschrift für das Standesamtswesen
YPIL	Yearbook of Private International Law

General Introduction

§1. Historical Development

1. Poland is a country located in Central Europe. The country covers an area of 312,696 square kilometres and has approximately 38.4 million inhabitants. Poland is a republic formed on the democratic basis. The Republic of Poland is based on the separation of powers principle. The legislative power is vested in the Parliament consisting of the lower house (*Sejm*) and the upper house (*Senat*). The President of Poland and the Council of Ministers exercise the executive power. The judicial power is vested in courts and tribunals.[1]

2. The common courts in Poland are the district courts (*sądy rejonowe*), provincial courts (*sądy okręgowe*) and courts of appeal (*sądy apelacyjne*). They are competent to hear civil law cases, family and custody law cases, labour law cases and social insurance cases and criminal law cases. The Supreme Court (*Sąd Najwyższy*) is the highest central judicial organ in the Republic of Poland, and thus the highest Court of Appeal. As regards tribunals, the Constitution lists the Constitutional Tribunal and the Tribunal of the State. There are separate administrative district courts (*wojewódzkie sądy administracyjne*). The administrative judiciary falls under the Supreme Administrative Court (*Naczelny Sąd Administracyjny*), which has judicial control of public administration.[2]

3. Poland is a civil law legal jurisdiction and belongs to the continental law system, thus law is exclusively written. Polish legal system developed under the influence of Roman law, German law, French law and Russian/Soviet law.[3]

4. Since 1 May 2004 Poland has been a member of the European Union (EU), which is a regional integration organization in the form of a political and economic union of twenty-seven Member States.

---

1. L. Garlicki in: S. Frankowski, Introduction to Polish Law, Kluwer Law International, The Hague 2005, pp. 1–36.
2. U. Jaremba, *National Judges as EU Law Judges: The Polish Civil Law System*, Brill, Nijhoff 2014, pp. 114–127.
3. W. Dajczak, *Historical development of private law in Poland* in: W. Dajczak, A, Szwarc, P. Wiliński (eds), Handbook of Polish Law, Wydawnictwo Szkolne PWN, Warszawa 2011, pp. 42–58.

5. The development of Polish PIL dates back to the nineteenth century, when the first works were written by Polish legal scientists. They mainly concerned the legal orders of the partitioning states, which divided the territory of Poland among themselves in the eighteenth century (the Habsburg Monarchy, the Kingdom of Prussia and the Russian Empire) and other foreign states, for example, France, where the science of PIL developed.

6. After World War I, when Poland regained independence, the idea of creating its own conflict of laws emerged. In 1926, the Act on PIL was adopted (PILA 1926).[4] This act was considered a big achievement of Polish legislature and was well received by the jurists from other countries. At the same time, an act on the conflict of laws between the districts was adopted,[5] whose task was to settle conflicts between different legal systems that were in force in Poland. Thus, both legal acts were applied not only in Poland's external relations, but also in settling internal relations.

7. After the unification of substantive law, the act on the inter-local conflict of laws ceased to apply, while PILA 1926 was replaced by a new legal act[6] in 1965.[7] The new act was introduced mainly because of the social and economic changes that occurred in Poland and around the world, and the desire to face them with the modern regulation.[8] Private International Law Act of 1965 (PILA 1965) has been in force for over forty years, but some gaps and shortcomings in it were gradually pointed out in the literature.[9] Also Poland's accession to the EU in 2004 raised additional challenges in the field of PIL. Those challenges could be met in two ways: by amending the PILA 1965 or by adopting the new act. After the discussion in legal science of PIL, which presented the advantages and disadvantages of both solutions, it was decided to develop a new act. Works on the new act started in 2001. In 2004 the first version of the draft was presented.[10] Further changes to the projects

4. Act of 2 Aug. 1926 on the Law Applicable to International Private Relations, Dz. U. 1926 nr 101 poz. 581.
5. Act of 2 Aug. 1926 on the Law Applicable to Internal Private Relations, Dz. U. 1926 nr 101 poz. 580.
6. Act of 12 Nov. 1965 Private International Law, Dz. U. 1965 nr 46 poz. 290.
7. A. Mączyński, *Polish Private International Law*, YPIL 2004, vol. 6, pp. 203–220.
8. J. Rajski, *The New Polish Private International Law, 1965*, The International and Comparative Law Quarterly 1966, vol. 15, No. 2, pp. 457–469.
9. M. Pazdan in: M. Pazdan (ed.), *System Prawa Prywatnego. Tom 20 A. Prawo prywatne międzynarodowe*, Wydawnictwo C. H. Beck, Warszawa 2014, pp. 130–131.
10. M. Pazdan, *Recent Codifications of Private International Law. The Polish Experience* in: Rapport polonaise au XVIIIe Congrès international de droit comparé. Washington 25.VII-1.VIII .2010, Łódź 2010, pp. 49–68.

were forced by the adoption of new EU regulations.[11] Finally, the new PIL Act[12] was adopted on 4 February 2011 and entered into force on 16 May 2011.[13]

8. The Private International Law Act of 2011 (PILA) 2011 is the basis of domestic PIL and contains conflict-of-law rules indicating the applicable law. Rules on jurisdiction and recognition and enforcement of foreign judgments are part of international civil procedure and were therefore set out in the Civil Procedure Code of 1964 (CPC).[14]

9. Currently PIL is seen as a distinct discipline of law, closely connected with civil law. It is usually taught as a separate subject at universities in Poland that offers law studies.

§2. International and Supranational Legal Framework

10. The legal norms of PIL have been unified on international and supranational level by the EU legislation and international conventions. Therefore, domestic legal acts, international agreements binding on Poland and the EU law create the PIL system in Poland.

11. Poland is a member of the EU which, since the entry into force of the Amsterdam Treaty in 1999, has the competence to legislate in the field of judicial cooperation in civil matters having cross-border implications (*see* Part I., Chapter 1, §2). From 1 May 2004, which is the date of Polish accession, EU law has direct effect in Poland, being a source of law, and takes precedence over national law.

12. Poland was a party to the Rome Convention (1980) on the law applicable to contractual obligations[15] (an international convention opened only to EU Member

---

11. T. Pajor, *Introduction to the New Polish Act on Private International Law of 4 February 2011*, YPIL, vol. 13 (2011), pp. 381–388.
12. Act of 2 Feb. 2011, Private International Law, Dz. U. 2011 nr 80 poz. 432. The PILA 2011 has no official English translation. Unofficial English translation by M. Zachariasiewicz is available in YPIL, vol. 13 (2011), pp. 641–656. Available online at https://www.isdc.ch/en/publications/yearbook. Translations into other languages: U. Ernst, *Polen. Gesetz vom 4. Februar 2011: Internationales Privatrecht*, RabelsZ 2012, pp. 639–653; P. Twardoch, M. Zachariasiewicz, *Loi du 4 février 2011 – Droit international privé. The Act on Private International Law dated 4 February 2011*, PPPM 2011, t. 8, pp. 108–138; M. Zachariasiewicz, A. Wowerka, *Das Gesetz vom 4.2.2011 – Das Internationale Privatrecht*, IPRax 2011, z. 6, pp. 609–619, reprint, PPPM 2012, t. 10, pp. 174–204; G. Zou, *Chinese Translation of Private International Law Act 2011*, PPPM 2012, t. 10, pp. 174–204.
13. A. Mączyński in: J. Basedow, G. Rühl, F. Ferrari, P. de Miguel Asensio, *Encyclopedia of Private International Law*, Cheltenham 2017, pp. 2421–2433.
14. Act of 17 Nov. 1964 – Civil Procedure Code, Dz. U. 1964 nr 43 poz. 296.
15. Convention 80/934/EEC on the law applicable to contractual obligations opened for signature in Rome on 19 Jun. 1980.

States) from 1 August 2007. This Convention was replaced by the Rome I Regulation[16] (contractual obligations) on 17 December 2009. In Poland, from the date of their entry into force, the Rome II Regulation[17] (non-contractual obligations), the Maintenance Regulation[18] and the Succession Regulation[19] have also been applicable.

13. Poland is also bound by the Brussels I *bis* Regulation[20] (jurisdiction and judgments in civil and commercial matters) and the Brussels II *bis* Regulation[21] (jurisdiction and judgments in family matters).

14. Certain EU regulations in the field of PIL have been adopted within the enhanced cooperation, which is a mechanism provided for by the Treaties for situations where it is not possible to achieve the required unanimity. The accession of a Member State to enhanced cooperation is voluntary, and those that do not choose to do so are not bound by the legal acts adopted within it.[22] For this reason, the following regulations do not apply in Poland: the Divorce Regulation,[23] the Matrimonial Property Matters Regulation[24] and the Property Consequences of Registered Partnerships Regulation.[25]

15. Poland has been a member of the Hague Conference on PIL (HCCH) since 29 May 1984. Since that date Poland has acceded to several conventions adopted within this organization.

---

16. Regulation (EC) No 593/2008 of the European Parliament and of the Council of 17 Jun. 2008 on the law applicable to contractual obligations (Rome I), OJ L 177, 4.7.2008, pp. 6–16.
17. Regulation (EC) No 864/2007 of the European Parliament and of the Council of 11 Jul. 2007 on the law applicable to non-contractual obligations (Rome II), OJ L 199, 31.7.2007, pp. 40–49.
18. Council Regulation (EC) No 4/2009 of 18 Dec. 2008 on jurisdiction, applicable law, recognition and enforcement of decisions and cooperation in matters relating to maintenance obligations, OJ L 7, 10.1.2009, pp. 1–79.
19. Regulation (EU) No 650/2012 of the European Parliament and of the Council of 4 Jul. 2012 on jurisdiction, applicable law, recognition and enforcement of decisions and acceptance and enforcement of authentic instruments in matters of succession and on the creation of a European Certificate of Succession, OJ 2012 L 201, pp. 107–134.
20. Regulation (EU) No 1215/2012 of the European Parliament and of the Council of 12 Dec. 2012 on jurisdiction and the recognition and enforcement of judgments in civil and commercial matters, OJ L 351, 20.12.2012, pp. 1–32.
21. Council Regulation (EC) No 2201/2003 of 27 Nov. 2003 concerning jurisdiction and the recognition and enforcement of judgments in matrimonial matters and the matters of parental responsibility, repealing Regulation (EC) No 1347/2000, OJ L 338, 23.12.2003, pp. 1–29.
22. A. Wysocka-Bar, *Enhanced cooperation in property matters and non-participating Member States*, ERA Forum 2019, vol. 20, pp. 187–200.
23. Council Regulation (EU) No 1259/2010 of 20 Dec. 2010 implementing enhanced cooperation in the area of the law applicable to divorce and legal separation, OJ L 343, 29.12.2010, pp. 10–16.
24. Council Regulation (EU) 2016/1103 of 24 Jun. 2016 implementing enhanced cooperation in the area of jurisdiction, applicable law and the recognition and enforcement of decisions in matters of matrimonial property regimes, OJ L 183, 8.7.2016, pp. 1–29.
25. Council Regulation (EU) 2016/1104 of 24 Jun. 2016 implementing enhanced cooperation in the area of jurisdiction, applicable law and the recognition and enforcement of decisions in matters of the property consequences of registered partnerships, OJ L 183, 8.7.2016, pp. 30–56.

16. Apart from multilateral treaties Poland is also a party to numerous bilateral agreements, which contain conflict-of-law rules, rules on jurisdiction, rules on procedural matters and provisions relating to the recognition and enforcement of foreign judgments (*see* Part I., Chapter 1, §1 and §2).

§3. Nature and Scope

17. PIL is a part of Polish domestic law. In Polish legal science PIL has two definitions. In a narrow sense it is defined as a discipline of law responsible for designating the law applicable to certain situations or facts considered being within the private law (e.g., contract, delict/tort, employment, marriage, succession, adoption). The problem of determining the applicable law arises because such situation has international or cross-border character, which means that it is related to the legal order of more than one state and may potentially be subject to the law of each of them.[26]

18. In a wider sense PIL is seen as a discipline of law containing both the rules of the PIL in the narrow sense (conflict-of-law rules) as well as the provisions of substantive law rules of civil and commercial law, which govern cross-border situations (e.g., Convention on Contracts for the International Sale of Goods (CISG)[27]). It contains also the norms specifying how foreign natural and legal persons (law of aliens) should be treated in a country and whether they are subject to certain restrictions while exercising rights in the field of private law (e.g., rules on the acquisition of real estate by foreigners[28]).[29]

19. International civil procedure in Poland is perceived as a separate discipline, which is the reason for codifying the conflict-of-law rules in PILA and rules on jurisdiction and recognition and enforcement of foreign judgments in CPC.[30] However, in some international conventions and in recent EU legislation there is a tendency to regulate these issues together in one legal act, which increasingly causes convergence of those disciplines, as is also present in Polish legal science.

§4. Characteristic of National PIL

20. The provisions of PIL are mandatory. Law enforcement authorities have a duty to apply national law, and thus also PIL, which is part of it. This means there is a principle of ex officio application of the conflict-of-law rules. Therefore, the

---

26. M. Pazdan in: M. Pazdan (ed.), *System Prawa Prywatnego. Tom 20 A. Prawo prywatne międzynarodowe*, Wydawnictwo C. H. Beck, Warszawa 2014, pp. 11–12.
27. Dz. U. 1997 nr 45 poz. 286.
28. Act of 24 Mar. 1920 on the acquisition of real estate by foreigners, Dz. U. 2017 poz. 2278.
29. M. Pazdan in: M. Pazdan (ed.), *System Prawa Prywatnego. Tom 20 A. Prawo prywatne międzynarodowe*, Wydawnictwo C. H. Beck, Warszawa 2014, pp. 12–13.
30. M. Pazdan in: M. Pazdan (ed.), *System Prawa Prywatnego. Tom 20 A. Prawo prywatne międzynarodowe*, Wydawnictwo C. H. Beck, Warszawa 2014, p. 29.

court is obliged to ascertain which law is designated as applicable by PIL rule, which (at least theoretically) does not depend on the parties' request in this matter. [31] Parties are not obliged to prove the content of foreign law either. Also, in the event of a choice of law by the parties, the court should independently determine the effectiveness of its implementation based on the rules of PIL. If, during the proceedings, the court finds the existence of circumstances indicating the applicability of a foreign law, it should apply it in a given case as the basis for a substantive decision.

21. Foreign law is treated as a law, not as a fact.[32] When applying it, the court should take into account its place in the catalogue of sources of law of a foreign legal order and apply appropriate rules of interpretation in the same way as a foreign court would do it. The consequence of non-application of the applicable law or its incorrect application constitutes a breach of substantive law and may be the basis for an appeal to a court of second instance or a cassation appeal.[33]

22. PILA contains provisions relating to situations in which it is not possible to find the applicable law or determine its content. Article 10(1) states that if the circumstances on which the applicability of a law depends cannot be established, then the law which is the most closely connected with the relationship shall apply. These circumstances constitute facts to be proven, just like other facts adduced in court proceeding. So when there are no facts that are necessary for the application of a specific conflict-of-law rule or it is impossible to prove these facts (e.g., lack of proof of citizenship of a given person or of his habitual residence in a specific country), then Article 10(1) PILA indicates a substitute solution.[34]

23. Another type of problem occurs if the content of the applicable foreign law cannot be ascertained within reasonable time. In such a case, according to Article 10(2) PILA Polish law applies. This solution helps to prevent excessive length of the proceedings. In each case, the court should try to determine the content of the applicable law based on the available sources. Only when it is not feasible in time allowing for effective granting of legal protection to the parties, the court should apply Polish law.[35]

---

31. Judgment of Supreme Court of 23 May 2013, II CKS 250/12; Decision of Supreme Court of 9 Apr. 2015, II CKS 550/14.
32. P. Rodziewicz, *Stwierdzenie treści oraz zastosowanie prawa obcego w sądowym postępowaniu cywilnym*, Warszawa 2015, pp. 6–11.
33. Article 368 § (2) and (3) CPC and article 398^3 § 1 CPC.
34. K. Sznajder-Peroń in: M. Pazdan (ed.), *Prawo prywatne międzynarodowe. Komentarz*, Wydawnictwo C. H. Beck, Warszawa 2018, pp. 172–173.
35. K. Sznajder-Peroń in: M. Pazdan (ed.), *Prawo prywatne międzynarodowe. Komentarz*, Wydawnictwo C. H. Beck, Warszawa 2018, pp. 173–174.

24. There is also separate solution provided for the situation in which the conflict-of-law rule provides for the applicability of the law of nationality of a person, and it is not possible to establish the content of this law. Then, pursuant to Article 3(1) PILA, the law of the state in which the given person is domiciled should apply (*see* Part I., Chapter 2, §1., V).

§5. Domestic Authorities Involved, Interpretation and Application of PIL

25. In the Polish science of PIL, it is assumed that the ex officio application of conflict-of-laws rules by judicial bodies is the rule. This principle was expressed directly in Article 1143 §1 CPC.[36] This provision was repealed, but a similar provision was added to the Act on the System of Common Courts.[37] Article 51a of that law provides that the court shall determine and apply the appropriate foreign law. This norm requires the court to determine the content of the law applicable to a given case and the circumstances constituting connecting factors that designate, which law is applicable in a given case (e.g., habitual residence of the deceased).[38]

26. For this purpose, the court can use all available sources of information on foreign law, such as foreign official publications, official documents, law books or data obtained through the European Judicial Network (EJN).[39]

27. The court may also apply to the Minister of Justice for the text of the law and to clarify the foreign judicial practice. In order to determine the content of foreign law or foreign judicial practice, the court may as well apply other measures, including consultation of experts.

28. An arbitration court established in Poland should, pursuant to Article 1194 §1 CPC, apply the law determined by the adequate conflict-of-law rule, unless the parties have authorized it to settle according to general principles of law or principles of equity.

29. The public administration bodies are also obliged to apply ex officio conflict-of-law rules and foreign law indicated as appropriate. In practice, this is especially relevant for civil registrars.[40]

---

36. P. Czubik, *Rzecz o praktyce sądów krajowych badających prawo obce zgodnie z art. 1143 kpc*, NPN 2010, nr 3, pp. 5–19.
37. Dz. U. 2001 nr 98 poz. 1070.
38. K. Sznajder-Peroń, *Zagadnienia związane z pojmowaniem i stosowaniem prawa właściwego*, Studia Prawa Prywatnego 2012, z. 2, pp. 3–30.
39. P. Rodziewicz, *Stwierdzenie treści oraz zastosowanie prawa obcego w sądowym postępowaniu cywilnym*, Warszawa 2015, pp. 72–113.
40. M. Wojewoda, *Problematyka kolizyjnoprawna w praktyce urzędów stanu cywilnego oraz w ustawie – Prawo o aktach stanu cywilnego z 2014 roku*, PPPM 2015, t. 17, pp. 25–67.

30. The notary public is also obliged to apply conflict-of-law rules and foreign law.[41] Pursuant to Article 95da §2 of the Notary Law,[42] the notary may request the Minister of Justice to provide the text of the applicable foreign law. In order to determine the content of the applicable foreign law, the notary may also take other appropriate measures. The disadvantage of the above provision is that it is included in Chapter 3a of the Notary Law, which, according to the principles of legal interpretation, means that its application is therefore limited to the activities of drafting certificates of succession and European certificates of succession, since that is the scope of Chapter 3a.[43] It is debated whether this possibility should be available to a notary also when he performs other notarial activities.[44]

41. M. Pazdan, *Notariat a prawo prywatne międzynarodowe (uwagi ogólne)*, Rejent 1995, nr 9, pp. 197–209; M. Pazdan, *Czynności notarialne w międzynarodowym prawie spadkowym*, Rejent 1998, nr 4, pp. 99–115; M. Pazdan, *Cudzoziemiec klientem polskiego notariusza*, Rejent 2001, nr 7–8, pp. 172–189.
42. Act of 14 Feb. 1991, Notary law, Dz. U. 1991 Nr 22 poz. 91.
43. P. Rodziewicz, *Stwierdzenie treści oraz zastosowanie prawa obcego przez notariusza wykonującego zawód w Rzeczypospolitej Polskiej*, PPPM 2015, t. 17, pp. 125–160.
44. P. Czubik, *Czy polskiemu notariuszowi jest potrzebny status inicjującego postępowanie celem ustalenia treści prawa obcego?*, NPN 2014, nr 4 (62), pp. 23–30.

Part I. General Principles (Choice of Law Technique)

Chapter 1. Sources of PIL

§1. Public International Law

31. PIL rules are nowadays often contained in international conventions, and as a result, take the form of rules which are part of and governed by public international law.[45] This is also the truth for Poland, which is a party to numerous international agreements. In Poland, pursuant to Article 87(1) Constitution of the Republic of Poland (1997), the sources of universally binding laws are the Constitution itself, statutes (*ustawy*), ratified international agreements and regulations (*rozporządzenia*). An international agreement which deals with matters covered by statutes (e.g., PIL) may be ratified if the consent to such ratification is granted by the Parliament in the form of a separate statute. An international agreement that was ratified and officially promulgated may be applied directly. Such agreements take precedence over domestic legislation (statues and regulations).

32. As mentioned above, Poland is party to numerous international agreements prepared under auspices of international organizations, in particular the HCCH. Poland has been a HCCH member since 1984.[46] Poland is a contracting party to the following Hague Conventions: Convention on Civil Procedure (1954),[47] Convention on the Protection of Infants (1961),[48] Convention on Form of Wills (1961),[49] Convention on Apostille (1961),[50] Convention on the Service Abroad (1965),[51]

45. A. Mills in: *Encyclopedia of Private International Law*, p. 1448.
46. A. Wysocka-Bar, *Stodwudziestopięciolecie Haskiej Konferencji Prawa Prywatnego Międzynarodowego*, KPP 2019, nr 2, pp. 379–416.
47. Convention of 1 Mar. 1954 on civil procedure, Dz. U. 1963 r. nr 17 poz. 90.
48. Convention of 5 Oct. 1961 concerning the powers of authorities and the law applicable in respect of the protection of infants, Dz. U. 1995 r. nr 106 poz. 519.
49. Convention of 5 Oct. 1961 on the Conflicts of Laws Relating to the Form of Testamentary Dispositions, Dz. U. 1969 r. nr 34 poz. 284.
50. The Convention of 5 Oct. 1961 Abolishing the Requirement of Legalisation for Foreign Public Documents, Dz. U. 2005 r. nr 112 poz. 938.
51. Convention of 15 Nov. 1965 on the Service Abroad of Judicial and Extrajudicial Documents in Civil or Commercial Matters, Dz. U. z 2000 r. nr 87 poz. 968.

Convention on the Recognition of Divorces and Legal Separations (1970),[52] Convention on Traffic Accidents (1971),[53] Convention on the Taking of Evidence Abroad (1970),[54] Convention on the Recognition and Enforcement of Decisions Relating to Maintenance Obligations (1973),[55] Convention on the Law Applicable to Maintenance Obligations (1973),[56] Convention on Child Abduction (1980),[57] Convention on International Access to Justice (1980),[58] Convention on Intercountry Adoption (1993)[59] and Convention on Protection of Children (1996).[60] Poland is also a party to the Hague Conventions which were approved by the EU in the name of EU Member States: Convention on Choice of Court Agreements (2005),[61] Convention on Maintenance (2007)[62] and Hague Protocol (2007).[63] Poland has also signed Convention on the Protection of Adults (2000),[64] but has not yet ratified it.

33. Poland is also a contracting party to conventions concluded under auspices of the United Nations, for example, Convention on the Recovery Abroad of Maintenance (1956), Convention on the Recognition and Enforcement of Foreign Arbitral Awards (1958), European Convention on International Commercial Arbitration (1961), Convention on Contracts for the International Sale of Goods (1980), and

---

52. Convention of 1 Jun. 1970 on the Recognition of Divorces and Legal Separations, Dz. U. 2001 r. nr 53 poz. 561.
53. Convention of 4 May 1971 on the Law Applicable to Traffic Accidents, Dz. U. 2003 r. nr 63 poz. 585.
54. Convention of 18 Mar. 1970 on the Taking of Evidence Abroad in Civil or Commercial Matters, Dz. U. 2000 r. nr 50 poz. 582.
55. Convention of 2 Oct. 1973 on the Recognition and Enforcement of Decisions Relating to Maintenance Obligations, Dz. U. z 2000 nr 2 poz. 13.
56. Convention of 2 Oct. 1973 on the Law Applicable to Maintenance Obligations, Dz. U. 2000 r. nr 39 poz. 444.
57. Convention of 25 Oct. 1980 on the Civil Aspects of International Child Abduction, Dz. U. z 1999 r. nr 93 poz. 1085.
58. Convention of 25 Oct. 1980 on International Access to Justice, Dz. U. 1995 r. nr 18 poz. 86.
59. Convention of 29 May 1993 on Protection of Children and Co-operation in Respect of Intercountry Adoption, Dz. U. 2002 r. nr 1 poz. 17.
60. Convention of 19 Oct. 1996 on Jurisdiction, Applicable Law, Recognition, Enforcement and Co-operation in Respect of Parental Responsibility and Measures for the Protection of Children, Dz. U. 2010 r. nr 172 poz. 1158.
61. Convention of 30 Jun. 2005 on Choice of Court Agreements, *see* Council Decision 2009/397/EC of 26 Feb. 2009 on the signing on behalf of the European Community of the Convention on Choice of Court Agreements, OJ L 133, 29.5.2009, pp. 1–13 and Council Decision 2014/887/EU of 4 Dec. 2014 on the approval, on behalf of the European Union, of the Hague Convention of 30 Jun. 2005 on Choice of Court Agreements, OJ L 353, 10.12.2014, pp. 5–8.
62. Convention of 23 Nov. 2007 on the International Recovery of Child Support and Other Forms of Family Maintenance, *see* Council Decision 2011/220/EU of 31 March 2011 on the signing, on behalf of the European Union, of the Hague Convention of 23 November 2007 on the International Recovery of Child Support and Other Forms of Family Maintenance OJ L 93, 7.4.2011, p. 9 and Council Decision of 9 Jun. 2011 on the approval, on behalf of the European Union, of the Hague Convention of 23 Nov. 2007 on the International Recovery of Child Support and Other Forms of Family Maintenance, OJ L 192, 22.7.2011, pp. 39–50.
63. Protocol of 23 Nov. 2007 on the Law Applicable to Maintenance Obligations, 2009/941/EC: Council Decision of 30 Nov. 2009 on the conclusion by the European Community of the Hague Protocol of 23 Nov. 2007 on the Law Applicable to Maintenance Obligations, OJ L 331, 16.12.2009, pp. 17–18.
64. Convention of 13 Jan. 2000 on the International Protection of Adults.

Council of Europe, for example the European Convention on Information on Foreign Law (1968). Please note that the above list should not be perceived as being an exhaustive list of all the multilateral international agreements relating to private law matters that Poland is party to.

34. Poland is also a party to numerous bilateral agreements (*see* the list of Bilateral Agreements under Table of International Treaties). They differ among each other when it comes to the scope of regulated matters. Some bilateral agreements, to which Poland is a party to, regulate only international civil procedure matters (e.g., legal aid, service of documents, taking of evidence and recognition and enforcement of judgments). Such agreements were concluded with Algeria (1976), China (1987), Cyprus (1996), Egypt (1992), Greece (1979), Iraq (1988), Italy (1989), Mongolia (1998), Syria (1985), Turkey (1998) and the United Kingdom (1931). The latter agreement also covers some member countries of Commonwealth. Other bilateral agreements, apart from procedural matters, provide also for some conflict-of-law rules. Such agreements were concluded with Belgium (1986), Finland (1980) and Libya (1985). Poland has denounced the agreement with Finland as of 2021. More comprehensive agreements, which cover procedural matters, including rules on jurisdiction and also conflict-of-law rules were concluded with Austria (1963), Belarus (1994), Bulgaria (1961), Cuba (1982), Estonia (1998), Hungary (1959), Latvia (1994), Lithuania (1983), North Korea (1986), Romania (1999), Russia (1996), Ukraine (1993) and Vietnam (1993). The agreement concluded with Yugoslavia (1960) applies nowadays to Bosnia and Herzegovina, Croatia, North Macedonia, Serbia and Slovenia. The agreement concluded with Czechoslovakia (1987) applies to the Czech Republic and Slovakia. The agreement concluded with France (1969) covers only personal and family law matters.

35. It is suggested in the legal literature that there is no substantial relationship between public international law and PIL.[65] However, an influence of public international law on PIL might be observed in certain instances. An example may be the functioning of a public policy clause, which serves as a protection shield to the fundamental principles of the *forum*, including those resulting from human rights (*see below* Part I. Chapter 3. §7 Ordre Public (Public Policy)).[66] Another sphere in which a connection between public and PIL is observed is the doctrine of comity, meaning respectful relations between states. An important decision of the Supreme Court concerning state immunity from claims brought by individuals for damages caused by the armed forces during the Second World War may serve as an example.[67] In this case the Supreme Court referred on several occasions to the current state of development of the customary public international law.

---

65. *See* A. Mills in: *Encyclopedia of Private International Law*, p. 1448. For this view expressed in Polish literature on private international law, *see* M. Pazdan, *Prawo prywatne międzynarodowe*, Wolters Kluwer, Warszawa 2017, p. 32.
66. A. Mills in: *Encyclopedia of Private International Law*, p. 1451 and M. Pazdan, *Prawo prywatne międzynarodowe*, Wolters Kluwer, Warszawa 2017, p. 32.
67. Decision of the Supreme Court of 29 Oct. 2010, IV CSK 465/09. On the lack of such immunity in civil matters, namely claims concerning compensation for the de facto use of immovable property, *see* Judgment of the Supreme Court of 19 Jun. 2018, I CSK 45/18.

§2. SUPRANATIONAL LAW

36. Poland has been a member of the European Union (EU) since 1 May 2004. Nowadays EU is an economic and political union between twenty-seven Member States. The predecessor of the EU was the European Economic Community (EEC) created in 1958 to foster economic cooperation between its first members. Over decades EEC gradually welcomed new Member States, evolved into an organization competent with respect to different branches of law, including even PIL, and after few transformations ended up as EU. On 1 February 2020, the UK left the EU. The EU law consists of EU treaties[68] (international agreements concluded between Member States), which set its objectives, provide rules on the functioning of its institutions and regulate the relationship between the EU and its Member States. These treaties are amended from time to time.

37. Other sources of EU law, which are enacted by EU institutions (in particular, European Commission, European Council and European Parliament) include, *inter alia*, regulations, which are legal acts that apply, in general, automatically and uniformly to all EU Member States, and directives, which oblige EU Member States to achieve a certain result (e.g., certain level of protection of consumers), but allows them to choose how to proceed. EU countries adopt measures (e.g., in Poland domestic statutes are passed) to incorporate directives into their domestic (national) laws. EU legal acts are promulgated in the Official Journal of the EU (which is accessible online in all EU Member States' languages).

38. The Court of Justice of the European Union (CJEU) is an institution, which among other is dedicated to interpreting EU law. This is done in the form of judgments issued within the preliminary ruling proceedings,[69] which are initiated by national courts of EU Member States when in doubt about the interpretation of a provision of EU law. Sometimes, before issuing a judgment, CJEU asks an advocate general to prepare an opinion, which provides suggestion on this interpretation, but it is in no way binding on CJEU. It is submitted that the general principles on which EU is based support the standpoint that CJEU judgments are binding not only on the court, which referred a question to CJEU, but also on all other courts in the EU.

39. When looking at the EU through the lens of PIL, it should be indicated that Article 81(1) of the Treaty on the Functioning of the EU provides that EU may develop judicial cooperation in civil matters having cross-border implications and may adopt legal acts in that respect. In other words, it means that EU Member States gave EU competences to adopt legal acts binding on them in the field of PIL and international civil procedure. Such possibility has been existing since 1999 (entry

68. Treaty on the Functioning of the European Union, OJ C 326, 26.10.2012, pp. 47–390 and consolidated version of the Treaty on European Union, OJ C 326, 26.10.2012, pp. 13–390.
69. *See* Article 267 of Treaty on the Functioning of the European Union, OJ C 326, 26.10.2012, pp. 47–390.

into force of Amsterdam Treaty). However, even before 1999 EU played an important role in the unification of PIL of EU Member States by influencing EU Member States to sign international conventions concerning jurisdiction, applicable law, recognition and enforcement of judgments in civil and commercial matters among themselves and with third states (Brussels Convention[70] (1968), Rome Convention[71] (1980), which are no longer in force in Poland, and Lugano Convention[72] (1988), which is currently replaced by Lugano II Convention[73] (2007) in force in EU Member States, including Poland and Switzerland, Norway and Iceland).

40. Over the last twenty years EU used this competence in judicial cooperation in civil matters quite extensively adopting regulations in different subject matters (*see* Principal EC/EU Regulations in the PIL Field in Table of Statutory Instruments). These regulations are applied uniformly in EU Member States, including Poland. They are very often interpreted by CJEU in its judgments (which are also published online in all EU languages).

41. Even though, in general, EU regulations apply directly and uniformly to all EU Member States, there exist certain exceptions to this rule, which are important in the field of PIL. First, when negotiating Amsterdam Treaty three EU Member States obtained a special status to this respect. The UK (now, no longer a Member State) and Ireland negotiated a right not to apply regulations concerning judicial cooperation in civil matters with the possibility to opt-in. Hence, certain regulations are not applied in those states, whereas others are. Denmark negotiated the right not to apply these regulations, without the right to opt-in. As a result, in general, EU regulations in this field are not applied in Denmark.[74] Second, in accordance with Article 81(3) TFEU regulations concerning family law matters need to be adopted in accordance with a different legislative procedure requiring unanimity among EU Member States. As this unanimity is sometimes lacking, three regulations in the field of PIL were adopted in another special procedure – enhanced cooperation. A specific feature about this procedure is that such regulations are binding not on all EU Member States, but only on interested ones.[75] Poland applies none of these three regulations.

---

70. Convention on jurisdiction and the enforcement of judgments in civil and commercial matters done at Brussels on 27 Sep. 1968, OJ L 299, 31.12.1972, pp. 32–42.
71. Convention 80/934/EEC on the law applicable to contractual obligations opened for signature in Rome on 19 Jun. 1980, OJ L 266, 9.10.1980, pp. 1–19.
72. Convention on jurisdiction and the enforcement of judgments in civil and commercial matters done at Lugano on 16 Sep. 1988, OJ L 319, 25.11.1988, pp. 9–48.
73. Convention on jurisdiction and the recognition and enforcement of judgments in civil and commercial matters done at Lugano on 30 Oct. 2007, OJ L 339, 21.12.2007, pp. 3–41.
74. P.A. Nielsen, *EU PIL and Denmark*, IPRax 2019, vol. 5, pp. 449–452.
75. A. Wysocka-Bar, *Enhanced cooperation in property matters and non-participating Member States*, ERA Forum 2019, vol. 20, pp. 187–200.

§3. National Law

42. Domestic (national) law in this monograph means law adopted by the Polish legislator, and therefore, in general applicable only on the territory of the Republic of Poland as opposed to EU law, which is adopted by the EU legislator and equally applicable in all EU Member States. As both legislators adopt instruments on PIL (and international civil procedure) the distinction between domestic and EU law is necessary in order to properly assess priority between these instruments.

43. In domestic law rules designating law applicable to private law cases are contained in the Private International Law Act 2011 (PILA).[76] It entered into force on 16 May 2011 and repealed its predecessor PILA 1965. The PILA of 2011 has eighty-one articles subdivided into nineteen chapters: (1) General provisions, (2) Natural persons, (3) Legal persons and unincorporated entities, (4) Representation, (5) Making a juridical act and its form, (6) Prescription of claims and the lapse of time, (7) Obligations, (8) Arbitration agreement, (9) Ownership and other property rights. Possession, (10) Intellectual property, (11) Matrimonial matters, (12) Relationships between the Parents and the Child, (13) Adoption, (14) Guardianship and care, (15) Maintenance obligations, (16) Inheritance Matters, (17) Other legal relationships, (18) Amendments to the provisions being in force and (19) Final provisions.

44. Certain specific rules on the applicable law are also contained in other statutes (e.g., Bills of Exchange Law,[77] Cheque Law,[78] Maritime Code[79] and Aviation Law[80]). The provisions on international civil procedure are provided for in a separate statute – the CPC. It entered into force on 1 January 1965. Important amendments to the rules on international civil procedure entered into force in 2009. The Bankruptcy Law[81] provides for rules on international insolvency proceedings.

45. As flows from the above, PIL rules in Poland are contained in domestic law statutes, international agreements, both multilateral and bilateral, as well as EU regulations. The above creates quite complicated mosaic of legal sources. Locating an adequate conflict-of-law rule might seem like a challenge. The below rules, generalized for the purpose of simplicity, allow to assess which PIL rule is adequate in a given case. International agreements (to the extent of their material scope) take precedence over domestic law. Similarly, EU regulations take precedence (to the extent of their material scope) over domestic law. Fortunately, PILA does not regulate subject matters covered by EU regulations. The legislator decided that such

76. Act of 4 Feb. 2011 – Private International Law, Dz. U. 2011 nr 80 poz. 432.
77. Act of 28 Apr. 1936 – Bill of Exchange Law, Dz. U. 1936 nr 37 poz. 282.
78. Act of 28 Apr. 1936 – Cheque Law, Dz. U. 1936 nr 37 poz. 283.
79. Act of 18 Sep. 2001 – Maritime Code, Dz. U. 2018 poz. 2175.
80. Act of 3 Jul. 2002 – Aviation Law, Dz. U. 2019 poz. 1580.
81. Act of 28 Feb. 2003 – Bankruptcy Law, Dz. U. 2003 nr 60 poz. 535.

rules should be repealed. PILA only reminds about the applicability of EU regulations in articles devoted to particular subject matters. For example, when the Succession Regulation[82] started to be applied from 17 August 2015, rules on succession matters contained in Articles 64–66 PILA were repealed and a new Article 66a was added to inform about the applicability of the Succession Regulation.[83] EU regulations take precedence (to the extent of their material scope) over bilateral agreements concluded between EU Member States. Bilateral agreements with non-EU states and multilateral agreements to which non-EU states are parties to take precedence over EU regulations. Hence, when looking for an adequate rule one should always look first to EU instruments, then international agreements, remembering that their relationship with EU law is nuanced depending on which countries are parties to it, and at the end to PILA. PILA is applied only if neither EU nor international law instruments cover a given case.

46. It should be noted that EU instruments and multilateral agreements to which Poland is party to are already subject to voluminous literature, and therefore, will only be mentioned or shortly summarized in this monograph. Similarly, the existence of bilateral agreements will be signalled. These conventions will not be analysed in detail due to their number and variety of their scopes, as well as solutions provided therein.

§4. Case Law

47. As mentioned above, Poland is a country with civil law tradition, and therefore, case law of common courts is not formally a source of law. Irrespective of the above, given an intensive growth in cross-border disputes and the fact that the written law is not always able to keep the pace with the real life, interpretations provided by the common courts and especially the Supreme Court are an important factor of the development of PIL.

48. In one of its judgments the Supreme Court[84] underlined that if there is no separate, clear rule for a given legal relationship, an *actio pauliana* in this case, it does not necessarily mean that there is a loophole in the legal system, but rather some other rule of a wider scope might be adequate. In this case the Supreme Court decided that Article 24 PILA 1965 indicating law applicable to ownership and other rights in rem is adequate, as related to the asset that was transferred by the debtor to a third party to the detriment of the creditor.

82. OJ 2012 L 201, pp. 107–134.
83. On the criticism on rules informing about applicability of EU instruments and international agreements, *see* Mączyński, A., *Ustawowe odesłania do umów międzynarodowych i rozporządzeń unijnych dotyczących prawa prywatnego międzynarodowego* in: A. Mączyński, Rozprawy i studia z prawa prywatnego międzynarodowego, Wolters Kluwer, Warszawa 2017, pp. 169–183. First published in J. Gołaczyński, P. Machnikowski (eds), Współczesne problemy prawa prywatnego. Księga pamiątkowa ku czci Profesora Edwarda Gniewka, Warszawa 2010, pp. 373–384.
84. Judgment of Supreme Court of 29 Nov. 2012, II CSK 96/12.

49. Another example may be a judgment[85] in which the Supreme Court had to decide which law is applicable to the voluntary assignment, as then in force PILA 1965 did not contain a separate rule in that respect. When looking for an adequate solution, the Supreme Court presented three different conceivable concepts, relied on comparative law (referring to rules present in the 1980 Rome Convention, not applicable to the case at stake, and domestic PILs of Switzerland, Austria and Germany) and standpoints presented in both 'domestic' and foreign legal literature. It was decided that voluntary assignment should be governed by the law applicable to the assigned claim (*lex causae*). Judgments of the Supreme Court are often cited by lower courts, as well as in its subsequent decisions.

§5. Doctrine

50. Doctrine, understood as views presented by legal scholars in the form of comprehensive commentaries, monographs, articles and annotations to judgments, is not a formal source of law in Poland. Nevertheless, it influences the interpretation of PIL provisions and its application in practice. It happens that standpoints presented in legal writings are mentioned in the reasoning parts of judgments, including those issued by the Supreme Court.

51. For example, in one of its judgments[86] the Supreme Court stated, underlining that such a view is presented in the literature on PIL, that Article 2(1) PILA concerning the understanding of the notion of 'national law' in case of multiple nationality, might not be applied in situations when interpreting the same notion ('national law') used in the bilateral agreement. Another example may be the judgment[87] in which the Supreme Court listed questions governed by the law applicable to ownership and other rights in rem (*lex rei sitae*) relying on the legal literature on PIL. Usually, while referring to the standpoint of legal scholars, the Supreme Court does not mention a particular work or the name of the author.

52. As PILA does not contain rules on its temporal scope, in one of its judgments[88] the Supreme Court remained, referring to the majority views presented in legal literature, that general rules relating to civil matters should apply. It stated that it is PILA 1965 (and not PILA 2011) that applies to a succession case, because its rules were in force at the time of the death of the testator, even though a court was seized when PILA 1965 has already been repealed.

53. Similarly, views of legal scholars from different EU Member States are taken into account in the opinions of Advocates Generals, which in turn might influence the CJEU while issuing a judgment in preliminary ruling proceeding relating to the

85. Judgment of Supreme Court of 19 Dec. 2012, III CK 80/02.
86. Decision of Supreme Court of 15 Apr. 2011, III CSK 223/10.
87. Judgment of Supreme Court of 11 Mar. 2011, II CSK 435/10.
88. Decision of Supreme Court of 14 Feb. 2013, II CSK 294/12.

EU PIL instruments.[89] It should be noted that important judgments of the Supreme Court (which are easily accessible, as published online, unfortunately only in Polish language) and the CJEU are read, analysed and commented by legal scholars in form of written annotations.[90] This shows that the inspiration flows in both directions.

§6. Customary Law

54. Customary law is not a source of law in Poland, including in the field of PIL. However, Brussels I *bis* Regulation[91] while providing requirements as to the form of a prorogation agreement refers to 'a usage' which in widely known and regularly observed by the parties (Article 25(1)(c)).

89. *See* for example: Opinion of Advocate General Szpunar delivered on 22 Feb. 2018, Case C-20/17 *Oberle*, Judgment of the Court (Second Chamber) of 21 Jun. 2018.
90. *See* for example: W. Kurowski, *Prawo właściwe dla przelewu wierzytelności. Glosa do wyroku Sądu Najwyższego z dnia 19 grudnia 2003 r. (III CK 80/02)*, PPPM 2007, pp. 145–152 and K. Weitz, *Wyłączenie fikcyjnych doręczeń krajowych w stosunkach między państwami członkowskimi? Glosa do wyroku Trybunału Sprawiedliwości Unii Europejskiej (ETS) z dnia 19 grudnia 2012 r., C-325/11 w sprawie Krystyna Alder i Ewald Alder przeciwko Sabina Orłowska i Czesław Orłowski,* Polski Proces Cywilny 2013, vol. 2, pp. 265–278.
91. OJ L 351, 20.12.2012, pp. 1–32.

Chapter 2. Determination of the Applicable Law

§1. Conflict-of-Law Rules

I. Types of Conflict-of-Law Rules

55. In Polish legal literature conflict-of-law rules are divided into the following four categories, based on the criterion of which law may be designated as applicable: unilateral, bilateral, multilateral and universal. A unilateral rule indicates only when Polish law is applicable. For example, Article 13(2) PILA provides that when Polish court decides on incapacitation of a foreigner, Polish law applies.

56. A bilateral rule indicates when Polish law or law of the other contracting state is applicable. It may not designate law of a third state as applicable. Such rules are contained in bilateral agreements. For example, in accordance with Article 24(1) bilateral agreement with Ukraine,[92] the form of marriage is governed by the law of this contracting party, on which territory marriage is concluded. As only Poland and Ukraine are contacting parties and a bilateral agreement applies to situations 'closed' within territories of those two states, only Polish or Ukrainian law may be designated as applicable.

57. Similarly, a multilateral rule may designate only a law of one of contracting states, including Polish law, as applicable. For example, such rules are included in Hague Guardianship Convention (1902).[93] In accordance with its Article 9 it applies only to minors having nationality of one of contracting states and habitual residence in another contracting state, whereas pursuant to Article 1 guardianship is governed by the national law of a minor. This shows that only the law of a contracting state may be designated as applicable.

58. Universal rules are the most commonly used and may be found in PILA, international agreements adopted under auspices of HCCH and all EU regulations. For example, 1971 Hague Convention on Traffic Accidents[94] provides that the applicable law is the internal law of the state where the accident occurred (Article 3). At the same time, Article 11 underlines that the application of the conflict-of-law rules of the Convention is independent of any requirement of reciprocity and it applies even if the applicable law is not that of a contracting state. Similarly, EU regulations containing choice of law rules underline their universal application. For example, Article 2 'Universal application' of the Rome I Regulation[95] indicates that any law specified by this Regulation is applied whether or not it is the law of an EU Member State.

---

92. Dz. U. 1994 r. nr 96 poz. 465.
93. Hague Convention of 12 Jun. 1902 on Guardianship (*Convention du 12 juin 1902 pour régler la tutelle des mineurs*), Dz. U. 1929 nr 80 poz. 596.
94. Dz. U. 2003 nr 63 poz. 585.
95. Regulation (EC) No 593/2008 of the European Parliament and of the Council of 17 Jun. 2008 on the law applicable to contractual obligations (Rome I), OJ L 177, 4.7.2008, pp. 6–16.

59. PILA does not provide for similar explanations; however, it was never put into doubts that its rules are also of universal application. For example, if Article 11(1) PILA provides that legal capacity is governed by the national law of a person concerned, it is obvious that this rule may indicate as applicable law of any state in the world (even though *renvoi* is possible, *see* Part I., Chapter 3, §4).

60. There is also a division into rules that are applied at the stage of designation of applicable law and rules that are applied at the stage of its application. At the stage of designation there are rules, which simply designate the law applicable and rules, which modify or specify this designation. For example, Article 11(1) PILA designates the national law of a person concerned as applicable, whereas Article 5(1) PILA may modify this designation, if foreign conflict-of-law rules use different connecting factor (e.g., habitual residence) and lead to *renvoi* back to Polish law. At the stage of application, rules which modify the substantive result of the application of designated law may come into play.[96] For example, public policy clause (Article 7) may impact the substantive result of the application of foreign law designated as applicable, if the result of this application is perceived as contrary to fundamental principles of Polish legal order (*see* Part I., Chapter 3, §7).

II. Connecting Factors

61. The designation of applicable law is often made with the use of a classical conflict-of-law rule and a connecting factor forming part of it. For example, Article 49(1) PILA is a classical conflict-of-law rule. It states that the formal validity of a marriage is governed by the law of the state in which it is concluded. Its structure may be divided into two main parts, a hypothesis and a disposition.[97] In the hypothesis a certain subject matter (here, a form of marriage) is described. The hypothesis designates a substantive law that should govern this matter. This designation is made with use of a certain circumstance, which, *in abstracto* in view of the legislator, presupposes the existence of the closest link between a subject matter and the law of a given country. This circumstance serves as a basis of a connecting factor (here, place of celebration of a marriage). As a result, Article 49 PILA obliges a court (or other public authority) to apply the law of the place, where marriage was celebrated.

62. It may happen that it is not possible to assess circumstances, which determine applicable law, and therefore it is not possible to designate applicable law. In such case Article 10(1) PILA provides for a solution. It states that if it is not possible to establish circumstances, which determines applicable law, the law most closely connected with a given legal relationship applies. It provides for a subsidiary connection and should be perceived as the very last step of the cascade. For

96. M. Czepelak, *Międzynarodowe prawo zobowiązań Unii Europejskiej*, LexisNexis, Warszawa 2012, pp. 441–444.
97. H. Trammer, *Z rozważań nad strukturą normy kolizyjnej prawa prywatnego międzynarodowego*, Studia Cywilistyczne 1964, pp. 399–405.

example, Article 51(1) PILA indicates the law applicable to property relations of the spouses. It is the law of their common nationality. Article 51(2) PILA provides also for next steps of the cascade. If Article 51(1) may not be applied (as spouses simply do not have a common nationality), the connecting factor of common domicile, than common habitual residence and at the end the law of a country with which spouses are together most closely connected come successively into play. If in a case relating to property matters of spouses the court is not able to ascertain what is the nationality of the spouses and whether there is any they have in common, it will not directly start to ascertain the law most closely connected based on Article 10(1) PILA, but should first try to apply laws indicated at the subsequent steps of the cascade provided for in Article 51(2) PILA. A court may make use of Article 10(1) PILA only if all steps of the cascade failed and there is no other solution in PILA that may be applied (e.g., Article 3(1) PILA which explains how to proceed if a national law is applicable, but a given person is stateless or it is not possible to determine this nationality). This shows that Article 10(1) PILA may be applied only in extremely rare cases.[98]

III. Time Factors

63. A classical conflict-of-law rule, in order to designate applicable law, makes use not only of a connecting factor but also a time factor. For example, Article 54(1) PILA states that the termination of marriage is governed by the common national law of the spouses at the time the termination is requested. The use of a connecting factor of nationality, without any time factor added could give rise to doubts as whether the nationality at the time of marriage or at the time of its termination should be decisive. Similarly, Article 41(2) PILA states that acquisition, loss, change in the content or priority of the rights in rem is governed by the law where the object of rights in rem was located at the moment that these legal consequences appeared. Sometimes, a conflict-of-law rule does not indicate the time factor literally. For example, Article 11(1) PILA provides that legal capacity is governed by the national law of the natural person concerned. In such case the time factor can be easily inferred from the rule. It is the national law at the time this legal capacity should be assessed, for example it is national law at the time the person concluded allegedly invalid contract. The above applies similarly to rules included in EU regulations and international agreements.

IV. *Dépeçage*

64. Dépeçage in the strict sense is a situation, when a formally uniform legal matter, which could have been governed by a single substantive law designated by one single conflict-of-law rule, becomes divided into partial matters, each governed

98. P. Mostowik, *O postępowaniu w razie nieustalenia łączników kolizyjnych lub treści prawa obcego* in M. Pecyna, J. Pisuliński (eds), *Rozprawy cywilistyczne: księga pamiątkowa dedykowana profesorowi Edwardowi Drozdowi*, LexisNexis, Warszawa 2013, pp. 714–716.

by a different applicable law. For example, there is no *dépeçage* when a sale contract is governed by the law of the habitual residence of the seller (*lex contractus*). *Dépeçage* exists if some questions (e.g., obligations of the parties to this contract) are governed by the law of one state, whereas some other questions (e.g., prescription periods) by the law of another state.

65. *Dépeçage* might result from the admissibility of a partial choice of applicable law (subjective *dépeçage*) or objective *dépeçage* (explained below).[99] Partial choice of applicable law is admissible in Article 3(1) *in fine* Rome I Regulation, which states that parties can select the law applicable only to a part of the contract. Objective *dépeçage* (not resulting from the freedom of choice granted to the parties) was admissible under Article 4(1) Rome Convention,[100] which is no longer in force. It stated that, in absence of choice of applicable law, the contract is governed by the law of the country with which it is most closely connected. Nevertheless, a severable part of the contract which has a closer connection with another country may by way of exception be governed by the law of that other country. Currently, Rome I Regulation allows only subjective *dépeçage*.

66. Other EU regulations do not provide for a partial choice of applicable law, and therefore *dépeçage*, is not possible.[101] When it comes to matters regulated in PILA, when a choice of applicable law is admissible (e.g., for matrimonial property matters, arbitration agreement and voluntary representation), PILA does not provide literally for the possibility of partial choice of law. It only states in respective articles (Article 23(1), Article 39(1) and Article 52(1) PILA) that the subject matter is governed by law chosen by the parties. As a result, it might be inferred that partial choice of applicable law and *dépeçage* are not admissible in PILA.[102]

67. It might be signalled that *depeçage* is sometimes understood in the broader sense, so that apart from the *dépeçage* itself (as described above) it includes also the situation, when a given matter (e.g., a contract of sale) is governed by different laws because different conflict-of-law rules exist to designate law applicable to different aspects of this matter. For example, it might happen that legal capacity and formal validity are governed by different substantive laws than legal obligations of

99. M. Wojewoda, *Rozszczepienie statutu kontraktowego w Konwencji rzymskiej o prawie właściwym dla zobowiązań umownych*, PPPM 2008, pp. 64–65; P. Mankowski in: J. Basedow, G. Rühl, F. Ferrari, P. de Miguel Asensio (eds), *Encyclopedia of Private International Law*, pp. 526–528.

100. Rome Convention 80/934/EEC on the law applicable to contractual obligations opened for signature in Rome on 19 Jun. 1980, OJ L 266, 9.10.1980, pp. 1–19.

101. With respect to successions, *see* A. Wysocka-Bar, *Wybór prawa w międzynarodowym prawie spadkowym*, LexisNexis, Warszawa 2013, p. 212. With respect to successions and non-contractual obligations, *see* M. Pazdan, w: M. Pazdan (ed.), *System Prawa Prywatnego. Tom 20A. Prawo prywatne międzynarodowe*, Wydawnictwo C. H. Beck, Warszawa 2015, p. 204.

102. With respect to matrimonial property matters, *see* A. Sapota, *Wybór prawa w międzynarodowym prawie rodzinnym*, Wydawnictwo C. H. Beck, Warszawa 2016, pp. 235–238.

the parties, which are governed by *lex contractus.*[103] Some authors underline that such situation should be distinguished from *dépeçage*. In the above example formal validity or legal capacity constitute so-called partial question (German *Teilfrage*,[104] Polish *kwestia cząstkowa*[105]), which might lead to the situation, where different substantive laws are applied to different legal issues relating to one single contract.

V. Legal Consequences

68. In accordance with Article 51a Act on the System of Common Courts,[106] the court determines on its own motion (ex officio) which law is applicable to a legal matter.[107] This means that the court has to proceed with characterization and find the adequate conflict-of-law rule for a question at hand (e.g., decide if a claim should be characterized as relating to contractual or non-contractual obligations). Then, the court must determine the circumstances which constitute the basis of the connecting factor (e.g., habitual residence of the seller).[108] If foreign law is designated as applicable, the court, again ex officio, has to apply it to a case at hand. Hence, the legal consequence of applying conflict-of-law rule is this obligation addressed to the court to apply the law that was designated as applicable. This shows that the addressees of conflict-of-law rules are courts (and other state authorities).

69. The court is therefore obliged to ascertain properly the content of foreign law in order to apply it. Article 51a Act on the System of Common Courts provides that the court may ask the Ministry of Justice for the text of foreign law and explanations as to the foreign legal practice. In order to ascertain the content of foreign law and foreign legal practice the court may also use other means, including asking for opinion of an expert witness. The use of word 'may' suggest that the court is not obliged to use these means indicated in Article 51a, but may instead ascertain content of foreign law using such means as it finds appropriate.

---

103. M. Pazdan, w: M. Pazdan (ed.), *System Prawa Prywatnego. Tom 20A. Prawo prywatne międzynarodowe*, C. H. Beck, Warszawa 2015, pp. 201–202; M. Wojewoda, *Rozszczepienie statutu kontraktowego w Konwencji rzymskiej o prawie właściwym dla zobowiązań umownych*, PPPM 2008, p. 64.
104. P. Mankowski in: J. Basedow, G. Rühl, F. Ferrari, P. de Miguel Asensio (eds), *Encyclopedia of Private International Law*, p. 526.
105. M. Pazdan, w: M. Pazdan (ed.), *System Prawa Prywatnego. Tom 20A. Prawo prywatne międzynarodowe*, C. H. Beck, Warszawa 2015, pp. 341–342.
106. Dz. U. 2001 Nr 98 poz. 1070.
107. For the overview of the treatment of foreign law in Poland, *see* M. Wojewoda, *Poland: Proof and Information About Foreign Law – Theory and Reality* in: Y. Nishitani, *Treatment of Foreign Law – Dynamics Towards Convergence?*, Springer, Cham 2017, pp. 289–308.
108. M. Czepelak, *Międzynarodowego prawo zobowiązań Unii Europejskiej*, LexisNexis, Warszawa 2012, pp. 461–465.

70. Here it should be mentioned that Poland has been party to 1968 European Convention on Information on Foreign Law[109] and its 1978 Additional Protocol[110] since 1992. The Convention foresees that contracting states supply to each other information concerning their law and procedure in civil and commercial fields as well as on their judicial system. Each contracting state is supposed to appoint bodies called a 'receiving agency', to receive requests for information and to respond to these requests, and a 'transmitting agency' to receive requests for information from its judicial authorities and to transmit them to foreign agencies. In Poland it is the Ministry of Justice that assumes the role of both agencies. Also, bilateral agreements often contain provisions on mutual assistance with that respect. Within EU the EJN in civil and commercial matters (EJN)[111] may also serve as a medium of exchange of information.[112]

71. While dealing with the case the court is obliged to identify within the applicable substantive law all these norms, which regulate the question at hand, irrespective of the legal act, in which these norms are located. For example, even though the applicable law was designated by the conflict-of-law rule relating to contract of sale, it may happen that within the applicable substantive law also provisions concerning unjust enrichment or delicts should be applied.[113] The court should apply the foreign law taking into account not only the wording of foreign law but also foreign legal practice, including methods of interpretation used and foreign courts' jurisprudence.[114] In case of any amendments to the applicable substantive law, the intertemporal rules of this law decide which version of substantive law applies to the case at hand. The above is truth also with respect to public law rules.

72. In PILA, the question of public law is dealt with a specific provision. In accordance with 6(1) PILA the law designated as applicable includes public law rules, which under the applicable law should be applied to a given legal situation. This provision seems to encompass both foreign public law and public law of the *forum* if the law of the *forum* is applicable in a given case.[115] The qualification of a given provision as part of the public law should be done in accordance with the law applicable. In practice this provision requires that first a conflict-of-law rule of PILA indicates the law applicable to the given situation, then within this law (*lex causae*) one should find the answer to the question whether and to what extent its public law rules should be applied. They will be applied only if applicable law (*lex*

109. Dz. U. 1994 r. nr 64 poz. 272.
110. Dz. U. 1994 r. nr 64 poz. 274.
111. Council Decision of 28 May 2001 establishing a European Judicial Network in civil and commercial matters OJ L 174, 27.6.2001, pp. 25–31.
112. M. Cichomska, *Metody ustalania treści prawa obcego a Europejska Sieć Sądownicza*, Polski Proces Cywilny 2012, vol. 2, pp. 292–311.
113. M. Czepelak, *Międzynarodowego prawo zobowiązań Unii Europejskiej*, LexisNexis, Warszawa 2012, pp. 321–332.
114. *See* Judgment of Supreme Court of 11 Aug. 2004, II CK 489/03.
115. J. Poczobut in: J Poczobut (ed.), *Prawo prywatne międzynarodowe. Komentarz*, Wolters Kluwer, Warszawa 2017, p. 199.

causae) wishes so.[116] It seems that the above provision does not provide for any grounds on which the application of foreign public law could be refused (e.g., when the public law of the applicable law serve only the interest of the state, which issued it). It is suggested this would be possible only based on the general institution of PIL, *id est* public policy clause.[117] It was underlined in the legal literature that this provision transforms the understanding of PIL, as now law applicable to the given situation covers also public law and, therefore, the distinction between private and public law becomes less relevant.[118] There were no similar rules in the previous PILA 1965 and PILA 1926.

73. A mistake in designating applicable law and therefore application of the law, which in fact was not applicable, as well as mistakes in applying foreign law correctly designated as applicable constitute a violation of substantive law with the same consequences as violation of Polish substantive law in a purely domestic case.[119] A foreign law in this respect is not treated differently than Polish law. A violation of substantive law serves as a basis for appeal (Article 268 §1(2) CPC), as well as appeal in cassation to the Supreme Court (Article 398^3 §1(1) CPC).

74. At the end it might be mentioned that pursuant to Article 10(2) PILA if it is not possible to ascertain the content of applicable law in a reasonable time, Polish law applies. It provides for a subsidiary connection and should be perceived as the very last step of the cascade (just like Article 10(2) PILA presented above in section II. Connecting Factors). For example, if Article 51(1) PILA which uses connecting factor of common nationality of the spouses may not be applied, as spouses simply do not have a common nationality, the connecting factor of common domicile, than common habitual residence, and at the end the law of a country with which spouses are together most closely connected come successively into play. If in such case the court is not able to ascertain the content of the law of common nationality of the spouses, it will not directly apply Polish law based on Article 10(2) PILA, but should first try to apply laws indicated at the subsequent steps of the cascade provided for in Article 51(2) PILA. Similarly, in accordance with Article 3(1) PILA, if it is not possible to ascertain the content of the national law of a given person, the law of the domicile applies. In case a person does not possess the domicile, the law of the state of habitual residence applies. A court may make use of Article 10(2) PILA only if all previous solutions failed, which, as one can imagine, will be an extremely rare case.[120]

116. J. Poczobut in: J Poczobut (ed.), *Prawo prywatne międzynarodowe. Komentarz*, Wolters Kluwer, Warszawa 2017, p. 200.
117. J. Poczobut in: J Poczobut (ed.), *Prawo prywatne międzynarodowe. Komentarz*, Wolters Kluwer, Warszawa 2017, p. 200.
118. J. Poczobut in: J Poczobut (ed.), *Prawo prywatne międzynarodowe. Komentarz*, Wolters Kluwer, Warszawa 2017, p. 201.
119. P. Rodziewicz, *Stwierdzenie treści oraz zastosowanie prawa obcego w sądowym postępowaniu cywilnym*, Wydawnictwo C. H. Beck, Warszawa 2015, pp. 257–297.
120. P. Mostowik, *O postępowaniu w razie nieustalenia łączników kolizyjnych lub treści prawa obcego* in M. Pecyna, J. Pisuliński (eds), *Rozprawy cywilistyczne: księga pamiątkowa dedykowana profesorowi Edwardowi Drozdowi*, LexisNexis, Warszawa 2013, pp. 714–716.

§2. Relevant Contact and Evasion of the Law

75. Evasion of the law (*fraude à la loi*) is a concept that is not regulated either in PILA or EU PIL instruments,[121] with the sole exception of the Succession Regulation.[122] The latter mentions it in its Recital 26 suggesting that nothing in the regulation prevents a court of an EU Member State from applying mechanisms designed to tackle the evasion of the law, such as *fraude à la loi*. It is not regulated in bilateral agreements either. Currently, *fraude à la loi* in the context of PIL is not discussed in the jurisprudence of Polish courts. This institution is elaborated on by legal scholars in commentaries or monographs devoted to PIL (*see below* Chapter 3 Basic Terms, §9. Evasion of the Law). It is underlined that some connecting factors might be more susceptible to manipulations than others[123] (e.g., it is far easier to change the place of habitual residence than nationality).

§3. Choice of Law

76. Party autonomy, understood as competence given by the legislator to interested parties to choose the law applicable to a given legal relationship, has been present within PIL in Poland since PILA 1926. In the last years it expanded greatly to new subject matters. Under PILA 1926 the choice of applicable law was admitted only for contractual obligations. Parties were allowed to choose between laws provided for in an exhaustive list (the law of their nationality, law of their domicile and law of the place where the contract was concluded, place where the obligation was supposed to be performed or place where the property was located). Under PILA 1965 the choice of law was still admitted only for contractual obligations. Parties could choose a law which had connection with the obligations in question. The concept of the connection was not defined. Choice of applicable law as admitted by PILA 1926 and later in PILA 1965 was perceived as too limited.[124]

77. In PILA party autonomy is further extended. PILA contains a general rule devoted to party autonomy in Article 4. It states that choice of applicable law is admissible when this law so provides (Article 4(1) PILA). This provision seems to explain that party autonomy is not a universal principle of PIL, and therefore, is not admissible universally in all kind of cases. PILA admits choice of applicable law to voluntary representation (Article 23(1) PILA), obligations resulting from unilateral

121. *See* Opinion of Advocate General Szpunar of 2 March 20171, Case C-54/16 *Vinyls Italia*, Judgment of the Court (Fifth Chamber) of 8 Jun. 2017.

122. Regulation (EU) No 650/2012 of the European Parliament and of the Council of 4 Jul. 2012 on jurisdiction, applicable law, recognition and enforcement of decisions and acceptance and enforcement of authentic instruments in matters of succession and on the creation of a European Certificate of Succession, OJ 2012 L 201, pp. 107–134.

123. M. Pilich, *Zasada obywatelstwa w prawie prywatnym międzynarodowym. Zagadnienia podstawowe*, Wolters Kluwer, Warszawa 2015, pp. 502–509.

124. J. Skąpski, *Autonomia woli w prawie prywatnym międzynarodowym w zakresie zobowiązań z umów*, Zeszyty Naukowe Uniwersytetu Jagiellońskiego, Kraków 1964, pp. 161–173.

acts (Article 32(1) PILA), arbitration agreements (Article 39(1) PILA) and matrimonial property matters (Article 52(1) PILA). It provided also for choice of applicable law to successions (Article 64(1) PILA), but this provision was repealed as a result EU Succession Regulation's universal rules. In most cases the choice is unlimited, which means that parties can choose the law of any state, irrespective of lack of any connection with the case. Only when it comes to matrimonial property matters Article 52(1) PILA provides for a list of laws, which parties may choose from (limited choice of law).

78. Pursuant to Article 4(2) PILA choice of applicable law should be made expressly or should unequivocally result from the circumstances of the case, unless a provision admitting it provides otherwise (e.g., Article 52(3) PILA concerning choice of law matrimonial property regime). Choice of applicable law made once a legal relationship was established is not affecting rights of third parties (Article 4(3) PILA). If while effecting a juridical act, but before a choice of law was made, requirements as to its form provided for in the applicable law were abided by, this validity may not be challenged in accordance with the chosen law (Article 4(4) PILA). In accordance with Article 4(5) PILA, when deciding whether a choice of law was made and whether it is valid other rules of PILA apply (e.g., Article 11 PILA relating to legal capacity). The above applies equally to modification or revocation of choice of law (Article 4(6) PILA).

79. Party autonomy is also provided for in EU regulations, which are applied in Poland (Article 3 Rome I Regulation, Article 14 Rome II Regulation, Article 22 Succession Regulation),[125] as well as in certain international instruments (e.g., Articles 7 and 8 Hague Protocol[126] or to a very limited extent Article 6(1) of the bilateral agreement with France).

§4. Objective Connecting Factor

I. Principle of the Closest Connection

80. The principle of the closest connection in PIL might be perceived from many different angles.[127] While choosing an adequate connecting factor to designate applicable law, the legislator must decide *a priori* which law has the closest connection with a given legal situation. For example, EU legislator decided that a succession case has the closest connection with the country in which the deceased had habitual residence (Article 21(1) Succession Regulation). Recital 23 Succession

125. M. Czepelak, *Autonomia woli w prawie prywatnym międzynarodowym Unii Europejskiej*, Poltext, Warszawa 2015.

126. Hague Protocol on the Law Applicable to Maintenance Obligations. The text of the Protocol is an annex to 2009/941/EC: Council Decision of 30 Nov. 2009 on the conclusion by the European Community of the Hague Protocol of 23 Nov. 2007 on the Law Applicable to Maintenance Obligations, OJ L 331, 16.12.2009, pp. 17–23.

127. M. Czepelak, *Zasada najściślejszego związku jako reguła kierunkowa prawa prywatnego międzynarodowego*, PPPM 2016, v. 18, pp. 81–97.

Regulation underlines that habitual residence as determined for the purpose of this regulation should reveal a close and stable connection between the deceased and a given state. Another example might be the use of nationality as a connecting factor in numerous provisions of PILA (e.g., Article 15(1) relating to name and surname). As explained in *travaux préparatoires*[128] this connecting factor is used because of its advantages, in particular stability and unambiguity of the connection, which it represents.

81. A connecting factor used by the legislator might designate the law, which in a particular case and under certain circumstances, turns out not to be the one, which is most closely connected to the case at hand. To mitigate the above, sometimes the legislator decides to make the designation more flexible by the use of the escape clause (also referred to as closer connection clause). In such case it is the court (or other public authority) that decides *a posterior*, which law is most closely connected with a case at hand. For example, Article 21(2) Succession Regulation provides that where, by way of exception, it is clear from all the circumstances of the case that the deceased was manifestly more closely connected with a state other than the state of the last habitual residence, this more closely connected law applies. Similar escape clauses might be found also in other EU regulations (e.g., Article 4(3) Rome I Regulation – for contracts covered by this provision, Article 5(3) Rome I Regulation – for contracts of carriage, Article 8(4) Rome I Regulation – for employment contracts, Article 4(3) Rome II Regulation – for torts covered by this provision, Article 10(4) Rome II Regulation – for unjust enrichment). Escape clause is also included in PILA in Article 32(2) PILA relating to obligations resulting from a unilateral juridical act and Article 43 PILA relating to goods in transit. There is no general escape close in PILA.

82. When it could be hard for the legislator to find an adequate connecting factor, the concept of the closest connection is also used to designate applicable law. Once again it is the court judge (or other public authority) that decides *a posterior*, which law is most closely connected with a case at hand. Such rule is provided for in Article 67 PILA, which states that if there is no conflict-of-law rule, which could designate applicable law in PILA, other statutes, international agreements and EU law, the law most closely connected to a given private law relationship is applied. A trust is given as an example of a relationship, which could be covered by this provision.[129] The concept of closest connection is also used as the last step of the conflict-of-law rule designed as a cascade (also referred to as Kegel's ladder). For example, Article 51(1) PILA provides that property relations of spouses are governed by the law of their common nationality. But if spouses simply do not have the nationality of the same state, the connecting factor of common domicile designates

128. Sejm Rzeczpospolitej Polskiej VI kadencji, Druk 1277 of 31 Oct. 2008, pp. 7–8.
129. M. Zachariasiewicz in: M. Pazdan (ed.), *Prawo prywatne międzynarodowe. Komentarz*, Wydawnictwo C. H. Beck, Warszawa 2018, pp. 547–559.

applicable law. If spouses do not have domicile in the same state, the law of common habitual residence applies and at the end, if spouses do not have habitual residence in the same state, the law of a country with which spouses are together most closely connected applies (Article 51(2) PILA).

II. Nationality

83. In accordance with commonly accepted paradigm of public international law, each state decides who and on the basis of which circumstances acquires (or losses) its nationality. Hence, nationality is always assessed in accordance with the supposedly national law (e.g., Polish law decides whether a given person is a Polish national or not, whereas French law decides whether this person is French national, which might be proven by an ID card or a passport). Nationality is a circumstance which is quite often used as a connecting factor in PILA and bilateral agreements. It is much less frequently used in multilateral agreements and in EU instruments (as sometimes perceived as irreconcilable with the EU principle of non-discrimination).

84. Nationality is an important connecting factor in PILA. As explained in *travaux préparatoires*[130] this connecting factor assures stability and therefore is used with respect to personal status of a person and in family matters (e.g., Article 11(1) – legal capacity, Article 15(1) – name and surname, Article 16(1) – personality rights, Article 48 – capacity to marry, Article 57(1) – adoption). It used to be a connecting factor in succession matters (Article 64 was repealed, once Succession Regulation started to be applied). In certain provisions PILA requires the existence of common nationality. Usually this is a first step of the cascade, so in case spouses do not have common nationality, other connecting factors come into play (e.g., in Article 51(1) – personal and property relations of spouses, Article 54(1) – dissolution of marriage, Article 57(2) – joint adoption by spouses).

85. PILA provides for specific rules for cases when a person possesses multiple nationalities or inversely possess none, whereas PILA indicates applicable law with use of nationality as a connecting factor.[131] Article 2 PILA deals with multiple nationalities. It provides that Polish nationality prevails over any foreign nationality a Polish national may possess (Article 2(1) PILA). When it comes to foreigners with multiple nationalities, the law of this state with which a foreigner is most closely connected prevails as national law (Article 2(2) PILA). Pursuant to Article 2(3) PILA, in cases when 'common nationality' is required for a conflict-of-law rule to be applied, the requirement is met if a law of a given state recognize both persons as its nationals.

---

130. Sejm Rzeczpospolitej Polskiej VI kadencji, Druk 1277 of 31 Oct. 2008, pp. 7–8.
131. M. Pilich, *Zasada obywatelstwa w prawie prywatnym międzynarodowym*, Wolters Kluwer Polska, Warszawa 2015, pp. 341–369.

86. PILA also regulates a case of stateless persons and refugees, as well as instances when it is not possible to determine the nationality of a given person whereas, a conflict-of-law rule indicates applicable law with use of nationality as a connecting factor. In both cases, in accordance with Article 3(1) PILA, the connecting factor of domicile indicates the applicable law and, if this person does not have a domicile, the law of the state of the habitual residence is applied.[132]

III. Residence

A. Domicile (of Origin, of Choice, of Dependence)

87. In Poland, the connecting factor of domicile (Polish *zamieszkanie*) is well known, as it was used successively in PILA 1926, PILA 1965[133] and now in PILA. In PILA 1926 and PILA 1965 the only personal connecting factors were nationality and domicile. Whereas, under PILA also a new connecting factor of habitual residence was introduced, which raises questions as to mutual relation between domicile and habitual residence.[134]

88. In accordance with *travaux préparatoires*[135] to PILA none of these connecting factors is deliberately defined. This is left to jurisprudence and legal literature. It is however explained that these concepts are close to one another but are not identical. Both should be understood in autonomous way, irrespective the way they might be defined in other branches of law (e.g., in substantive civil law). When assessing both domicile and habitual residence two elements should be considered – *corpus* (the place where one lives and where one established the centre of one's activity) and *animus* (intention to remain). The difference between two connecting factors lies in the intensity of the two above elements. Domicile constitutes a stronger connection of a person with a given country than habitual residence.

89. The concept of domicile of origin, of choice or of dependence is not used in Polish PIL, even though there are discussions as how to assess domicile of a child or a person mentally incapable. It was suggested that the intention of legal representatives could be taken into account.[136] Domicile is also present in international agreements and in some EU regulations, which are applied in Poland. For example,

---

132. M. Pilich, *Zasada obywatelstwa w prawie prywatnym międzynarodowym*, Wolters Kluwer Polska, Warszawa 2015, pp. 369–388.
133. A. Mączyński, *Zamieszkanie jako podstawa łącznika normy kolizyjnej* in: A. Mączyński, *Rozprawy i studia z prawa prywatnego międzynarodowego*, Wolters Kluwer, Warszawa 2017, pp. 184–202. First published in Zeszyty Naukowe Uniwersytetu Jagiellońskiego. Prace prawnicze 1978, pp. 41–62.
134. O. Bobrzyńska, P. Mostowik, *Zwykły pobyt dziecka jako postawa jurysdykcji krajowej oraz łącznik kolizyjny*, Zeszyty Naukowe Uniwersytetu Szczecińskiego. Acta Iuris Stetinensis 2014, no 2, pp. 540–544.
135. Sejm Rzeczpospolitej Polskiej VI kadencji, Druk 1277 of 31 Oct. 2008, pp. 8–9.
136. M. Świerczyński w: M. Pazdan (ed.), *System Prawa Prywatnego. Tom 20A. Prawo prywatne międzynarodowe*, C. H. Beck, Warszawa 2015, p. 231.

Article 4(1) Brussels I *bis* Regulation[137] provides for domicile of the defendant as the basis for jurisdiction. Articles 62, 63 Brussels I *bis* Regulation provide guidance as how this concept should be understood.

B. Habitual Residence

90. Habitual residence is a relatively new connecting factor in Polish domestic PIL, introduced for the first time in PILA. It is inspired by works of HCCH, which uses this connecting factor in numerous international agreements which Poland is also party to (e.g., Hague Convention on Form of Wills (1961)).[138] Similarly, it has been used in EU law (since Brussels Convention (1968)).[139] Now, it may be found in all EU regulations (e.g., in Article 4(1)(a) Rome I Regulation, in Article 4(2) Rome II Regulation or Article 21(1) Succession Regulation together with extensive explanations provided in its Recitals 23 and 24. The notion of habitual residence within EU PIL was interpreted by CJEU on several occasions.[140]

91. As explained in *travaux préparatoires*[141] habitual residence in PILA constitutes a weaker connection between a person and a state than domicile. Habitual residence does not require an intention to settle permanently in a given country. Settling for a definite period of time is enough (e.g., for the period of studies or work). Indication of certain periods of time to determine habitual residence (or domicile) was omitted purposefully. Residing in a given place temporarily or while travelling (e.g., stays during holidays or professional trainings) do not amount to habitual residence.

C. Temporary Residence

92. Temporary residence is not used as a connecting factor in PILA.[142] A presence in a given country is used as a connecting factor in Article 25(1) PILA, which states that if a contract is concluded between persons, who find themselves in two

---

137. Regulation (EU) No 1215/2012 of the European Parliament and of the Council of 12 Dec. 2012 on jurisdiction and the recognition and enforcement of judgments in civil and commercial matters (Brussels I bis), OJ L 351, 20.12.2012, pp. 1–32.
138. O. Bobrzyńska, P. Mostowik, *Zwykły pobyt dziecka jako postawa jurysdykcji krajowej oraz łącznik kolizyjny*, Zeszyty Naukowe Uniwersytetu Szczecińskiego. Acta Iuris Stetinensis 2014, no 2, pp. 509–524.
139. O. Bobrzyńska, P. Mostowik, Zwykły pobyt dziecka jako postawa jurysdykcji krajowej oraz łącznik kolizyjny, Zeszyty Naukowe Uniwersytetu Szczecińskiego. Acta Iuris Stetinensis 2014, no 2, pp. 524–540.
140. *See* for example: recent case concerning succession matters: Case C-80/19 *E. E.*, Judgment of the Court (First Chamber) of 16 Jul. 2020; cases concerning parental responsibility: Case C-393/18 *UD v. XB*, Judgment of the Court (First Chamber) of 17 Oct. 2018; Case C-111/17 *OL v. PQ*, Judgment of the Court (Fifth Chamber) of 8 Jun. 2017; Case C-523/07 *A.*, Judgment of the Court (Third Chamber) of 2 Apr. 2009; Case C-497/10 *Mercredi*, Judgment of the Court (First Chamber) of 22 Dec. 2010.
141. Sejm Rzeczpospolitej Polskiej VI kadencji, Druk 1277 of 31 Oct. 2008, pp. 8–9.
142. M. Świerczyński w: M. Pazdan (ed.), *System Prawa Prywatnego. Tom 20A. Prawo prywatne międzynarodowe*, C. H. Beck, Warszawa 2015, p. 236.

different states it is enough to abide by the form of the contract provided for in one of them. Connecting factors based on the simple presence might be found in other PIL instruments. For example, Article 13(1) Brussels II *bis* Regulation[143] provides that where a child's habitual residence cannot be established and jurisdiction cannot be determined on the basis of other provisions, the courts of the EU Member State where the child is present have jurisdiction in parental responsibility matters. This also apply to refugee children or children internationally displaced because of disturbances occurring in their country (Article 13(2) Brussels II *bis* Regulation).

IV. Registered Office

93. As will be explained below (*see* Part II. Conflict-of-Law Rules, Chapter 1. Persons, §2. Legal Persons), in accordance with Article 17(1) PILA, a legal person is governed by the law of the country, in which its seat is located. In the legal literature there is a lack of consensus as to the understanding of the concept of a 'seat' for the purpose of Article 17(1) PILA. Some authors advocate in favour of to the real seat theory,[144] some in favour of the statutory seat (registered office) theory,[145] some seem to leave the question deliberately open.[146] Some of bilateral agreements to which Poland is party to contain conflict-of-law rules concerning legal capacity of a legal person. At the EU level international company law is not unified, however numerous CJEU judgments concerning freedom of establishment have repercussions in PIL.[147]

V. *Lex Loci Delicti*

94. In accordance with Article 31 §1 PILA 1965 (which is no longer in force in Poland, as repealed by PILA), non-contractual obligation is governed by the law, where the event giving rise to this obligation occurred (*lex loci delicti commissi*). This rule is also provided for in Article 3 Hague Convention on Traffic Accidents,[148] which is in force in Poland since 2002. As underlined in the explanatory report to the Convention, by adopting the classical solution of the application of the

143. Council Regulation (EC) No 2201/2003 of 27 Nov. 2003 concerning jurisdiction and the recognition and enforcement of judgments in matrimonial matters and the matters of parental responsibility (Brussels II bis), repealing Regulation (EC) No 1347/2000, OJ L 338, 23.12.2003, pp. 1–29.
144. A. Wowerka w: M. Pazdan (ed.), *System Prawa Prywatnego. Tom 20A. Prawo prywatne międzynarodowe*, C. H. Beck, Warszawa 2015, pp. 633–638.
145. A. Opalski, A. Wiśniewski in: J. Poczobut (ed.) *Prawo prywatne międzynarodowe. Komentarz*, Wolters Kluwer, Warszawa 2017, pp. 336–353; M. Mataczyński, *Seat of the company in private international law. Selected issues*, Wydawnictwo naukowe UAM: Poznań 2018, pp.11–28.
146. W. Klyta in: M. Pazdan (ed.), *Prawo prywatne międzynarodowe. Komentarz*, Wydawnictwo C. H. Beck, Warszawa 2018, pp. 238–239, M. *Pazdan, Prawo prywatne międzynarodowe*, Wolters Kluwer, Warszawa 2017, pp. 144–146.
147. *See* M.-Ph. Weller, Ch. Thomale in: J. Basedow, G. Rühl, F. Ferrari, P. de Miguel Asensio (eds), *Encyclopedia of Private International Law,* pp. 408–411.
148. Hague Convention on the Law Applicable to Traffic Accidents signed at The Hague on 4 May 1971, Dz. U. 2003 nr 63 poz. 585.

lex loci commissi in tortious matters, the Convention conforms with the present practice in the majority of Member States of the HCCH. Please note, that the Hague Convention on Traffic Accidents takes in Poland precedence over Rome II Regulation, whereas the latter applies with respect to remaining delicts (*see* Part II., Chapter 2, §3).

95. It should be noticed that the principle of *lex loci delicti commissi* was partly abandoned within EU Member States as a result of the adoption of uniform rules of Rome II Regulation, which has been applied since 11 January 2009 to events giving rise to damage which occur starting from that date. Recital 15 stresses that even though this principle is the basic solution for non-contractual obligations in virtually all the Member States, the practical application of the principle varies, which in turn negatively affects certainty as to the law applicable. Recital 16 Rome II Regulation underlines that uniform rules should enhance the foreseeability of court decisions and ensure a reasonable balance between the interests of the person claimed to be liable and the person who has sustained damage. A fair balance between the interests of the person claimed to be liable and the person sustaining the damage is ensured if the law of the country where the direct damage occurred (*lex loci damni*) applies. The principle of *lex loci damni* reflects the modern approach to civil liability and the development of systems of strict liability (Recital 16 Rome II Regulation). Hence, the general rule provided for in Article 4(1) adopts *lex loci damni* principle. Recital 17 Rome II Regulation explains that in cases of personal injury or damage to property, the country in which the damage occurs should be the country where the injury was sustained, or the property was damaged, respectively.

VI. *Lex Rei (Cartae) Sitae*

96. The connecting factor of a place where an object is located is used in PILA for the purpose of designating law applicable to ownership, other rights in rem and possession, as well as their acquisition or loss (*see* Part II. Conflict-of-Law Rules, Chapter 3. Property, §1. *Lex rei sitae*). This connecting factor is also used in international agreements (e.g., Hague Convention on Form of Wills (1961) – with respect to immovable property) and EU instruments (e.g., Article 24(1) Brussels I *bis* Regulation or Article 4(1)(c) Rome I Regulation).

97. An interesting example of the applicability of *lex rei sitae* is provided for in Article 30 Succession Regulation. It states that if the law of the country in which certain immovable property, certain enterprises or other special categories of assets are located contains special rules which, for economic, family or social considerations, impose restrictions concerning or affecting the succession in respect of those assets, those special rules apply to the succession in so far as, under the law of that country, they are applicable irrespective of the law applicable to the succession. This concept seems similar to the idea of overriding mandatory rules (*see* Part I. General Principles, Chapter 3. Basic terms, §8. Overriding Mandatory Rules).

§5. Changes in the Connecting Factors; Changes in the *Lex Causae*

98. Changes in PIL in Poland resulting from the adoption of a new PILA in 2011, successive replacement of domestic PIL by EU regulations and entry into force of new international agreements (e.g., Hague Protocol on the Law Applicable to Maintenance Obligations (2007)[149]) might induce changes of connecting factors, and therefore changes in the designation of the applicable law.

99. When it comes to PILA it does not contain intertemporal provisions and it is submitted that general intertemporal rules provided for in substantive civil law should apply to its relations with PILA 1965.[150] For example, in general, in a succession case PIL rules in force at the time of death of the testator should be applied, hence PILA, in general, applies to succession cases of persons who died starting from its entry into force – 16 May 2011. When it comes to EU regulations they usually precisely indicate the date from which they should be applied and therefore at the same time indicate when PILA stops to be applied (e.g., Succession Regulation applies to succession cases of persons who died starting from 17 August 2015, hence PILA might only be applied to those who have died on 16 August 2015 at the latest). Similarly, international agreements usually also indicate the moment from which they should be applied to a contracting state.

100. A separate issue is change by the parties of the circumstance, which serves as a connecting factor (French *conflict mobile*, Polish *konflikty ruchome*). For example, in accordance with Article 41(1) PILA ownership is governed by the law, where the object of this right is located (*lex rei sitae*). Hence, once the object is moved across a border, a different substantive law governs the ownership of this object. Such change of the governing law is not dealt with in a general way by PILA. Instead, some specific mechanisms are in place. Sometimes the legislator decides to fix permanently the applicability of a given substantive law. For example, in accordance with Article 48 PILA capacity to marry is governed by the national law of a given spouse at the time the marriage was concluded. If the spouse changed nationality few years later and applies for the annulment of the marriage, the national law at the time of concluding the marriage will be applied when assessing potential grounds for annulment and change of nationality has no impact on the applicability of this law (Article 50 PILA). In other cases, the applicable law is purposefully not fix, and therefore might change if the circumstance serving as basis of connecting factor (e.g., nationality) changes. For example, Article 51(1) PILA states that personal and property relations between spouses are governed by their currently common national law. Assuming that spouses changed their nationality few times in a row, all these laws were consecutively applicable. The above might have impact on the matrimonial property regime of the spouses, and therefore, also on

149. OJ L 331, 16.12.2009, pp. 17–23.

150. M. Kłoda, *Zagadnienia międzyczasowe nowego prawa prywatnego międzynarodowego*, KPP 2011, no 2, pp. 507–560.

the situation of third parties (e.g., a spouse's creditor). To mitigate this impact a special conflict-of-law rule concerning opposability of matrimonial property regime against third parties is provided for in Article 53 PILA.

101. Another question, separate from the above one, are changes in the law applicable to a given matter (*lex causae*). It might be explained with use of the following example. The law applicable to the matrimonial property agreement between spouses, in accordance with Article 52(2) PILA is governed by the law applicable to their personal and property relations at the time of concluding the agreement (as designated by the cascade of Article 51 PILA). The time factor of 'at the time of concluding agreement' is supposed to fix in time a circumstance, which serves as the basis of connecting factor (e.g., it means common national law of the spouses at the time of concluding the agreement). The time factor does not mean that the applicable substantive law should be applied as it was at the time of concluding the agreement (e.g., twelve years ago). As already explained (*see above* V. Legal Consequences), applicable law is applied in accordance with its own intertemporal provisions. Hence, intertemporal provisions of the applicable law determine whether a new or an old provision of its substantive law should be applied. Similarly, it is not possible to choose as applicable a substantive law as it was at a certain point in time (e.g., Napoleon's Code as it was in 1804). This will not be treated as choice of applicable law within the meaning of this concept in PIL.

§6. Combination of Connecting Factors

102. As shown above often a conflict-of-law rule designates applicable law using a single connecting factor (e.g., in accordance with Article 41(1) PILA ownership and other rights in rem are governed by *lex rei sitae*). This however is not always the case. In many instances different combinations of connecting factors are used to indicate applicable law and serve also other purposes (e.g., a desired substantive result).[151]

103. Alternative connecting factors (Polish *wskazanie alternatywne*)[152] are used to achieve a substantive result of the validity of a given legal act (*favor validitatis*). This mechanism may be observed in EU instruments (e.g., Article 11(1) Rome I Regulation with respect to formal validity of a contract), international agreements (e.g., Article 1 Hague Convention on Form of Wills) and in PILA. For example, in accordance with Article 40(1) PILA formal validity of an arbitration agreement is governed by the law of the place of arbitration. It is enough however if the form of

151. H.-P. Mansel in: J. Basedow, G. Rühl, F. Ferrari, P. de Miguel Asensio (eds), *Encyclopedia of Private International Law*, pp. 441–452.

152. A. Mączyński, *Wskazanie kilku praw przez normę kolizyjną prawa prywatnego międzynarodowego* in: A. Mączyński, M. Pazdan, A. Szpunar (eds), Rozprawy z polskiego i europejskiego prawa prywatnego, Wydawnictwo i Drukarnia 'Secesja', Kraków 1994, pp. 236–238.

the agreement abides by the law, which governs arbitration agreement (*lex causae*). Similarly, Article 49(1) PILA states that formal validity of a marriage is governed by the law of the country where it is concluded (*lex loci celebrationis matrimonii*). Pursuant to Article 49(2) PILA, if the marriage is concluded outside Poland, it is enough if the form conforms to common national law of the spouses or the law of their common domicile or common habitual residence at the time of concluding the marriage. This desired substantive result does not have to be validity of a juridical act. It might be obtaining of maintenance (as in Article 4 Hague Protocol) or establishing filiation (Article 55(2) and 55(3) PILA).

104. Multiple connecting factors are also used in rules allowing for choice of applicable law (Polish *wskazanie opcyjne*). In such case parties may not choose any law as applicable, but instead their choice is limited to laws, which – in view of the legislator – have an adequate connection with the legal matter. For example, Article 52(1) PILA provides that spouses may choose as applicable to their matrimonial property relations the national law of either of them or law of the domicile or habitual residence of either of them.

105. Subsidiary connection (Polish *właściwość subsydiarna*)[153] is used in conflict-of-law rules designed as cascade (Kegel's ladder). Subsidiary connecting factors allow for the designation of applicable law, in cases the main connecting factor fails in this regard. For example, Article 54(1) PILA provides for the applicability of the common national law of the spouses to the dissolution of their marriage. If spouses do not have common nationality, the connecting factor is not able to designate the applicable law, and therefore subsidiary connection comes into play. In accordance with 54(2) and (3) PILA consecutive steps of the cascade are as follows: common domicile at the time the dissolution is requested, last common habitual residence provided that one of them still has habitual residence in this state and Polish law as the last step of the cascade.

106. Cumulative connection (Polish *wskazanie kumulatywne*)[154] requires that requirements of more than one law must be fulfilled cumulatively in order for the legal effect to take place, and therefore makes more than one law applicable. For example, Article 57(1) PILA provides that adoption is governed by the national law of the adopter. However, the adoption may not be established without abiding by the national law of the adoptee with respect to the consent of the adoptee, the consent of the legal representative or consent of the public authority, as well as with respect to limitations to the adoption resulting from the change of the domicile for the domicile in another state.

---

153. A. Mączyński, *Wskazanie kilku praw przez normę kolizyjną prawa prywatnego międzynarodowego* in: A. Mączyński, M. Pazdan, A. Szpunar (eds), Rozprawy z polskiego i europejskiego prawa prywatnego, Wydawnictwo i Drukarnia 'Secesja', Kraków 1994, pp. 245–246.

154. A. Mączyński, *Wskazanie kilku praw przez normę kolizyjną prawa prywatnego międzynarodowego* in: A. Mączyński, M. Pazdan, A. Szpunar (eds), Rozprawy z polskiego i europejskiego prawa prywatnego, Wydawnictwo i Drukarnia 'Secesja', Kraków 1994, pp. 236–238.

107. In accessory connection (Polish *wskazanie akcesoryjne*) a conflict-of-law rules does not designate applicable law directly, but points to the law applicable to another legal matter. For example, pursuant to Article 26 PILA prescription period is governed by the law applicable to the claim (*lex causae*).

Chapter 3. Basic Terms

§1. Characterization (Classification)

108. Characterization or classification (Polish *kwalifikacja*) in Polish PIL means interpretation of the legal concepts used in choice-of-law rules in order to determine which rule should apply to a given case. This interpretation should also lead to determination which juridical concept in a substantive law applicable is appropriate in the case and therefore which particular provisions should be applied.

109. PILA 2011 does not contain any provision on classification. That was also the case with PIL acts previously being in force – PILA 1926[155] and PILA 1965.[156] Creating a rule defining classification and specifying how it should be done for the use of all conflict-of-law rules included in PILA would be extremely difficult. Instead, an appropriate solution should be sought in every case, separately for each conflict-of-law rule.[157]

110. The Polish doctrine has undertaken the task to define what is classification. The Polish literature presents various ways that classification can be done.[158] According to the first of them, the terms used in the conflict-of-law rules should be given the same meaning as is given to them by the norms of substantive law belonging to *lex fori*. The second solution assumes that the interpretation of the concepts appearing in the conflict-of-law rules should be made according to the substantive law indicated as applicable (*lex causae*). In the third solution, it is assumed that the conflict-of-law rules have different character from substantive legal norms, which is related to their specific nature and goals. Thus, the terms used in the content of the conflict-of-law rules can be understood differently from their meaning under the substantive law. The fourth method is called 'autonomous qualification' and according to it the concepts used in the conflict-of-law rules should be interpreted independently from the meaning assigned to them under substantive law of a particular country. Instead, the meaning of those concepts should be established based on the legal science of PIL and comparative law studies.[159]

111. The most widespread view in Polish doctrine is that the concepts that appear in the hypothesis of conflict-of-law rules should be defined independently,

155. Act of 2 August 1926 on the Law Applicable to International Private Relations, Dz. U. 1926 nr 101 poz. 581.
156. Act of 12 Nov. 1965 Private International Law, Dz. U. 1965 nr 46 poz. 290.
157. M. Pazdan in: M. Pazdan (ed.), *System Prawa Prywatnego. Tom 20 A. Prawo prywatne międzynarodowe*, Wydawnictwo C. H. Beck, Warszawa 2014, p. 318.
158. K. Przybyłowski, *Prawo prywatne międzynarodowe. Część ogólna, Księgarnia Gubrynowicza i syna*, Lwów 1935, pp. 101–105; B. Walaszek, M. Sośniak, *Międzynarodowe prawo prywatne. Część ogólna*, Uniwersytet Jagielloński, Kraków 1965, pp. 77–82; M. Pazdan in: M. Pazdan (ed.), *System Prawa Prywatnego. Tom 20 A. Prawo prywatne międzynarodowe*, Wydawnictwo C. H. Beck, Warszawa 2014, pp. 311–315.
159. M. Pazdan in: M. Pazdan (ed.), *System Prawa Prywatnego. Tom 20 A. Prawo prywatne międzynarodowe*, Wydawnictwo C. H. Beck, Warszawa 2014, pp. 311–315.

apart from their meaning in the substantive law, in accordance with their goals and separate character. The classification should be made according to the *lex fori* conflict-of-law rule, but in accordance with the assumptions of the autonomous character of those norms. However, if a Polish court exceptionally in the case of *renvoi* (*see* Part I, Chapter 3, §4) and preliminary question (*see* Part I, Chapter 3, §2)) applies the conflict-of-law rules belonging to the legal system of a foreign country, then the terms and concepts used therein should be interpreted in accordance with the law of that country.[160]

112. It is also worth to mention that classification, as a part of applying the EU regulations in the field of PIL, should be done differently – according to the principle of autonomous interpretation of the EU law and all the guidelines given by the CJEU in the preliminary rulings.[161]

§2. Preliminary Question (Incidental Question)

113. In Polish PIL, a preliminary question (Polish *kwestia wstępna*, French *question préalable*, German *Vorfrage*) means a separate legal situation, distinct from the main case, the assessment of which affects the resolution of the main case. For example, the existence of a marriage may be a preliminary question in an inheritance case, when substantive succession law indicates a surviving spouse as an heir. The inheritance by a given person depends on whether this person can be classified as a 'surviving spouse', *id est* whether the marriage was validly contracted and whether it still lasted in the moment of spouse's death.

114. Preliminary question is disclosed only after the law applicable to the main question has been determined. The need to resolve a preliminary question arises from the content of the substantive rules of the law applicable to the main case. The substantive rules of the applicable law link certain legal effects with the existence of a relationship being a preliminary question. For the preliminary question, a separate assessment on the basis of conflict-of-law rules is needed. In other words, it is necessary to indicate the applicable law to it, which may be a different than the law that governs the main case.

115. No legal relationship is by its nature a main case or a preliminary question. It may take such a character in a given case. For example, the acknowledgement of a child can be a main case or a preliminary question in a maintenance case.

---

160. K. Przybyłowski, *Prawo prywatne międzynarodowe. Część ogólna*, Księgarnia Gubrynowicza i syna, Lwów 1935, pp. 101–105.

161. *See* for example, Case C-585/08 *Pammer and Hotel Alpenhof*, Judgment of the Court (Grand Chamber) of 7 Dec. 2010; Case C-350/14 *Lazar*, Judgment of the Court (Fourth Chamber) of 10 Dec. 2015; Case C-497/10 *Mercredi*, Judgment of the Court (First Chamber) of 22 Dec. 2010.

116. In PILA there is no special provision on preliminary question. Such provision was neither included in PILA 1926,[162] nor in PILA 1965.[163] The methods of resolving a preliminary question have been however examined in the doctrine.[164] The most widely recognized view was that the law designated by the *lex fori* conflict-of-law rule should be applied to the preliminary question.[165] Whether a given issue is a main case or a preliminary question, the same law will be indicated as applicable to it. The second solution assumes that to the preliminary question, the law specified by the *lex causae* conflict-of-law rules should be applied, *id est* the rules belonging to this system, which has been indicated as the law applicable to the main case. This solution ensures uniformity of decisions at the international level. In such a case, the preliminary question would be solved in the same was as if it belonged to the court whose law is applicable to the main case. Thus, it cannot be ruled out that in some situations the latter solution should apply.[166]

117. The jurisprudence of courts in the cases in which a preliminary question has arisen is not fully consistent. Usually the courts stand in favour of applying the *lex fori* conflict-of-law rule for preliminary question. For example, in a ruling where the preliminary question concerned whether a valid contract on transfer of rights in rem had been concluded, and the main case was the acquisition of property, the court used the *lex fori* conflict-of-law rule to the preliminary issue.[167] However, in another ruling on granting a pension in respect of the death of a relative, where the preliminary question was the existence of a maintenance obligation between the deceased and the person potentially entitled to the pension, the court stated that the *lex causae* conflict-of-law rule should govern the preliminary question, even though at the end it applied the conflict-of-law rule of bilateral agreement between Poland and Ukraine.[168]

---

162. Act of 2 Aug. 1926 on the Law Applicable to International Private Relations, Dz. U. 1926 nr 101 poz. 581.
163. Act of 12 Nov. 1965 Private International Law, Dz. U. 1965 nr 46 poz. 290.
164. B. Walaszek, M. Sośniak, *Międzynarodowe prawo prywatne. Część ogólna*, Uniwersytet Jagielloński, Kraków 1965, pp. 82–84; J. Balicki, *Międzynarodowe prawo prywatne*, Uniwersytet Marii Curie-Skłodowskiej, Lublin 1976, pp. 67–69; M. Pazdan in: M. Pazdan (ed.), *System Prawa Prywatnego. Tom 20 A. Prawo prywatne międzynarodowe*, Wydawnictwo C. H. Beck, Warszawa 2014, pp. 338–353.
165. K. Przybyłowski, *Z problematyki stosowania obcych norm kolizyjnych*, Państwowe Wydawnictwo Naukowe, Kraków 1959, pp. 6–7; P. Rodziewicz, *Stwierdzenie treści oraz zastosowanie prawa obcego w sądowym postępowaniu cywilnym*, Wydawnictwo C. H. Beck, Warszawa 2015, pp. 165–168.
166. M. Pazdan in: M. Pazdan (ed.), *System Prawa Prywatnego. Tom 20 A. Prawo prywatne międzynarodowe*, Wydawnictwo C. H. Beck, Warszawa 2014, p. 345.
167. Judgment of Supreme Court of 22 Mar. 2002, I CKN 1137/99.
168. Judgment of Supreme Court of 19 Dec. 2003, III CK 155/02.

§3. Substance and Procedure

118. The distinction between substance law and procedure law is a characteristic feature of most legal systems of PIL. Polish law is not an exception in this matter. Issues of procedure are governed by *lex fori processualis*, which for Polish court means mainly the rules included in CPC.[169] Whereas, the substantive legal provisions, and sometimes also conflict-of-law rules,[170] belonging to a legal system of a particular country, are applied to a legal relationship with an international element.[171]

119. On the practical problems with distinguishing between material law questions and procedural law questions, *see* Part III, Chapter 2.

§4. *Renvoi*

120. In Polish PIL, *renvoi* is understood in a traditional way. It is a situation in which the conflict-of-law rules of the state whose law has been indicated as applicable regulate a given issue differently, by using another connecting factor. Thus, the conflict-of-law norm of the state whose law was designated as applicable refers to another legal order. If it refers back to the legal order of the adjudicating court, then it is called 'remission' (Polish *odesłanie zwrotne*, French *renvoi au premier degré*, German *Rückverweisung*).[172] And if it refers to the legal order of a third country, it is called 'transmission' (Polish *odesłanie dalsze*, French *renvoi au second degré*, German *Weiterverweisung*).[173]

121. Pursuant to Article 5(1) PILA, if the foreign law that is indicated as applicable law by this act, refers back to the Polish law, Polish law applies. This provision therefore regulates remission. Such solution has a significant advantage as it allows the court to apply *lex fori*, which is best known to the court. Additionally, the acceptance of the remission by the law indicated by the conflict-of-law rule is irrelevant (meaning that it is not relevant if in accordance with conflict-of-law rules of that state it is its own law that would be applied).[174]

122. However, in some cases *renvoi* is not allowed. According to Article 5(2) PILA renvoi does not apply if the applicable law: was determined by the parties'

---

169. Act of 17 Nov. 1964 – Civil Procedure Code, Dz. U. 1964 nr 43 poz. 296.
170. In the case of *renvoi* (*see* Part I Chapter 3, §4) and preliminary question (*see* Part I Chapter 3, §2).
171. J. Poczobut in: J. Poczobut (ed.), *Prawo prywatne międzynarodowe. Komentarz*, Wolters Kluwer, Warszawa 2017, p. 136.
172. Decision of Supreme Court of 26 Jan. 2006, II CSK 124/05.
173. B. Walaszek, M. Sośniak, *Międzynarodowe prawo prywatne. Część ogólna*, Uniwersytet Jagielloński, Kraków 1965, pp. 87–95.
174. W. Popiołek in: M. Pazdan (ed.), *System Prawa Prywatnego. Tom 20 A. Prawo prywatne międzynarodowe*, Wydawnictwo C. H. Beck, Warszawa 2014, pp. 373–377.

choice of law; concerns the formal validity of a juridical act; or concerns the contractual or non-contractual obligations, or obligations arising out of a unilateral juridical act, which are governed by the law determined in accordance with the provisions of this act.

123. There is also specific case of *renvoi* included in PILA 2011 concerning the law applicable to legal persons. Article 17(2) states that if the law of the state, in which the legal person has its seat, refers to the law of the state according to which the legal person has been incorporated, that law applies. In practice this provision can cause especially transmission to a third law, as remission is possible in accordance with the general provision of Article 5(1) PILA.[175]

124. In PILA 2011 there is no general provision on transmission, therefore this type of *renvoi* is not allowed. Such provision was included in PILA 1926[176] (Article 36) and PILA 1965[177] (Article 4§2). According to those provisions transmission to a third state's law was allowed only if the applicable law which referred to the law of a third country was the national law. In other words, transmission was only possible when the indication of the applicable law (which referred to a third state's law) was made by the PILA conflict-of-law rule, which was based on the nationality as a connecting factor. Moreover, only a single transmission was allowed, because in the case of transmission to a third state's law, the substantive law of this legal system should have been applied, disregarding the conflict-of-law rules.[178]

125. The provision on transmission has not been included in PILA 2011 primarily for practical reasons. In the case of transmission, it is necessary to research on conflict-of-law rules of at least two foreign systems, which cause difficulties for the courts.[179] Another argument against it was that it is usually included neither in international conventions, nor in the EU regulations.[180] Moreover, provisions on transmission in PILA 1926 and PILA 1965 were based on the assumption that national law as a law applicable should be privileged over law indicated by other personal connecting factors, which resulted from the approach to the national law itself.[181]

---

175. *See* A. Wowerka in: *System Prawa Prywatnego. Tom 20 A. Prawo prywatne międzynarodowe*, Wydawnictwo C. H. Beck, Warszawa 2014, pp. 639–641.
176. Act of 2 Aug. 1926 on the Law Applicable to International Private Relations, Dz. U. 1926 nr 101 poz. 581.
177. Act of 12 Nov. 1965 Private International Law, Dz. U. 1965 nr 46 poz. 290.
178. K. Przybyłowski, *Prawo prywatne międzynarodowe. Część ogólna*, Księgarnia Gubrynowicza i syna, Lwów 1935, pp. 142–146; F. Zoll, *Międzynarodowe prawo prywatne w zarysie*, Księgarnia Powszechna, Kraków 1947, pp. 90–93, A. Mączyński, *Stosowanie norm kolizyjnych obcego prawa prywatnego międzynarodowego*, Wolters Kluwer, Warszawa 2017, pp. 223–231. First published in A. Matlak (ed.), *Spory o własność intelektualną. Księga jubileuszowa dedykowana Profesorom Januszowi Barcie i Ryszardowi Markiewiczowi*, Warszawa 2013, pp. 571–595.
179. *See* M. Pazdan, *Stosowanie obcych norm kolizyjnych*, PPPM 2016, t.18, p. 22.
180. Exceptions are for example: Article 21(2) of 1996 Hague Convention on jurisdiction, applicable law, recognition, enforcement and co-operation in respect of parental responsibility and measures for the protection of children (Dz. U. 2010 nr 172 poz. 1158) and Article 34(1) of the Regulation 650/2012 on succession (OJ 2012 L 201, pp. 107–134).
181. K. Przybyłowski, *Z problematyki stosowania obcych norm kolizyjnych*, Państwowe Wydawnictwo Naukowe, Kraków 1959, p. 21.

Currently, however, this argument is much weaker, as the importance of citizenship as a connecting factor has decreased in recent decades.[182]

126. *Renvoi* is also included in provisions of legal acts on bills of exchange and cheques. According to Article 77 of the Bill of Exchange Law [183] a person's ability to incur bill obligations shall be assessed according to his or her national law, but if this law indicates as applicable the law of another country, this law should apply. Analogous provision is provided for in the Cheque Law.[184] Pursuant to Article 62 a person's ability to incur cheques is assessed according to his or her national law, but if this law indicates as applicable the law of another country, this law should apply. Both provisions can serve as a basis for remission and transmission.

§5. General Conflict Rule/Special Conflict Rule

127. PILA 2011 is a detailed regulation, including many special conflict-of-law rules. Nevertheless, it is possible to identify several conflict-of-law rules of a more general character. Those norms apply when there are no special norms concerning the given situation, in accordance with the classic rule *lex specialis derogat legi generali.* The conflict-of-law rules of a general nature concern: capacity of natural persons; representation; making a juridical act and its form; and prescription of claims and the lapse of time (*see below*).

I. Capacity of Natural Persons

128. According to the general conflict-of-law rule in Article 11(1) PILA, the capacity of natural person is subjected to the person's nationality. In PILA 2011 there are several special conflict-of-law rules on the legal capacity to perform a specific legal action, which prevail over the general rule (*see* Part II., Chapter 1, §1). For example, the law applicable to the capacity to enter into marriage is determined on the basis of Article 48 PILA, not Article 11(1) PILA[185]

II. Representation

129. PILA includes the general conflict-of-law rule indicating the law applicable to representation. Pursuant to Article 22 the statutory representation is subject to the law applicable to the legal relationship resulting in the power to act on behalf

182. *See* M. Pilich, *Zasada obywatelstwa w prawie prywatnym międzynarodowym*, Wolters Kluwer Polska, Warszawa 2015, p. 51.
183. Act of 28 Apr. 1936 – Bill of Exchange Law, Dz. U. 1936 nr 37 poz. 282.
184. Act of 28 Apr. 1936 – Cheque Law, Dz. U. 1936 nr 37 poz. 283.
185. M. Pilich in: J. Poczobut (ed.), *Prawo prywatne międzynarodowe. Komentarz*, Wolters Kluwer, Warszawa 2017, pp. 281–282.

of another. This provision can be used to many different types of the statutory representations, for example, parents towards the child, spouses towards each other or guardian towards the pupil.

130. In the case of the voluntary representation, the law applicable is determined in accordance with Article 23 PILA. Pursuant to Article 23(1) the voluntary representation is governed by the law chosen by the principal. The chosen law may, however, be invoked in regard to the third person only where the latter knew or could readily have known about the choice. The principal may invoke the chosen law against the representative only if the latter was aware or could have easily learned about the choice of law. In the absence of a choice, in accordance with Article 23(2), the voluntary representation is governed, respectively, by: (1) the law of the state in which the representative has a seat where he constantly operates, or (2) the law of the state in which the principal's business is located, if it also constitutes the place where the representative constantly operates, or (3) the law of the state in which the representative actually acted while representing the principal or in which the representative should have acted according to the intention of the principal.[186]

131. Article 23 PILA has a general character, as it indicates the law applicable to voluntary representation in many situations when the representative performs a juridical act on behalf of the principal, unless there is a special conflict-of-law rule. For example, law applicable to entering into marriage by proxy should be indicated by the Article 23, as there is no special conflict-of-law rule on that matter.[187] The same is true for the law applicable to conclusion of the contract by representative on behalf of the principle. It should be determined according to the conflict-of-law rules included in Article 23 PILA, as according to Article 1(2)(g) of the Rome I Regulation[188] on the law applicable to contractual obligations the question whether the representative is able to bind a principal in relation to a third party is excluded from the scope of the regulation.

III. Making a Juridical Act and Its Form

132. The conflict-of-law rules concerning making a juridical act can also be considered of general nature. They apply to different types of juridical act (e.g., acknowledgement of a child), unless there are other conflict-of-law rules that can be applied to the particular type of the juridical act for example, entering into marriage (Article 48 PILA) or making a will (Article 24–26 Succession Regulation).

186. J. Pazdan in: J. Poczobut (ed.), *Prawo prywatne międzynarodowe. Komentarz*, Wolters Kluwer, Warszawa 2017, pp. 414–428.
187. J. Pazdan, *Zawarcie małżeństwa przez pełnomocnika w prawie prywatnym międzynarodowym* in: L. Ogiegło, W. Popiołek, M. Szpunar (eds), *Rozprawy prawnicze. Księga pamiątkowa Profesora Maksymiliana Pazdana*, Zakamycze, Kraków 2005, pp. 263–268; E. Kamarad, *Matrimonium per procura – uwagi na tle prawa materialnego i prawa kolizyjnego*, PWPM 2013, vol. XI, pp. 31–42.
188. Regulation (EC) No 593/2008 of the European Parliament and of the Council of 17 Jun. 2008 on the law applicable to contractual obligations (Rome I), OJ L 177, 4.7.2008, pp. 6–16.

133. According to Article 24(1) PILA when determining whether the juridical act has been made, the law governing that juridical act applies (e.g., to determine if the acknowledgement of a child was made, the law applicable to this acknowledgement should apply, *id est* the child's law of nationality as of the time of acknowledgement in accordance to Article 55(3)). A party claiming that he or she has not made a declaration of intent (e.g., remained silent), may invoke, in accordance with Article 24(2), the law of the state in which he or she has habitual residence, if it appears from the circumstances that it would not be justified to determine the effects of his or her conduct in accordance with *lex causae*.[189]

134. Similarly, the conflict-of-law rules indicating the law applicable to the form of a juridical act have rather general character. Pursuant to Article 25(1) PILA the form of a juridical act is governed by the law applicable to that juridical act. However, it suffices to satisfy the formal requirements provided in the law of the state in which the juridical act has been made. If a contract is concluded between persons who are in different states at the time when making the declarations of intent, it suffices to satisfy the formal requirements provided for such a contract in the law of either of these states. Nevertheless, according to Article 25(2) PILA only the main rule stated in Article 25(1) applies to disposition of immovable property, or to juridical acts that relate to the formation, merger, division, transformation and dissolution of a legal person or an unincorporated entity without legal personality. Therefore, the form of those juridical acts should be governed by *lex causae* only.[190]

135. Conflict-of-law rules stated in Article 25 PILA should be used to determine the law applicable to form of a judicial act, if there are no other special rules. For example, the law applicable to the form of the contract, which only transfer rights in rem, should be determined in accordance with the general rule of Article 25 PILA, as such contracts do not fall into scope of the Rome I Regulation.[191] However, if there is a special rule, for example, Article 40 PILA, which states that the form of the arbitration agreement shall be subject to the law of the country of the place of the arbitration, or Article 49 PILA, according to which the form of the marriage is governed by the law of the country in which it is celebrated, those special rules should apply instead of general rule of Article 25 PILA.

IV. Prescription of Claims and the Lapse of Time

136. Conflict-of-law rules concerning the influence of the lapse of time on the possibility of pursuing claims may be regarded as general rules, as they can be

189. M. Pazdan in: M. Pazdan (ed.), *Prawo prywatne międzynarodowe. Komentarz*, Wydawnictwo C. H. Beck, Warszawa 2018, pp. 279–283.
190. J. Pazdan in: M. Pazdan (ed.), *Prawo prywatne międzynarodowe. Komentarz*, Wydawnictwo C. H. Beck, Warszawa 2018, pp. 283–293.
191. Regulation (EC) No 593/2008 of the European Parliament and of the Council of 17 Jun. 2008 on the law applicable to contractual obligations (Rome I), OJ L 177, 4.7.2008, pp. 6–16.

applied in many different types of cases, including both proprietary claims and non-proprietary claims. Pursuant to Article 26 PILA the prescription of a claim is subject to the law applicable to the claim in question. Therefore, it should be governed by *lex causae*. The same rule, in accordance with Article 27 PILA, *mutatis mutandis* applies to other legal institutions concerning lapse of time.[192] For example, the question whether a certain right in rem might be acquired as a result of long term possession in good faith will be governed by *lex causae*, which in this case will be *lex rei sitae* indicated by Article 41(2) PILA.[193]

§6. ASSIMILATION

137. Assimilation (Polish *dostosowanie*, French *l'adaptation*, German *Anpassung*), in English also known as adjustment or adaptation, has been understood in Polish PIL as a general instrument which helps to avoid unintended results caused by the fragmentation of applicable law in cases connected to more than one legal system. For example, transfer of movable property across border and related to it problem of change of *lex rei sitae* and therefore law applicable to rights in rem, which can regulate it in a different way than the law previously applicable (*see* Part II., Chapter 3, §2).

138. In PILA there is no provision on adaptation, therefore it had to be defined by the doctrine.[194] It is a procedure that takes place at the certain stage of application of law and is a remedy for the discrepancy in legal norms in the legal systems that are parallelly indicated by the conflict-of-law rules as law applicable for a given situation. These discrepancies can lead to a few types of difficulties. First, it may happen that in none of the legal systems indicated as applicable there is a legal norm that would regulate a given issue. Second, there may be an 'overlap' of several legal norms which regulate a given issue differently. Third, the parallel application of the norms indicated as law applicable is not possible as they provide for completely different legal effects for a given situation.[195]

139. In practice, the number of possible discrepancies is very large, hence it is difficult to create a single pattern of conduct. Everything depends on the court (or other state authority applying the law) that decides the case.[196]

---

192. M. Tomaszewski in: J. Poczobut (ed.), *Prawo prywatne międzynarodowe. Komentarz*, Wolters Kluwer, Warszawa 2017, pp. 451–461.
193. M. Tomaszewski in: J. Poczobut (ed.), *Prawo prywatne międzynarodowe. Komentarz*, Wolters Kluwer, Warszawa 2017, p. 460.
194. B. Walaszek, M. Sośniak, *Międzynarodowe prawo prywatne. Część ogólna*, Uniwersytet Jagielloński, Kraków 1965, pp. 128–130.
195. P. Rodziewicz, *Stwierdzenie treści oraz zastosowanie prawa obcego w sądowym postępowaniu cywilnym*, Wydawnictwo C. H. Beck, Warszawa 2015, pp. 228–231.
196. *See* Resolution of Supreme Court of 30 Mar. 1992, III CZP 17/92; Judgment of Supreme Court of 22 Mar. 2002, I CKN 1137/99.

140. Undoubtedly, the adaptation may be made at the level of conflict-of-law rules, by modifying their scopes, so as to enable a case to be resolved on the basis of norms belonging to a single legal system or at the level of the substantive applicable law, by modifying, for the purposes of an individual decision, the manner of applying the norms governing the issue under consideration.[197]

141. Currently the provision that serves as a legal basis for adaptation is included in the Succession Regulation.[198] According to Article 31 where a person invokes a right in rem to which this person is entitled under the law applicable to the succession and the law of the Member State in which the right is invoked does not know the right in rem in question, that right should be adapted to the closest equivalent right in rem under the law of that state, taking into account the aims and the interests pursued by the specific right in rem and the effects attached to it.

§7. Ordre Public (Public Policy)

142. The public policy clause (Polish *klauzula porządku publicznego*), as a traditional mechanism of PIL, was regulated in PILA 1926[199] (Article 38) and in PILA 1965[200] (Article 6) and in detail analysed in the Polish doctrine of PIL.[201]

143. Currently, the basis for the application of the public policy clause is Article 7 PILA. It states that a foreign law shall not be applied, if this application would lead to the consequences that are incompatible with the public policy of the Republic of Poland.

144. The public policy clause is therefore intended to exclude the application of foreign law, which has been indicated as applicable by the provisions of PILA, in a situation where the application of this law would cause effects contrary to Polish public order. This may happen when foreign law regulates a given issue in a different way than Polish substantive law. However, dissimilarity alone is not a sufficient premise. It may happen that, despite the different wording of a foreign law provision, its application may have the same effects as the application of Polish substantive law. As it is noted in Polish doctrine, the public policy clause is not directed

---

197. K. Sznajder-Peroń in: M. Pazdan (ed.), *System Prawa Prywatnego. Tom 20 A. Prawo prywatne międzynarodowe*, Wydawnictwo C. H. Beck, Warszawa 2014, pp. 537–544.
198. Regulation (EU) No 650/2012 of the European Parliament and of the Council of 4 Jul. 2012 on jurisdiction, applicable law, recognition and enforcement of decisions and acceptance and enforcement of authentic instruments in matters of succession and on the creation of a European Certificate of Succession, OJ 2012 L 201, pp. 107–134.
199. Act of 2 Aug. 1926 on the Law Applicable to International Private Relations, Dz. U. 1926 nr 101 poz. 581.
200. Act of 12 Nov. 1965 Private International Law, Dz. U. 1965 nr 46 poz. 290.
201. K. Przybyłowski, *Prawo prywatne międzynarodowe. Część ogólna*, Księgarnia Gubrynowicza i syna, Lwów 1935, pp. 164–180; M. Sośniak, *Klauzula porządku publicznego w prawie międzynarodowym prywatnym*, Państwowe Wydawnictwo Naukowe, Warszawa 1961; M. Zachariasiewicz, *Klauzula porządku publicznego jako instrument ochrony materialnoprawnych interesów i wartości fori*, Wydawnictwo C. H. Beck, Warszawa 2018.

against the very institution of foreign law, but against its effects, which would be grossly contrary to Polish legal order.[202] Moreover, even if the effects of applying foreign law would be different, they do not have to be contrary to the fundamental principles of the Polish legal order. Foreign law may achieve the same goal by means of institutions or legal structures other than those in Polish law. Hence, a simple analysis of the content of the foreign applicable law is not sufficient. The court should 'simulate' the application of foreign law, checking what effects it will have in a given case.[203]

145. The term 'public policy' used in Article 7 PILA means the fundamental principles of the legal order of Poland. These principles may be derived from national legislation and acts of international and EU law, like the European Convention on Human Rights[204] or the Charter of Fundamental Rights of the European Union.[205] The importance of the fundamental principles of Polish legal order is twofold. On the one hand, they constitute the Polish public order and thus specify when public policy clause should be applied in order to protect them.[206] On the other hand, they may lead to the limitation of the possibility of invoking the public policy clause if the refusal to apply foreign law would violate the provisions contained in these acts, including in particular norms of human rights.

146. The fundamental principles of the legal order of a given state are not immutable, therefore public policy should always be interpreted dynamically. When making the aforementioned 'simulation', the court should take into account the fundamental principles of *lex fori* that are in force at the time of adjudication.[207]

147. Polish doctrine of PIL distinguishes between two types of effects of invoking the public policy clause. This distinction is made from the point of view of the party, whose case is judged by the court.[208] If the result of invoking the clause is the refusal to apply the foreign law that imposed restrictions on the party, then it is referred to as 'permitting effect'. Thanks to the application of the public order clause, the party is given the opportunity to perform a specific action that it could not have performed on the basis of foreign law. For example, if the law of a state does not allow its citizens to marry foreigners, those forbidding provisions will not be applied by Polish authority, therefore granting the citizen of this country right to

---

202. M. Sośniak in: M. Sośniak, B. Walaszek, E. Wierzbowski (eds), Międzynarodowe prawo rodzinne, Wydawnictwo PAN, Wrocław-Warszawa-Kraków 1969, p. 36.
203. M. Sośniak, *Klauzula porządku publicznego w prawie międzynarodowym prywatnym*, Państwowe Wydawnictwo Naukowe, Warszawa 1961, pp. 187–190.
204. The Convention for the Protection of Human Rights and Fundamental Freedoms opened for signature in Rome on 4 Nov. 1950, Dz. U. 1993 nr 61 poz. 284.
205. OJ C 326, 26.10.2012, pp. 391–407.
206. M. Zachariasiewicz, *Klauzula porządku publicznego jako instrument ochrony materialnoprawnych interesów i wartości fori*, Wydawnictwo C. H. Beck, Warszawa 2018, pp. 324–325 and 342–345.
207. M. Sośniak, *Klauzula porządku publicznego w prawie międzynarodowym prywatnym*, Państwowe Wydawnictwo Naukowe, Warszawa 1961, pp. 133–135.
208. M. Zachariasiewicz in: M. Pazdan (ed.), *System prawa prywatnego. Tom 20A. Prawo prywatne międzynarodowe*, Wydawnictwo C. H. Beck, Warszawa 2014, p. 499.

marry a foreigner. On the other hand, 'prohibiting effect' will occur when non-application of foreign law will worsen the situation of the party. In other words, under foreign law, the party has certain rights, which, however, will not be able to exercise, because it would result in effects inconsistent with Polish public policy. For example, if the foreigner, according to his national law, is allowed to enter into polygamic marriage, Polish authority will allow him to marry, but only if he is unmarried and if he is not, then he will not be allowed to enter into another marriage.[209]

148. The law on civil status records[210] also contains a couple of provisions concerning public policy clause. According to Article 103 the head of the registry office refuses to register the event if the registration of the event would be contrary to the fundamental principles of Polish legal order. Similar provision concerns the transcription of civil status record. Pursuant to Article 107 the head of the registry office refuses to make a transcription if it would be contrary to the fundamental principles of Polish legal order.[211]

149. Provisions on public policy clause are also included in CPC.[212] According to Article 1135 §2 (1) Polish court may refuse to take evidence or deliver a document at the request of courts and other authorities of foreign countries, if this would be contrary to the fundamental principles of the Polish legal order. Article 1146 §1 (7) CPC states that the judgment shall not be recognized if its recognition would be contrary to the fundamental principles of the legal order of Poland.[213] Similar provision, Article 1152 CPC, concerns a settlement in civil cases concluded before courts and other authorities of foreign countries and stipulates that their enforceability is not to be found if they are contrary to the fundamental principles of the legal order in Poland. Finally, pursuant to Article 1206 §1 (2) CPC an arbitration award is set aside when the court finds that it is inconsistent with the fundamental principles of Polish legal order of.[214]

150. Public policy clause can be found in all EU regulations adopted in the field of PIL and in multilateral conventions ratified by Poland, for example Article 7 of

209. M. Sośniak, *Klauzula porządku publicznego w prawie międzynarodowym prywatnym*, Państwowe Wydawnictwo Naukowe, Warszawa 1961, pp. 210–212.

210. Act of 28 Nov. 2014 – Law on civil status records, Dz. U. 2014 poz. 1741.

211. *See* J. Gajda, *Klauzula porządku publicznego w prawie o aktach stanu cywilnego z 29 września 1986 r. oraz z 28 listopada 2014 r.*, Administracja: teoria, dydaktyka, praktyka 2015, nr 4, pp. 5–46; M. Wojewoda, *Transkrypcja aktu stanu cywilnego sporządzonego za granicą*, KPP 2009, nr 4, pp. 1089–1124; M. Zachariasiewicz, *Transkrypcja aktów urodzenia dzieci par jednopłciowych*, Studia Prawno-Ekonomiczne 2019, t. CXI, pp. 143–170.

212. Act of 17 Nov. 1964 – Civil Procedure Code, Dz. U. 1964 nr 43 poz. 296.

213. *See* K. Zawada, *Klauzula porządku publicznego w międzynarodowym postępowaniu cywilnym (na tle orzecznictwa Sądu Najwyższego w sprawach z zakresu prawa rodzinnego i spadkowego)*, Nowe Prawo 1979, nr 5, pp. 73–79.

214. *See* M. Zachariasiewicz, *Klauzula porządku publicznego jako podstawa odmowy uznania lub wykonania orzeczenia sądu polubownego w polskim prawie arbitrażowym na tle prawnoporównawczym*, PPPM 2010, t. 6, p. 61–114; M. Pilich, *Klauzula porządku publicznego w postępowaniu o uznanie i wykonanie zagranicznego orzeczenia arbitrażowego*, KPP 2003, z. 1, pp. 157–187.

Hague Convention (1961) on the conflicts of laws relating to the form of testamentary dispositions[215] or Article 10 of Hague Convention (1971) on the law applicable to traffic accidents.[216] In some bilateral agreements that Poland is a party to are included provision on refusal to recognize or enforce a judgment on the grounds that it is contrary to fundamental principles of public order of the contracting state, for example, Article 20 (f) in the bilateral agreement with China.[217]

151. The public order clause has the broadest application in the fields of family and inheritance law, which is also evident in the jurisprudence of Polish courts.[218]

152. The court for example decided that the provision of the foreigner's national law providing for the prohibition of marrying people of other nationality cannot be applied in Poland due to its contradiction to the fundamental principles of Polish public order.[219]

153. Public policy clause has been recently evoked also in the cases involving registering children born out of surrogacy arrangements in Polish civil register and transcription of the foreign birth certificates with two people of the same sex entered into certificate as child's parents. Some authors agree with the use of public policy clause in those cases, others criticized it.[220]

154. As an example of the use of public policy clause in the field on international civil procedure is the judgment in which the foreign judgment on divorce was not recognized. The reason for that was that the dissolution of the marriage was a

---

215. Dz. U. 1969 nr 34 poz. 284.
216. Dz. U. 2003 nr 63 poz. 585.
217. Dz. U. 1988 r. nr 9 poz. 65.
218. *See* J. Cieszewski, *Zakazy i ograniczenia małżeństw z cudzoziemcami a klauzula porządku publicznego*, Państwo i Prawo 1984, z. 3, pp. 90–101; A. Mączyński, *Działanie klauzuli porządku publicznego w sprawach dotyczących zawarcia małżeństwa z cudzoziemcami* in: E. Łętowska (ed.), *Proces i prawo. Rozprawy prawnicze, Zakład Narodowy im.* Ossolińskich, Wrocław 1989, pp. 157–167; K. Zawada, *Klauzula porządku publicznego w prawie prywatnym międzynarodowym (na tle orzecznictwa Sądu Najwyższego w sprawach z zakresu prawa rodzinnego i spadkowego)*, Nowe Prawo 1979, Nr 4, pp. 71–84; M. Gocek, *Podstawowe zagadnienia zastosowania klauzuli porządku publicznego w orzecznictwie Sądu Najwyższego*, Rejent 2005, nr 6, pp. 56–73; E. Kamarad, *Zastosowanie klauzuli porządku publicznego w sprawach dotyczących zawarcia małżeństwa – wybrane zagadnienia*, PWPM 2012, vol. 10, pp. 106–118.
219. Resolution of Supreme Court 20 Jan. 1983, III CZP 37/82.
220. M. Pilich, *Mater semper certa est? Kilka uwag o skutkach zagranicznego macierzyństwa zastępczego z perspektywy stosowania klauzuli porządku publicznego*, PWPM 2018, vol. XVI, pp. 7–37; A. Wysocka-Bar, *Nabycia polskiego obywatelstwa a urodzenie przez matkę zastępczą – uwagi na tle wyroków Naczelnego Sądu Administracyjnego z 6 maja 2015 r., sygnatura akt: II OSK 2372/13 oraz II OSK 2419/13*, PWPM 2018, vol. XVI, pp. 38–54; P. Mostowik, *Problem obywatelstwa dziecka prawdopodobnie pochodzącego od obywatela polskiego niebędącego mężem surrogate mother. Uwagi aprobujące wyroki NSA z 6 maja 2015 r. (II OSK 2372/13 i II OSK 2419/13)*, PWPM 2018, vol. XVI, pp. 55–75; M. Wojewoda, *Uznanie rozstrzygnięć organów państw obcych a przesłanki transkrypcji zagranicznych aktów stanu cywilnego*, Studia Prawno-Ekonomiczne 2018, t. CIX, pp. 159–172.

result of the husband's unilateral declaration, without taking into account the position of the wife, which contradicts the principle of the durability of the marriage and the equality of spouses, which is one of the fundamental principles of Polish family law.[221]

155. There were also examples of judgments in which the public policy clause was used incorrectly. For example, in the judgment the court decided not to allow a marriage between a Polish woman and a foreigner, as the national law of the foreigner allowed polygamy, the lack of equality between a woman and a man in a marriage, a great ease of dissolution of a marriage by a man and the lack of any maintenance guarantees by the ex-husband for the ex-wife in the event of dissolution of marriage. [222] This judgment was criticized by the representatives of the doctrine, who argued that the unfavourable legal status of a Polish citizen under the foreigner's national law after marriage did not justify invoking the public order clause in order to prevent this marriage.[223]

156. Outside the field of family law, the public policy clause has been evoked by the courts much less often. There was also a decision in which the court stated that a foreign court decision excluding inheritance between divorced spouses is not contrary to the fundamental principles of the Polish legal system. [224] In other judgments the court found that the provisions of civil law expressing the principle of *pacta sunt servanda*[225] and guaranteeing compensation for damage under *ex delicto* and *ex contractu* liability[226] belong to the basic principles of the Polish legal system.

§8. Overriding Mandatory Rules

157. Overriding mandatory rules (Polish *przepisy wymuszające swoją właściwość*, French *lois d'application immédiate*, German *Eingriffsnormen*) are relatively new concept in Polish PIL. They were regulated neither in the PILA 1926, nor in the PILA 1965. Nonetheless, before 2011 they were defined by the Polish doctrine as provisions of key importance for the protection of public order in the state, which due to their purpose or nature are applicable irrespective of the law applicable to the given situation.[227]

---

221. Decision of Court of Appeal in Katowice of 20 Aug. 2009, I ACa 410/09.
222. Resolution of Supreme Court of 22 Jun. 1972, III CZP 34/72.
223. *See* K. Zawada, *Klauzula porządku publicznego w prawie prywatnym międzynarodowym (na tle orzecznictwa Sądu Najwyższego w sprawach z zakresu prawa rodzinnego i spadkowego)*, Nowe Prawo 1979, Nr 4, pp. 81–83; K. Pietrzykowski, *Zawarcie małżeństwa i przesłanki jego ważności w prawie prywatnym międzynarodowym*, Warszawa 1985, pp. 55–58.
224. Decision of Supreme Court of 26 Feb. 2003, II CK 13/03.
225. Judgment of Supreme Court of 11 Aug. 2005, V CK 86/05.
226. Judgment of Supreme Court of 15 Mar. 2012, I CSK 286/11.
227. *See* discussions on the applicability of a special inheritance regime concerning an agricultural land located in Poland, even if foreign law was applicable to the succession case: M. Tomaszewski, *Przepisy szczególne o dziedziczeniu gospodarstw rolnych a prawo prywatne międzynarodowe*, PiP 1970, nr 12, p. 925; M. Pazdan, *Glosa do uchwały Sądu Najwyższego – Izba Cywilna z 28 maja*

158. Currently PILA 2011 also does not consist of a legal definition of overriding mandatory rules, but there are some provisions on how they should be applied. Those provisions distinguish between overriding mandatory rules of Polish and foreign overriding mandatory rules.

159. According to Article 8(1) PILA the designation of a foreign applicable law does not prevent the application of the rules of Polish law, if it clearly results from their content or purpose that they should be applied to a given legal relationship irrespective of the law otherwise applicable.

160. Pursuant to Article 8(2) PILA when applying the law determined under PILA, effect may be given to mandatory rules of another state whit which the considered legal relationship has a close connection, if under the law of that state the rules in question should be applied irrespective of the law otherwise applicable to that legal relationship. In considering whether to give effect to these provisions, regard shall be had to their nature and purpose and to the consequences of their application or non-application.

161. The regulation on overriding mandatory rules in the Article 8 PILA 2011 is based on the Article 7 of the 1980 Rome Convention on the law applicable to contractual obligations.[228] Therefore, this definition is different from the one included in Rome I Regulation,[229] if it comes to giving effect to the overriding mandatory provisions of the third country (Article 9(3) Rome I Regulation). Article 8(2) PILA 2011 allows to give an effect to the mandatory provisions of the law of another country with which the given legal relationship has a close connection, even if those provisions are not a part of the law of the country where the obligations arising out of the contract have to be or have been performed and even if they do not render the performance of the contract unlawful. In other words, the possibility of application the overriding mandatory provisions of the third country upon Article 8(2) PILA 2011 is much broader than the one given by the Article 9(3) Rome I Regulation.[230]

162. While applying Article 8(1) PILA it is important to determine which Polish imperative provisions fall into the category of overriding mandatory provisions. According to Article 8(1) such a determination should arise undoubtedly from the content or the purpose of the relevant provisions. Establishing that a particular imperative provision is primarily intended to protect the public interest will strongly support its overriding feature, especially when only granting it such character will

1969 r. (III CZP 23/69), Orzecznictwo Sądów Powszechnych i Komisji Aritrażowych 1970, item. 196, p. 424 and A. Mączyński, *Glosa do uchwały Sądu Najwyższego – Izba Cywilna z 28 maja 1969 r. (III CZP 23/69)*, Nowe Prawo 1970, nr 12, p. 1862.

228. M. Czepelak, *Międzynarodowe prawo zobowiązań Unii Europejskiej*, Warszawa 2012, p. 485.

229. Regulation (EC) No 593/2008 of the European Parliament and of the Council of 17 Jun. 2008 on the law applicable to contractual obligations (Rome I), OJ L 177, 4.7.2008, pp. 6–16.

230. M. A. Zachariasiewicz in: M. Pazdan (ed.), *Prawo prywatne międzynarodowe. Komentarz*, Wydawnictwo C. H. Beck, Warszawa 2018, p. 164.

ensure that that provision has maximum effectiveness in international cooperation.[231] However, overriding mandatory provisions can include also norms serving merely or predominantly private interests. As an example of such provisions those that providing protection to 'weaker' party of civil law relations can be given.[232]

163. So far in Poland there is rather limited case law on the overriding mandatory provisions. There is a judgment in which the court confirmed that the provisions of Polish Civil Code (CC)[233] – Article 359 §2^3 on maximal interest in capital and Article 481 §2^3 on maximal interest for delay – should be treated as overriding mandatory provisions, as they state that contractual clauses may not exclude or limit the provisions on maximum interest for delay, also in the event of a choice of foreign law, and if they do – the provisions of the CC apply.[234] Moreover, in the literature it was suggest that abovementioned provisions of CC apply not only in the case of choice of foreign law made by the parties, as it is literally stated in the text of the provisions, but also in the case when the foreign law was indicated by the conflict-of-law rule of PILA, other national legal act or EU Regulation Rome I.[235]

§9. Evasion of Law

164. The evasion of law (Polish *obejście prawa, fraude à la loi, Gesetzesumgehun*) is traditionally associated with conflict of laws in family matters. This is because the concept of the evasion of law refers to mandatory provisions, which are quite common in substantive family law, for example, rules on capacity to marry, on form of marriage or admissibility and consequences of divorce.

165. There are no regulations governing evasion of law in Polish PIL. The concept of evasion of law was thus defined by the representatives of the Polish doctrine of PIL.[236] It is understood as the party's behaviour to avoid the consequences of the application of the law that would be otherwise applicable in a given situation. This behaviour of the party can manifest itself in linking the legal relationship with another system legal in such a way that, with the application of the conflict-of-law rules, norms belonging to this legal system are indicated as law applicable to this legal relationship.[237]

---

231. M. Mataczyński, *Przepisy wymuszające swoje zastosowanie – wybrane zagadnienia*, PPPM 2016, t. 18, pp. 62–63.
232. K. Pacuła, *Przepisy wymuszające swoje zastosowanie jako instrument ochrony „strony słabszej" umowy ubezpieczenia*, PPPM 2014, t. 15, pp. 31–48.
233. Act of 23 Apr. 1964 – Civil Code, Dz. U. 1964 nr 16 poz. 93.
234. Judgment of the Supreme Court of 6 Apr. 2017, III CSK 174/16.
235. M. Czepelak, *Międzynarodowe prawo zobowiązań Unii Europejskiej*, LexisNexis, Warszawa 2012, p. 489.
236. K. Przybyłowski, *Prawo prywatne międzynarodowe. Część ogólna*, Księgarnia Gubrynowicza i syna, Lwów 1935, pp. 157–163; Walaszek, B., Sośniak, M., *Międzynarodowe prawo prywatne. Część ogólna*, Uniwersytet Jagielloński, Kraków 1965, pp. 109–114; J. Balicki, *Międzynarodowe prawo prywatne*, Uniwersytet Marii Curie-Skłodowskiej, Lublin 1976, pp. 72–75.
237. M. Jagielska in: M. Pazdan (ed.), *System Prawa Prywatnego. Tom 20 A. Prawo prywatne międzynarodowe*, Wydawnictwo C. H. Beck, Warszawa 2014, pp. 426–427.

166. Therefore, circumvention of the law takes place when the conflict-of-law rule requires that a given law be applied as applicable, but it is not applied because of the activity of the parties that have taken specific actions for this purpose. Parties can in such a way, cause non-application of *lex fori* in favour of the foreign law or, on the contrary, cause non-application of the foreign law in favour of *lex fori*. It is also possible to cause application of the foreign law instead of application of the foreign law of another state. Usually the first situation is the most presented in literature. It also causes a stricter reaction from the courts, as it aims at excluding the application of *lex fori*.[238]

167. If the court finds that the law has been circumvented, it should, in principle apply the law that would be applicable had the parties not acted in order to form the basis for the application of another law. In such situation, the court should consider not only the actions of the parties and their intention, but also the structure of the conflict-of-law norm. If for a given situation, it is possible to choose the law applicable or indication of the applicable law is an alternative connection or is based on the connecting factor, which is not permanent (e.g., habitual residence), then the action of the parties should be rated as less objectionable.[239]

168. Moreover, it can happen that the effect bypassing the law may be consistent with *lex fori*. Such a situation may take place when the parties, by the evasion of law, cause non-application of the discriminatory provisions, which would have been blocked by the court anyway by evoking the public policy clause. For example, the parties will get married in a country where *lex loci celebrationis matrimonii* governs the capacity to marry, instead of the national law of the spouses, because the law of their country of origin does not allow concluding interfaith or interracial marriages.

169. As already mentioned, evasion of law is not regulated in the PILA 2011. However, the provision on the circumvention of law was provided for in the act on the conflict of laws between the districts[240] of 1926. Pursuant to Article 2 of this act, the persons changing their place of residence were subject to the new law in the matters of legal capacity, family relations and inheritance only after one year. *Ratio legis* of this provision was to make it difficult to circumvent the law by changing the place of residence in order to cause the application of the more favourable law.[241]

---

238. K. Przybyłowski, *Prawo prywatne międzynarodowe. Część ogólna*, Księgarnia Gubrynowicza i syna, Lwów 1935, pp. 157–159.
239. M. Jagielska in: M. Pazdan (ed.), *System Prawa Prywatnego. Tom 20 A. Prawo prywatne międzynarodowe*, Wydawnictwo C. H. Beck, Warszawa 2014, p. 433.
240. Act of 2 Aug. 1926 on the Law Applicable to Internal Private Relations, Dz. U. 1926 nr 101 poz. 580.
241. F. Zoll, *Międzynarodowe prawo prywatne w zarysie*, Księgarnia Powszechna, Kraków 1947, pp. 44–45.

170. PILA 1926[242] also contained the provision on evasion of law. Article 17(2) stated that if the spouses changed citizenship in order to get the divorce, the fact that was a ground for a divorce according to new applicable law (e.g., infidelity) could be taken into account only if it justified the divorce also in accordance with the law applicable prior to this change.[243]

171. So far, no decision has been issued by the Polish court in which it would invoke the doctrine of evasion of law in order to apply another law.

§10. References to the Law of States with Multiple Legal Orders

172. The phenomenon of multiple legal orders can manifest itself in two ways. First, there may be a situation where different legal norms apply in different territorial units within one state. Such a situation occurs in countries where federal states or districts have autonomous competence to legislate (e.g., in the USA, Spain). Second, different legal norms may apply to different categories of people, for example, due to their religious affiliation or social position.

173. In such situation indication of the law of a state as the law applicable does not provide an answer as to which law should actually be applied to a given situation. Because of that additional solutions are needed. PILA 2011 includes special provision on situations in which the conflict-of-law rule refers to the law of a state with multiple legal orders. According to Article 9 if, in the state whose law is applicable, there are different legal systems in force, the law of that state determines which of the legal systems should apply. Therefore, the relevant internal conflict-of-law rules of the state whose law is indicated as applicable should be applied, delimiting the spheres of application of the substantive rules of this law.

174. Article 9 PILA also states that if there is no such determination in *lex causae*, the legal system that has the closest connection with the legal relationship in question applies. This means that, having regard to all the circumstances of the case, it is necessary to consider which legal system the situation is most closely related to.[244]

175. Similar solutions were provided in PIL acts that were previously in force in Poland. In PILA 1926 there was Article 37 and in PILA 1965 – Article 5.[245]

---

242. Act of 2 Aug. 1926 on the Law Applicable to International Private Relations, Dz. U. 1926 nr 101 poz. 581.
243. *See* K. Przybyłowski, *Prawo prywatne międzynarodowe. Część ogólna*, Księgarnia Gubrynowicza i syna, Lwów 1935, pp. 147–151; F. Zoll, *Międzynarodowe prawo prywatne w zarysie*, Księgarnia Powszechna, Kraków 1947, p. 93.
244. W. Popiołek in: M Pazdan (ed.), *System Prawa Prywatnego. Tom 20 A. Prawo prywatne międzynarodowe*, Wydawnictwo C. H. Beck, Warszawa 2014, pp. 389–390.
245. K. Przybyłowski, *Prawo prywatne międzynarodowe. Część ogólna*, Księgarnia Gubrynowicza i syna, Lwów 1935, pp. 159–161; F. Zoll, *Międzynarodowe prawo prywatne w zarysie*, Księgarnia

176. Apart from PILA 2011, provisions on the law of states with multiple legal orders can be found both in EU regulations and in international agreements. There are special provisions in Rome I Regulation[246] (Article 22) and Rome II Regulation (Article 25).[247] The Succession Regulation[248] contains two provisions on the law of states with multiple legal orders: Article 36 for interlocal conflicts and Article 37 to interpersonal ones. Similar solution was used in Hague Protocol (2007).[249] Article 16 concerns territorially non-unified legal systems and Article 17 – systems of law applicable to different categories of persons.

177. Provisions on the states with multiple legal orders can be found also in international agreements, which Poland is a party to. Usually those provisions state that every territorial entity forming part of a state having a non-unified legal system should be considered as a state for the purposes of application of the conflict-of-law rules of the Convention, for example, in Article 12 Hague Convention on Traffic Accidents (1971)[250] and in Articles 31–32 Hague Convention on child abduction[251] (1980). Sometimes other solutions can be found, like the rule that the law applicable should be determined by the rules in force in that system, for example, in Article 1 Hague Convention on Form of Wills (1961)[252] or requirement of the direct application of the law of a territorial unit determined according to the connecting factor provided for in the convention (e.g., any reference to habitual residence in that state should be understood as referring to habitual residence in a territorial unit of that state), for example, in Article 36 Hague Convention on intercountry adoption (1993).[253]

Powszechna, Kraków 1947, p. 93; B. Walaszek, M. Sośniak, *Międzynarodowe prawo prywatne. Część ogólna*, Uniwersytet Jagielloński, Kraków 1965, p. 96–100.

246. Regulation (EC) No 593/2008 of the European Parliament and of the Council of 17 Jun. 2008 on the law applicable to contractual obligations (Rome I), OJ L 177, 4.7.2008, pp. 6–16.
247. Regulation (EC) No 864/2007 of the European Parliament and of the Council of 11 Jul. 2007 on the law applicable to non-contractual obligations (Rome II), OJ L 199, 31.7.2007, pp. 40–49.
248. Regulation (EU) No 650/2012 of the European Parliament and of the Council of 4 Jul. 2012 on jurisdiction, applicable law, recognition and enforcement of decisions and acceptance and enforcement of authentic instruments in matters of succession and on the creation of a European Certificate of Succession, OJ 2012 L 201, pp. 107–134.
249. The text of the Protocol is an annex to 2009/941/EC: Council Decision of 30 Nov. 2009 on the conclusion by the European Community of the Hague Protocol of 23 Nov. 2007 on the Law Applicable to Maintenance Obligations, OJ L 331, 16.12.2009, pp. 17–23.
250. Dz. U. 2003 nr 63 poz. 585.
251. Dz. U. 1995 nr 108 poz. 528.
252. Dz. U. 1969 nr 34 poz. 284.
253. Dz. U. 2000 nr 39 poz. 448.

Part II. Conflict-of-Law Rules

Chapter 1. Persons

§1. Natural Persons

I. Legal Capacity

178. Pursuant to Article 11(1) PILA legal capacity of the natural person and his or her capacity to effect juridical acts shall be subject to the law of his or her nationality.[254] However, there are many exceptions to this rule. The first one is set in Article 11 (2), which states that if the natural person enters into a juridical act within the scope of his or her business activity, it shall be sufficient that his or her capacity be governed by the law of the country where his or her place of business is situated.[255]

179. The second exception is regulated in Article 11(3), which deals with specific legal capacity, *id est* specific capacity requirements for certain types of legal acts. This provision states that the Article 11(1) does not exclude the application of the law governing the juridical act, if this law establishes specific requirements as to the capacity to make such an act. This means that for the specific requirements relating to the capacity to perform a specific juridical act, the provisions of the law applicable to this legal action should apply, which take precedence over the law applicable to general legal capacity determined under Article 11 (1), for example, in the case of entering into marriage or acknowledgement of a child.[256]

180. The third exception is set in Article 12 PILA, which is a deviation from the general rule in favour of the law of the place of legal transaction (*lex loci actus*). Article 12 (1) provides for *Lizardi* rule. It states that if the contract is concluded between persons present in the same state, a natural person who would have capacity under the law of that state may invoke his or her incapacity resulting from the law specified in Article 11(1), only if at the time of entering into the contract the

254. On legal capacity under PILA 1965: M. Pazdan, *Zdolność do czynności prawnych osób fizycznych w polskim prawie prywatnym międzynarodowym*, Zeszyty Naukowe Uniwersytetu Jagiellońskiego, Kraków 1967.

255. M. Pazdan in: M. Pazdan (ed.), *System Prawa Prywatnego. Tom 20 A. Prawo prywatne międzynarodowe*, Wydawnictwo C. H. Beck, Warszawa 2014, pp. 604–605.

256. M. Pazdan in: M. Pazdan (ed.), *System Prawa Prywatnego. Tom 20 A. Prawo prywatne międzynarodowe*, Wydawnictwo C. H. Beck, Warszawa 2014, pp. 609–610.

other party was aware of that incapacity, or was not aware thereof as a result of negligence. Article 12 (2) provides for the similar solution for the unilateral judicial act. It states that a natural person is making a unilateral juridical act who would have capacity under the law of the state in which the judicial act was made, may invoke his or her incapacity under the law specified in Article 11(1) only if this does not adversely affect anyone, who despite having acted diligently, was convinced that the person making the judicial act had the capacity. If a natural person acts through a representative, it is the circumstances on the part of the representative that decide about the prerequisites of the application of Article 12(1) and (2). A similar exception to the general rule of the law applicable to legal capacity is provided for in Article 13 Rome I Regulation.[257]

181. If an incapacity is invoked pursuant to Article 12 (1) or (2), the consequences of the incapacity must be assessed according to the law indicated by the conflict-of-law rule in Article 11 (1) PILA, that is, according to the national law of the person concerned.[258] The provisions contained in Article12(1) and (2) PILA do not apply to juridical acts relating to family, guardianship and succession law, or to transfers concerning immovable property located elsewhere than in the state in which the juridical act was made.

182. The fourth group of exceptions concern legal capacity in the case of specific legal actions, namely capacity to enter into a marriage (Article 48 PILA), capacity to inherit (Articles 21, 22 and 23(2)(c) of Succession Regulation[259]), capacity of the person making the disposition of property upon death to make such a disposition (Articles 24, 25 and 26(1)(a) of Succession Regulation), capacity to incur bill obligations (Article 77 of Bills of Exchange Law[260]) and capacity to incur cheque obligations (Article 62 of Cheque law[261]) (*see* Part II., Chapter 2, §2., IX., A. and B.).

183. PILA also contains separate conflict-of-law rules indicating the law applicable to incapacitation, presumption of death or a declaration of the death of a natural person. Pursuant to Article 13(1) the legal incapacitation of a natural person is governed by the law of his or her nationality. Similarly, according to Article 14(1) the presumption of death or the declaration of the death of a natural person is governed by the law of his or her nationality. Articles 13(2) and 14(2) PILA state that if the Polish court decides about the legal incapacitation, the presumption of death or the declaration of death of a foreign citizen, Polish law applies. Such a case may

257. Regulation (EC) No 593/2008 of the European Parliament and of the Council of 17 Jun. 2008 on the law applicable to contractual obligations (Rome I), OJ L 177, 4.7.2008, pp. 6–16.
258. M. Pazdan in: M. Pazdan (ed.), *System Prawa Prywatnego. Tom 20 A. Prawo prywatne międzynarodowe*, Wydawnictwo C. H. Beck, Warszawa 2014, p. 608.
259. Regulation (EU) No 650/2012 of the European Parliament and of the Council of 4 July 2012 on jurisdiction, applicable law, recognition and enforcement of decisions and acceptance and enforcement of authentic instruments in matters of succession and on the creation of a European Certificate of Succession, OJ 2012 L 201, p. 107.
260. Act of 28 Apr. 1936 – Bill of Exchange Law, Dz. U. 1936 nr 37 poz. 282.
261. Act of 28 Apr. 1936 – Cheque Law, Dz. U. 1936 nr 37 poz. 283.

be decided by the Polish court when the foreigner had the last place of residence or the last place of habitual residence in Poland, when the case shows a sufficient connection with the Polish legal order, or if the death took place in Poland.[262] The scope of the rule of Article 14 (1) PILA should be understood broadly, as it covers institutions similar to the presumption of death or the declaration of the death, *id est* recognition as missing or absent.

184. Conflict-of-law rules on legal capacity, the legal incapacitation, the presumption of death and the declaration of death are also included in some of bilateral agreements to which Poland is a party. In this respect, they most often provide for the application of national law in these matters.[263]

185. Poland is also a party to Hague Convention Deprivation of Civil Rights (1905)[264] since 23 August 1929.[265] Poland has also signed Convention on the Protection of Adults (2000),[266] but has not yet ratified it.

II. Name

186. There was no conflict-of-law rule in PILA 1965 regarding the law applicable to a name of a person. In legal science it was assumed that the name and surname should be governed by the national law of a given person.[267] The discrepancies concerned the issue of the law applicable to the acquisition and change of surname as a result of family law events, such as marriage or divorce.[268] Hence, a separate conflict-of-law rule has been added to the new PILA.[269]

187. Pursuant to Article 15(1) PILA the name and surname of a natural person is governed by the national law of the concerned person. The applicable law indicated by the above-mentioned conflict-of-law rule determines whether the right to

---

262. Article 1106 CPC.
263. M. Pazdan in: M. Pazdan (ed.), *Prawo prywatne międzynarodowe. Komentarz*, Wydawnictwo C. H. Beck, Warszawa 2018, pp. 189–190, pp. 190–191, p. 194.
264. Convention du 17 juillet 1905 concernant l'interdiction et les mesures de protection analogues.
265. Dz. U. 1929 nr 80 poz. 598.
266. Convention of 13 Jan. 2000 on the International Protection of Adults.
267. E. Wierzbowski in: M. Sośniak, B. Walaszek, E. Wierzbowski (eds), Międzynarodowe prawo rodzinne, Wydawnictwo PAN, Wrocław-Warszawa-Kraków 1969, pp. 88–91; P. Wypych, *Prawo właściwe dla nabycia i zmiany nazwiska* in: P. Kasprzyk (ed.) *Prawo rodzinne w Polsce i Europie*. Zagadnienia wybrane, Lublin 2005, p. 570.
268. M. Pazdan, *Nazwisko w prawie prywatnym międzynarodowym* in: P. Machnikowski, J. Gołaczyński (eds), Współczesne problemy prawa prywatnego. Księga pamiątkowa ku czci Profesora Edwarda Gniewka, Warszawa 2010; A. Mączyński, *Kolizyjna problematyka nazwiska* in: J. Gudowski, K. Weitz (eds), *Aurea praxis, aurea teoria*. Księga pamiątkowa ku czci Profesora Tadeusza Erecińskiego, t.2, Warszawa 2011.
269. F. Nowak, *Kilka uwag na temat wskazania prawa właściwego dla imienia i nazwiska osoby fizycznej w ustawie z dnia 4 lutego 2011 r. – Prawo prywatne międzynarodowe*, Metryka 2015, nr 1, pp. 79–100.

have a name is treated as a subjective right, what features it has and what rights and obligations a given person has in connection with this right.[270]

188. In accordance with Article 15(2) PILA the acquisition or alternation of a name or surname is governed by the law applicable to the consequences of an event that leads to this acquisition or alternation. Therefore, Article 51 PILA concerns the impact of entering into marriage on the names of future spouses; Article 54 determines the effect of divorce on the surname of ex-spouses; Article 55 PILA regulates the impact of the determination of child's filiation on the child's name, and Article 57 PILA determines the impact of the adoption on the adoptee's name. However, the choice of surname (if such possibility exits) made by the spouse or ex-spouse at the time of concluding or terminating marriage are governed by the law of the nationality of each of the spouses.

III. Nationality/Habitual Residence/Domicile

189. According to the rule of public international law, the nationality of a natural person is to be determined according to the law of the state which nationality is being ascertained.[271] Such rule is also present in the Hague Convention on Certain Questions relating to the Conflict of Nationality Laws (1930) to which Poland is a party since 1934.[272] In the field of PIL, nationality is therefore indicated according to the *lex causae*, that is, the law of the presumable nationality. Nationality serves as a connecting factor in numerous conflict-of-law rules included in PILA, for example, Article 11(1) on person's legal capacity; Article 13(1) on the legal incapacitation of ta natural person; Article 14(1) on a presumption of death or a declaration of the death of a natural person; Article 15(1) on the name and the surname of a natural person; Article 16(1) on the personal rights of a natural person; Article 48 on the capacity to marry; Article 51(1) on the personal relations between spouses and the matrimonial property regime; Article 54(1) on the termination of marriage; Article 55(1) on the determination and challenge of the child's filiation; Article 57(1) on adoption and Article 60(1) on establishing a guardianship, curatorship or other protective measures for an adult. If the person has multiple nationalities, indication of the applicable law may be problematic. Article 2 PILA provides a solution for this problem (*see* Part I., Chapter 2, §4., II).

190. Domicile is treated as an autonomous concept of PIL, the interpretation of which under PILA is separate from the interpretation of this concept in substantive law. It is assumed that a person has a domicile in the state where he or she resides with the intention of permanent residence. Domicile is used as an additional connecting factor in some conflict-of-law rules in PILA: for example, Article 49(2) on formal validity of a marriage concluded outside Poland; Article 52(1) on choice of

270. K. Mikša, *Nazwisko w prawie prywatnym międzynarodowym*, Technika IT, Gliwice 2015, p. 149.
271. M. Pilich, *Zasada obywatelstwa w prawie prywatnym międzynarodowym. Zagadnienia podstawowe*, Wolters Kluwer Polska, Warszawa 2015, pp. 115–132.
272. Dz. U. 1937 nr 47 poz. 361.

law applicable to matrimonial property regime; Article 54(2) on the termination of marriage; Article 57(2) on the adoption by a married couple. It is also used as an alternative connecting factor when the nationality fails to serve its function (*see below*).

191. In the field of PIL, a person has habitual residence in a country where his or her life activity is cantered in a given period. In the PILA habitual residence plays either a subsidiary role for the other two personal connecting factors (e.g., Article 3(1) on stateless persons; Article 49(2) on formal validity of a marriage concluded outside Poland; Article 51(2) on the personal relations between spouses and the matrimonial property regime; Article 54(2) on the termination of marriage; Article 57(2) on the adoption by a married couple) or is used as a sole connecting factor (e.g., Article 16(3) on the infringement of a natural person's personal rights in the media; Article 24(2) on the making a juridical act; Article 32(2) in the obligation resulting out of a unilateral juridical act; Article 53(1) on a special rule aimed at protecting the good faith of third parties entering into relations with a spouse or spouses; Article 56(2) and Article 59(2), both on the transfer of child's habitual residence to another state and its influence on, respectively, the law applicable to parental authority and access to child and the law applicable to guardianship or curatorship.

IV. Stateless Persons and Refugees

192. Pursuant to Article 3(1) PILA if the conflict-of-law rule provides for the applicability of the law of nationality and it is not possible to establish the nationality of a given person, or if he or she does not have the nationality of any state (stateless person), then the law of the state in which the given person is domiciled applies. If the person does not have domicile, then the law of the state in which he or she has habitual residence applies. This provision applies to stateless persons, who did not acquire citizenship at birth or who lost their previous citizenship and did not acquire a new one.

193. With regard to refugees, who formally hold nationality but have left their country of origin, Article 3(2) applies. It states that with respect to a person who has been afforded protection in a state other than the state of his or her nationality, and whose links with the latter state have been permanently broken, as a result of violation of the fundamental human rights therein.

V. Transsexuals

194. There is no provision on transsexuality in PILA. It is most likely related to the fact that the situation of transsexual people has not yet been specifically regulated in substantive law either.

195. In Polish law there is no right to self-determination of sex. Polish law also does not provide for recognition of non-binary. From a legal point of view, gender must therefore always be determined as male or female. Changing legal sex, which is recorded in civil status register as a part of birth certificate, can be done in judicial proceeding. In the absence of separate provisions on the change of the gender as recorded in civil status register, general Article 189 CPC serves as a legal basis for it.[273] This provision says that the plaintiff having a legal interest may request the court to establish the existence or non-existence of a legal relationship or a right. The procedure currently involves filing a lawsuit against own parents for incorrect sex determination after birth. In view of the absence of a separate conflict-of-law rule it can be assumed that in such proceedings the Polish court applies *lex fori*, therefore Polish law.

196. During this proceeding, the court should ex officio appoint an expert doctor to determine whether the request to determine the sex is justified. The justification of the claims should also include elements indicating that the claimants have lived in their identified gender role for some time (so-called Real Life Test). Medical certificates as a proof of undergone hormone therapy are also very important.

197. After obtaining a favourable judgment, the court sends its content to the competent registry office, which makes an annotation in the transsexual's birth certificate. The transsexual receives a new PESEL number (national identification number used in Poland) because one of its digits indicates the sex of the person. After assigning a new PESEL number, it is necessary to replace the documents in which it is listed, for example, national ID and passport. Issuing new documents is also necessary when there is a change of the person's first name.

§2. Legal Persons

I. Incorporated Organizations

198. Pursuant to Article 17(1) PILA a legal person is governed by the law of the state, in which it has its seat. However, Article 17(2) states that if the law determined under Article 17(1) refers to the law of the state according to which the legal person has been incorporated, that law applies. Abovementioned regulation is a compromise between the two main concepts present in PIL of different countries: the seat theory and the incorporation theory. The Polish solution of *lex societatis* is therefore based on the seat theory but allows reference to the law of the state based on which the legal entity was created. The provision does not prejudge whether it is a real or statutory seat (registered office). The views of the doctrine on this subject differ[274]: some believe that when determining the seat of a legal person, the overall circumstances of a given case should be taken into account, including the

273. Resolution of Supreme Court of 22 Sep. 1995 r., III CZP 118/95.

274. *See* K. Oplustil, *Łącznik siedziby spółki w nowym Prawie Prywatnym międzynarodowym – uwagi na tle prawa europejskiego*, KPP 2011, z. 3, pp. 635–680.

registered office of the legal person and the place where the governing bodies of the legal person are permanently operating.[275] Others claim that the concept of 'seat' used in Article 17 PILA has to be understood as statutory seat.[276] There is also opinion that the real seat, *id est* the place where the management board usually conducts the company's affairs, should be decisive.[277]

199. In the bilateral agreements concluded by Poland, which regulate this matter, both solutions are used with regard to the capacity of legal persons: the provisions of some international agreements refer to the theory of the seat of a legal person, others – to the theory of the formation of a legal person.

200. PILA also contains specific provisions on legal capacity which are an exception to the principle of Article 17. In accordance with Article 18(1) PILA if a legal person makes a juridical act within the scope of its business, it suffices that it has the capacity to make such an act under the law of the state in which the business is operated. This provision applies when the legal person has permanent, additional centres of its economic activity outside the state in which its main seat is located. Article 18 (1) PILA provides for the subsidiary application of the law of the country in which the legal person is established. If a legal person fails to comply with the requirements of this law when making a juridical act, then the final assessment of the action should be made according to the law designated in accordance with the general rule, *id est* Article 17 (1) and (2) PILA.

201. Article 18(2) PILA provides for another exception from the general rule. It states that a legal person may invoke limitations as to its capacity or representation resulting from the law indicated by Article 17(1) and (2) as against the other party, if such limitations are not known under the law of the state in which the judicial act has been made, only if the other party was aware of them or was not aware thereof as a result of its negligence. This does not apply to dispositions of immovable property located in a state other than a state in which the judiciary act has been made. This provision mirrors the one that applies to natural persons (Article 12(1) and (2)). It aims at protecting the good faith of a legal person's contractor.[278]

II. Unincorporated Organizations

202. In accordance with Article 21 PILA the provisions of Article 17–20 *mutatis mutandis* apply to unincorporated entities without legal personality.

---

275. M. Pazdan, *Prawo prywatne międzynarodowe*, LexisNexis, Warszawa 2012, p. 106.
276. A. Opalski, A. Wiśniewski in: J. Poczobut (ed.), *Prawo prywatne międzynarodowe. Komentarz*, Wolters Kluwer, Warszawa 2017, p. 350; M. Mataczyński, *Seat of the company in private international law. Selected issues*, Wydawnictwo naukowe UAM, Poznań 2018, pp.11–28.
277. A. Wowerka in: M. Pazdan (ed.), *System Prawa Prywatnego. Tom 20 A. Prawo prywatne międzynarodowe*, Wydawnictwo C. H. Beck, Warszawa 2014, p. 636.
278. W. Klyta in: M. Pazdan (ed.), *Prawo prywatne międzynarodowe. Komentarz*, Wydawnictwo C. H. Beck, Warszawa 2018.

III. Scope of the Lex Societatis

203. The scope of the *lex societatis* is defined in Article 17(3) PILA. Interestingly, this is the only provision in PILA which lists matters governed by the law applicable as designated by PILA. It states that the law determined under Articles 17(1) and (2) PILA governs in particular: (1) the formation, merger, division, transformation and dissolution of a legal person; (2) the nature of a legal person; (3) the name and business name; (4) the capacity of a legal person; (5) the competences and rules of functioning, as well as appointment of the members of the corporate bodies; (6) representation; (7) the acquisition and loss of the status of a shareholder or a membership and the rights and obligations pertaining thereto; (8) the liability of the shareholders or members for the obligations of the legal person; (9) the consequences of a breach of law, the act of incorporation or the articles of association by a representative of the legal person.

IV. Liability

204. The liability of the shareholders or board members for the obligations of the legal person is governed by the law indicated by the conflict-of-law rules of Article 17(1) and (2) PILA. Therefore, it is regulated by the law of the state, in which it has its seat or if this law refers to the law of the state according to which the legal person has been incorporated – by the latter.

V. Relocation

205. The choice of the theory of the seat of a legal person when constructing a conflict-of-law rule means that the transfer of the seat of its management board essentially changes *lex societatis*.

206. According to Article 19(1) PILA upon the transfer of the seat to another state, a legal person is governed by the law of that state. The legal personality acquired under the law of the state of the previous seat is preserved if the laws of each interested states so provides. The transfer of the seat within the European Economic Area[279] does not result in the loss of legal personality.

207. Above solution is consistent with the thesis of the CJEU judgment in *Überseering* case,[280] concerning the company formed in accordance with the law of one EU Member State and having its registered office there, which transferred its actual

279. The European Economic Area is an agreement between the EU Member States and three European Free Trade Association (EFTA) states (Iceland, Liechtenstein, and Norway) that creates an internal market.

280. Case C-208/00 *Überseering BV v Nordic Construction Company Baumanagement GmbH (NCC)*, Judgment of the Court of 5 Nov. 2002.

centre of administration to another Member State under the law of that state. The court decided that the new host Member State is obliged to recognize the company legal capacity.

208. In this context it is also worth to mention a case of a Polish company *POLBUD* that was brought to the CJEU.[281] *POLBUD* was a limited liability company based in Poland. The general meeting of shareholders of this company adopted a resolution on transferring the company's seat to Luxembourg. However, it was not mentioned in this resolution that the seat of the management board of the company and the place where the company actually conducts business was also transferred to Luxembourg. The CJEU decided that the transfer of the registered office of a company formed in accordance with the law of one EU Member State to the territory of another Member State, even when there is no change in the location of the real head office of that company, is guaranteed by the freedom of establishment enshrined in the EU treaties (Article 49 TFEU). Therefore, national legislation of the EU Member State cannot make such a transfer conditional on the prior liquidation of the first company.[282]

VI. Cross-Border Transformation

209. Pursuant to Article 19(2) PILA a merger of legal persons having their seats in different states is completed if the requirements provided for in these states are cumulatively satisfied.

281. Case C-106/16 *POLBUD*, Judgment of the Court of 25 Oct. 2017.
282. *See* annotation to Judgment: G. Kozieł, Dopuszczalność i zasady przeniesienia siedziby statutowej polskiej spółki handlowej do innego państwa członkowskiego Unii Europejskiej – glosa do wyroku Trybunału Sprawiedliwości z 25.10.2017 r., C-106/16, Polbud-Wykonawstwo sp. z o.o., EPS 2018, nr 2, pp. 25–32.

Chapter 2. Obligations

§1. Contractual Obligations

210. The main source of conflict-of-law rules on obligations is Rome I Regulation.[283] Article 28(1) PILA informs that the law applicable to the contractual obligation is determined in accordance with the Rome I Regulation. Conflict-of-law rules included in the regulation apply irrespective of whether the contract is in any way connected with the EU Member State and whether those rules indicate as applicable the law of an EU Member State or of the law of a non-EU country. Therefore, the Rome I Regulation is the main source of PIL in the matter of contractual obligations, while PILA provides for conflict-of-law rules on the contractual obligations excluded from the scope of application of the Rome I Regulation.

211. In the case of the Rome I Regulation it must be noted that the Regulation is not analysed in detail in this monograph, as it is the subject of numerous publications.[284]

212. The regulation is applied in Poland starting from 17 December 2009 to contracts concluded after this date (Articles 28 and 29). Poland was a party to the 1980 Rome Convention on the law applicable to contractual obligations[285] from 1 August 2007. Therefore, for contracts concluded between 1 August 2007 and 16 December 2009 provisions of Rome Convention apply. For contracts concluded before 1 August 2007 conflict-of-law rules of PILA 1965[286] apply.

213. It should be explained that PILA never contained its own rules on contractual obligations (with some exceptions on contractual obligations falling outside the scope of Rome I Regulation mentioned below) as it entered into force on 16 May 2011, once Rome I Regulation was already applied. Its predecessor PILA 1965 contained such rule in the Articles 25–30.

214. Rome I Regulation replaced the Rome Convention in EU Member States[287] (Article 24) (*see* Part I., Chapter 1, §2).

---

283. Regulation (EC) No 593/2008 of the European Parliament and of the Council of 17 Jun. 2008 on the law applicable to contractual obligations (Rome I), OJ L 177, 4.7.2008, pp. 6–16.
284. *See* for example: U. Magnus, P. Mankowski, *European Commentaries on Private International Law. Commentary. Volume II. Rome I Regulation*, OttoSchmidt: Köln 2017; F. Garcimartín Alférez in: J. Basedow, G. Rühl, F. Ferrari, P. de Miguel Asensio (eds), *Encyclopedia of Private International Law*, Edward Elgar Publishing, Cheltenham 2017, pp. 1553–1562 and the literature cited therein.
285. Rome Convention 80/934/EEC on the law applicable to contractual obligations opened for signature in Rome on 19 Jun. 1980, OJ L 266, 9.10.1980, pp. 1–19.
286. Act of 12 Nov. 1965 Private International Law, Dz. U. 1965 nr 46 poz. 290.
287. Rome I Regulation is not applied in Denmark, which still applies Rome Convention. *See* P.A. Nielsen, *EU PIL and Denmark*, IPRax 2019, v. 5, pp. 449–452.

215. According to Article 25 the international conventions to which one or more EU Member States are parties and which lay down conflict-of-law rules relating to contractual obligations can still be applied. Therefore, it should be remembered that the conflict-of-law rules on contractual obligations included in bilateral conventions signed by Poland with non-EU states are still applied, for example, Article 36(1) of bilateral agreement between Poland and Russia.[288] However, between EU Member States the regulation takes precedence over conventions concluded exclusively between two or more of them in so far as such conventions concern matters governed by the regulation.

216. Article 1 Rome I Regulation concerns its material scope. According to this provision the regulation applies in situations involving a conflict of laws, to contractual obligations in civil and commercial matters. It does not apply, in particular, to revenue, customs or administrative matters. Article 1(2) contains the list of matters excluded from the scope of the regulation, for example, obligations arising out of family relationships, obligations arising out of matrimonial property regimes or arbitration agreements and agreements on the choice of court.

217. For the obligations arising under bills of exchange and cheques the conflict-of-law rules are included in, respectively, Bill of Exchange Law[289] and Cheque Law.[290]

218. It is also worth to mention that PILA contains conflict-of-law rules on obligations resulting of a unilateral juridical act, which fall outside of the scope of Rome I Regulation.[291] An obligation, which is accepted by the doctrine to qualify as the example of an obligation resulting out of a unilateral juridical act, is a public promise. According to Article 919 CC[292] anyone who promised an award for the performance of a specified activity by public announcement is obliged to keep the promise.

219. According to Article 32(1) PILA an obligation resulting out of a unilateral juridical act is subject to the law chosen by the person making this act. From the time when both parties of the obligation are specified, the choice of law, its modification or revocation, requires the consent of both parties. In the absence of choice of law, according to Article 32(2), an obligation resulting out of a unilateral juridical act is subject to the law of the state, in which the person making this act has his or her habitual residence or seat. Where it results from the circumstances that the obligation is more closely connected with the law of a different state, the law of that state applies.

288. Dz. U. 2002 r. nr 83 poz. 750.
289. Dz. U. 1936 nr 37 poz. 282.
290. Dz. U. 1936 nr 37 poz. 283.
291. A. W. Wiśniewski in: J. Poczobut (ed.), *Prawo prywatne międzynarodowe. Komentarz*, Wolters Kluwer, Warszawa 2017, pp. 559–560.
292. Act of 23 Apr. 1964 – Civil Code, Dz. U. 1964 nr 16 poz. 93.

220. It is apparent that those conflict-of-law rules are very similar to those included in Rome I Regulation, which apply to contractual obligations.

I. Party Autonomy

221. The Rome I Regulation is based on the principle of party autonomy, allowing the parties to agree on which law should govern the contract concluded by them.[293] Pursuant to Article 3(1) Rome I Regulation a contract should be governed by the law chosen by the parties. The allowed choice of law has an unlimited character in general,[294] which means that the parties can choose the law of any country, whether or not it is the law of an EU Member State. However, parties may only choose as applicable the law of a particular country. Recital 13 explains that the regulation does not preclude parties from incorporating by reference into their contract a non-State body of law or an international convention. Therefore, reference to rules developed by non-state institutions or entities (e.g., Principles of European Contract Law (PECL) prepared by the 'Lando Commission', UNIDROIT Principles of International Commercial Contracts or Common Frame of Reference prepared under the auspices of the European Commission) is only possible under the freedom of contract defined by the applicable substantive law.

222. Provisions of Rome I Regulation do not require any specific form for the choice of law. The choice can be made expressly or clearly demonstrated by the terms of the contract or the circumstances of the case (so-called tacit choice of law). Recital 12 states that an agreement between the parties to confer on one or more courts or tribunals of a Member State exclusive jurisdiction to determine disputes under the contract should be one of the factors to be taken into account in determining whether a choice of law has been clearly demonstrated. Other situations in which there is tacit choice of law are when the wording of the provisions of the contract cannot let to assume that the parties wanted to subject the contract to a different law, and the behaviour of the parties during court proceedings which shows that they chose the law of the state, to which they implicitly refer.[295]

223. By their choice, the parties can select the law applicable to the whole or to part only of the contract. Partial choice of law is allowed according to the Article 3(1), which means that the parties can select the law applicable to part of the contract only or even choose several different legal orders to govern different parts of the contract. Such choice of law will lead to *depeçage* (*see* Part I., Chapter 2, §1., IV).

---

293. F. Garcimartín Alférez in: J. Basedow, G. Rühl, F. Ferrari, P. de Miguel Asensio (eds), *Encyclopedia of Private International Law*, Edward Elgar Publishing, Cheltenham 2017, p. 1556.

294. There are some exceptions to this rule in case of particular contracts (e.g., carriage contracts or insurance contracts). Those exceptions are analysed in the following subchapters.

295. M. Czepelak, *Międzynarodowe prawo zobowiązań Unii Europejskiej*, LexisNexis, Warszawa 2012, p. 139.

224. The parties can change the law applicable, as Article 3(2) states that they may at any time agree to subject the contract to a law other than that which previously governed it, whether as a result of an earlier choice of law. This provision also grants the protection of third parties, as any change in the law to be applied that is made after the conclusion of the contract should not adversely affect the rights of third parties.

225. Provisions of Rome I Regulation allow to choose law applicable in a purely domestic case, *id est* when the contract is connected with a single country. However, according to Article 3(3) where all other elements relevant to the situation at the time of the choice are located in a country other than the country whose law has been chosen, the choice of the parties should not prejudice the application of provisions of the law of that other country which cannot be derogated from by agreement. These provisions, which cannot be derogated by an agreement, mean *ius congens* within the substantive law and they should not be confused with overriding mandatory provisions (Article 9 Rome I). As a result, the application of Article 3(3) limits a choice of applicable law to merely a material incorporation (*materiellrechtliche Verweisung*) of foreign law provisions into the applicable law designated by an objective connecting factor.

226. Analogous provision, provided for in Article 3(4) Rome I Regulation, concerns intra-EU cases, where all other elements relevant to the situation at the time of the choice are located in one or more EU Member States. The result of the choice of applicable law in such situation is also similar – it should not prejudice the application of provisions of community law (EU law), where appropriate as implemented in the Member State of the forum, which cannot be derogated from by agreement (*ius cogens*).

227. Choice of law applicable is a legal act. Thus, as with every legal act, questions arise about its substantive validity (e.g., fraud, duress, mistake). Article 3(5) refers on these points to the *lex contractus*, stating that the existence and validity of the consent of the parties as to the choice of the applicable law shall be determined in accordance with the provisions of Rome I Regulation. Therefore, in those matters the same rules apply to the choice of law and to the contract itself. However, it must be remembered, that the existence and validity of the choice of law applicable should be assessed separately from the existence and validity of the contract.

II. Form

228. Law applicable to the form of a contract is indicated by the conflict-of-law rule of Article 11 Rome I Regulation. According to Article 11(1) a contract concluded between persons who are in the same country at the time of its conclusion is formally valid if it satisfies the formal requirements of the law which governs it in substance (*lex contractus*) or of the law of the country where it is concluded (*lex loci contractus*). Article 11(2) adds that a contract concluded between persons who are in different countries at the time of its conclusion is formally valid if it satisfies the formal requirements of the law which governs it in substance (*lex contractus*) or of the law of either of the countries where either of the parties is present at the time of conclusion, or of the law of the country where either of the parties had his habitual residence at that time.

229. If the contract is concluded by the representative (agent), who acts on behalf of a principal, the circumstances mentioned in Article 11(1) and (2), like the presence in a certain place at the time of conclusion of the contract, on the part of the representative (agent) should be taken into consideration.

230. Article 11(3) Rome I Regulation includes conflict-of-law rules indicating law applicable to the form of unilateral acts. According to this provision a unilateral act intended to have legal effect relating to an existing or contemplated contract (e.g., a proposal) is formally valid if it satisfies the formal requirements of the law which governs or would govern the contract in substance (*lex contractus*), or of the law of the country where the act was done (*lex loci actus*), or of the law of the country where the person by whom it was done had his habitual residence at that time.

231. Articles 11(1), (2) and (3) Rome I Regulation do not apply to consumer contracts (*see* Part II., Chapter 2, §2., III). The form of such contracts is governed by the law of the country where the consumer has his habitual residence.

232. There are also some exceptions in regard to contracts the subject matter of which is a right in rem in immovable property or tenancy of immovable property. According to Article 11(5) the form of such contracts is subject to the requirements of form of the law of the country where the property is situated (*lex rei sitae*) if by that law those requirements are imposed irrespective of the country where the contract is concluded and irrespective of the law governing the contract; and those requirements cannot be derogated from by agreement. The purpose of this provision is to take into account the unilateral conflict-of-law rules of the state in which the real estate is located, which impose the application of substantive rules applicable in that state relating to the form in every situation where real estate situated in that state is the subject of a legal transaction. It is irrelevant whether such unilateral conflict-of-law rules are expressed directly in the conflict-of-law provisions, or whether they result from the wording of the substantive provision establishing formal requirements.[296] Polish law, however, does not provide for the conflict-of-law rules like this[297] and because of that the law applicable to the form of contracts the subject matter of which is a right in rem in immovable property or tenancy of immovable property located in Poland is determined according to the conflict-of-law rules of Rome I Regulation, which can indicate the foreign law to govern it.

296. M. Czepelak, *Międzynarodowe prawo zobowiązań Unii Europejskiej*, LexisNexis, Warszawa 2012, pp. 395–396.
297. M. Czepelak, *Międzynarodowe prawo zobowiązań Unii Europejskiej*, LexisNexis, Warszawa 2012, p. 397.

233. It is also worth to mention, that according to Article 3(2) any change in the law to be applied that is made after the conclusion of the contract shall not prejudice its formal validity under Article 11. Therefore, the formal validity of the contract is assessed in accordance with the law applicable indicated by the abovementioned conflict-of-law rules at the moment of its conclusion and it is not affected by the subsequent choice of law.

234. Law applicable to the form of contracts, which are excluded from the scope of the Rome I Regulation should be indicated by the domestic conflict-of-law rules. In general, those rules are included in PILA (Article 25) (*see* Part I., Chapter 3, §5., III).

III. Validity and Formation

235. Article 10(1) Rome I Regulation concerns the existence and material validity of a contract. According to this provision those issues should be determined by the law which would govern the contract if the contract was valid (*lex contractus*). The same rule applies to any term of a contract.

236. Moreover, there is an additional rule, set in Article 10(2), which states that a party, in order to establish that he did not consent, may rely upon the law of the country in which he has his habitual residence if it appears from the circumstances that it would not be reasonable to determine the effect of his conduct in accordance with *lex contractus*.

IV. Performance

237. The contractual performance is, in accordance with Article 12(1)(b) Rome I Regulation, governed by the law applicable to a contract. Article 12(2) adds that in relation to the manner of performance and the steps to be taken in the event of defective performance, the law of the country in which performance takes place should be also taken into regard.

238. Similar provision was included in Rome Convention (1980) on the law applicable to contractual obligations. The Report on the convention[298] noted that the term 'manner of performance' of an obligation does not seem to have any precise and uniform meaning. Quite opposite, this concept has different meaning in the various laws and in the views of learned writers. Giving it a strict legal definition seemed like an inaccurate solution. Therefore, the *lex fori* should determine what is meant by 'manner of performance'. Among the matters normally falling within the

298. Report on the Convention on the law applicable to contractual obligations by Mario Giuliano, Professor, University of Milan, and Paul Lagarde, Professor, University of Paris I, O.J. C 282, 31/10/1980, pp. 1–50.

description of 'manner of performance' the Report mentions the rules governing public holidays, the manner in which goods are to be examined, and the steps to be taken if they are refused.

239. It is also worth to mention that Polish domestic PILA contains the provisions on performance of an obligation involving the payment of a sum of money. According to Article 38 PILA the impact of a change in the value of currency on the amount due under the obligation is governed by the law applicable to that obligation (*lex causae*).

V. Breach of Contractual Obligations (Including Damages)

240. According to Article 12(1)(c) Rome I Regulation, the consequences of a total or partial breach of obligations is governed by the law applicable to contract, however within the limits of the powers conferred on the court by its procedural law. Among the consequences of breach, the provision lists the assessment of damages in so far as it is governed by rules of law.

241. Thus, *lex contractus* regulates, first of all, the conditions of contractual liability, the rules of this liability, and the method of determining damage. It also governs the measures to be taken by the creditor in the event of improper performance of the obligation and his rights in this situation. For example, if *lex contractus* grants the creditor the right to demand non-pecuniary benefits in kind, then it is possible to claim that right in court, as long as the court can – in accordance with *lex fori processualis* – issue a judgment granting such request.[299]

VI. Rescission

242. Rescission, understood as a right of a contractual party to cancel the contract and as a way of extinguishing of obligation, is governed, according to Article 12(1)(d) Rome I Regulation, by the law applicable to the contract.

VII. Representation

243. In the case of conclusion of the contract by a representative, either as part of statutory representation or voluntary representation (*see* Part I., Chapter 3, §5., II), it is important to mention that the provisions of Rome I Regulation apply only to some issues of this legal relationship. For sure they apply to the contract concluded between the representative and the third person.

---

299. M. Czepelak, *Międzynarodowe prawo zobowiązań Unii Europejskiej*, LexisNexis, Warszawa 2012, pp. 351–352.

244. Regarding the statutory representation, conflict-of-law rules of Rome I Regulation apply only to the relation between the representative and the person with whom the contract is concluded. However, they do not apply to the relationship which allows such statutory representation, for example, parents towards the child, spouses towards each other or guardian towards the pupil. The law applicable to this relation is indicated by the conflict-of-law rules included in PILA (Article 22) (*see* Part I., Chapter 3, §5., II).[300]

245. When it comes to voluntary representation, conflict-of-law rules of Rome I Regulation apply only to the internal relationship between the representative agent and the principal. Depending on the case, those are the conflict-of-law rules on employment contracts or contracts for the provision of services. Nevertheless, those rules do not apply to the authority of the representative to represent the principal. This issue is not covered by the Regulation, due to Article 1(2)(g) which states that the question whether an agent is able to bind a principal, or an organ to bind a company or other body corporate or unincorporated, in relation to a third party is excluded from the scope of the Regulation. Because of that, the law applicable to this issue is determined according to provisions of PILA (Article 23) (*see* Part I., Chapter 3, §5., II). [301]

246. It is also worth to mention that the law applicable to *negotiorum gestio*, meaning a form of spontaneous voluntary representation in which an intervenor (*gestor*) acts on behalf and for the benefit of a principal (*dominus negotii*), but without the latter's prior consent, is covered by Rome II Regulation[302] (Article 11) (*see* Part II., Chapter 2, §3., V).

VIII. Interpretation

247. According to Article 12(1)(a) Rome I Regulation, interpretation of a contract is governed by the law applicable to contract. Interpretation of a contract should be understood as a process of determining the content of the legal relationship based on the declarations of intent of the parties. Interpretation should not be reduced only to the question of determining the meanings of words by using the linguistic guidelines but should also encompass the rules of interpretation used in the applicable legal system. Usually, these rules cover two types of issues: the circumstances of the conclusion of the contract relevant for interpretation and the rules for

300. Ł. Żarnowiec in: M. Pazdan (ed.), *System Prawa Prywatnego. Tom 20 A. Prawo prywatne międzynarodowe*, Wydawnictwo C. H. Beck, Warszawa 2014, pp. 820–832.
301. J. Pazdan in: M. Pazdan (ed.), *System Prawa Prywatnego. Tom 20 A. Prawo prywatne międzynarodowe*, Wydawnictwo C. H. Beck, Warszawa 2014, pp. 857–876.
302. Regulation (EC) No 864/2007 of the European Parliament and of the Council of 11 Jul. 2007 on the law applicable to non-contractual obligations (Rome II), OJ L 199, 31.7.2007, pp. 40–49.

determining the meaning of these circumstances.[303] Therefore, if the contract is governed for example by Polish law, Article 65 CC,[304] including the principles of interpretation of a declaration of intent, should be applied. It states that the declaration of intent should be interpreted in the view of the circumstances in which it was made, as required by the principles of community life and established customs. Additionally, when interpreting the contracts, one should rather examine what the parties' intention and purpose of the contract were, rather than rely on its literal wording.

IX. Third Parties and Multiparty Agreements

248. Rome I Regulation contains provision on protection of third parties in case of subsequent choice of law applicable to the contract. Article 3(2) *in fine* states that any change in the law to be applied that is made after the conclusion of the contract should not adversely affect the rights of third parties.

249. Similar provision can be found in PILA. According to Article 4(3) the choice of law made after the conclusion of a legal relationship shall not adversely affect the rights of third parties. This provision can be applied to the choice of law for contracts that fall outside the scope of the Rome I Regulation.

250. There is no conflict-of-law provision *explicite* referring to multiparty agreements. However, Rome I Regulation contains provision on multiple liability. Pursuant to Article 16, if a creditor has a claim against several debtors who are liable for the same claim, and one of the debtors has already satisfied the claim in whole or in part, the law governing the debtor's obligation towards the creditor also governs the debtor's right to claim recourse from the other debtors. The other debtors may rely on the defences they had against the creditor to the extent allowed by the law governing their obligations towards the creditor.

X. Assignment and Subrogation

251. Rome I Regulation contains special provisions on assignment and subrogation (both contractual and legal). The concept of assignment upon the Regulation, according to Article 14(3), includes outright transfers of claims, transfers of claims by way of security and pledges or other security rights over claims.

252. According to Article 14(1) Rome I Regulation the relationship between assignor and assignee under a voluntary assignment or contractual subrogation of a claim against another person (the debtor) is governed by the law that applies to the contract between the assignor and assignee. The law applicable to this contract

303. M. Czepelak, *Międzynarodowe prawo zobowiązań Unii Europejskiej*, LexisNexis, Warszawa 2012, pp. 346–347.
304. Act of 23 Apr. 1964 – Civil Code, Dz. U. 1964 nr 16 poz. 93.

should be indicated by the conflict-of-law rules of the regulation. The law governing the assigned or subrogated claim, according to Article 14(2), determines its assignability, the relationship between the assignee and the debtor, the conditions under which the assignment or subrogation can be invoked against the debtor and whether the debtor's obligations have been discharged.

253. Article 15 Rome I Regulation concerns legal subrogation. Pursuant to this provision, where a person (the creditor) has a contractual claim against another (the debtor) and a third person has a duty to satisfy the creditor, or has in fact satisfied the creditor in discharge of that duty, the law which governs the third person's duty to satisfy the creditor shall determine whether and to what extent the third person is entitled to exercise against the debtor the rights which the creditor had against the debtor under the law governing their relationship.

254. Conflict-of-law rules indicating law applicable to those matters are included also in domestic PILA. Article 36 PILA states the law governing the assigned claim determines the effects of the assignment as against third parties. And according to Article 37 the assumption of a debt is subject to the law of the state that governs the assumed debt. Those provisions apply to the matters that fall outside the scope of the Rome I Regulation.[305]

§2. Particular Contracts

I. Sales Contract

255. The law applicable to sales contract is determined by the conflict-of-law rules of Rome I Regulation. According to Article 3 parties are free to choose the law applicable to sales contract. In the absence of choice of law, the regulation indicates in Article 4(1)(a) that a contract for the sale of goods is governed by the law of the country where the seller has his habitual residence. If the seller is a legal person, then according to Article 19(1) the law of the country where the place of its central administration is located should apply. The law applicable to the contract for the sale of goods by auction is indicated by the rule in Article 4(1)(g), which states that this type of contract is governed by the law of the country where the auction takes place, if such a place can be determined.

256. In both cases, contracts for the sale of goods and contracts of the sale of goods by auction, Rome I Regulation provides for an escape clause. Article 4(3) states that where it is clear from all the circumstances of the case that the contract is manifestly more closely connected with a country other than that indicated by the relevant conflict-of-law rule, the law of that other country applies to the contract.

305. W. Kurowski in: M. Pazdan, *Prawo prywatne międzynarodowe. Komentarz*, Wydawnictwo C. H. Beck, Warszawa 2018, p. 348, p. 350.

257. With regard to sales contracts it is worth to mention that Poland is a party to Vienna CISG[306] since 1996.[307] The Convention mainly aims at the unification of substantive law on sale of goods.[308]

258. Article 1(1) of the CISG states that it applies to contracts of sale of goods between parties whose places of business are in different states being contracting states bound by the convention or when the rules of PIL lead to the application of the law of a contracting state. Therefore, Polish court will apply the CISG if, according to the Rome I Regulation, the law of any CISG contracting state is designated as applicable to the contract of sale of goods. Certain issues are not regulated by CISG, for example material validity of a contract (Article 4(a) CISG), which will be governed by the law applicable indicated by Article 10(1) Rome I Regulation. However, Article 6 CISG allows the parties to exclude the application of the Convention or derogate from or vary the effect of its certain provisions.

II. Service Contract

259. According to Article 3 of Rome I Regulation parties are free to choose the law applicable to service contract. In the absence of choice of law, the regulation indicates in Article 4(1)(b) that a contract for the provision of services is governed by the law of the country where the service provider has his habitual residence, unless it is clear from all the circumstances of the case that the contract is manifestly more closely connected with other country. Then the law of that other country applies. If the service provider is a legal person, then according to Article 19(1) the law of the country where the place of its central administration is should apply.

III. Consumer Contract

260. Rome I Regulation contains special conflict-of-law rules on consumer contracts, based on the principle of most favourable law. The *ratio legis* of those provisions is the need to protect consumer, who is considered a weaker party of the contractual obligation.[309] It is confirmed in Recital 23, which states that in case of contracts concluded with parties regarded as being weaker, those parties should be protected by conflict-of-law rules that are more favourable to their interests than the general rules.

306. Dz. U. 1997 nr 45 poz. 286.
307. *See* Ł. Dyrda, *Konwencyjne prawo jednolite a normy kolizyjne*, KPP 2013, nr 2, pp. 483–512.
308. F. Ferrari in: J. Basedow, G. Rühl, F. Ferrari, P. de Miguel Asensio (eds), *Encyclopedia of Private International Law*, Edward Elgar Publishing, Cheltenham 2017, pp. 338–341.
309. *See* M. Jagielska, *Ewolucja ochrony konsumenta w prawie kolizyjnym Unii Europejskiej w zakresie zobowiązań umownych*, Wydawnictwo C. H. Beck, Warszawa 2010, pp. 6–11.

261. Consumer contract is defined in Article 6(1) as a contract concluded by a natural person for a purpose which can be regarded as being outside his trade or profession (the consumer) with another person acting in the exercise of his trade or profession (the professional).

262. According to Article 6(2) parties to the consumer contract are allowed to choose the law applicable to this contract, in accordance with the general rules on choice of law included in Article 3. Such a choice of law applicable may not, however, have the result of depriving the consumer of the protection afforded to him by provisions that cannot be derogated from by agreement by virtue of the law which, in the absence of choice, would have been applicable to it.

263. Article 6(1) Rome I Regulation indicates the law applicable to the consumer contract in the absence of choice of law. It states that the consumer contract should be governed by the law of the country where the consumer has his habitual residence, as long as two requirements are met: 1) the professional pursues his commercial or professional activities in the country where the consumer has his habitual residence, or 2) by any means, directs such activities to that country or to several countries including that country, and the contract falls within the scope of such activities.

264. Combining provisions of Article 6(1) and (2) together shows, that the conflict-of-law rules indicating the law applicable to consumer contracts are special because of two reasons. First, the concept of characteristic performance that is used in others conflict-of-law rules (e.g., for sales contracts and service contracts), is not used in those provisions. On the contrary, it is the law of the country where the consumer has his habitual residence, assuming that this law the consumer is most familiar with. Second, the choice of law is allowed only to limited extend. It is possible to choose the law applicable to the consumer contract, but since the consumer most likely will have little influence over what law is chosen as applicable, the EU legislator decided to protect him from the situations in which the professional chooses the law unfavourable for the consumer. Therefore, the provisions of the law of the country where the consumer has his habitual residence that grant him protection will be applicable to the contract, regardless of the choice of law and even if the law of other country will be applicable to the contract in general.

265. If the requirements stated in Article 6(1) are not met, then according to Article 6(3) then the general conflict-of-law rules on the choice of law (Article 3) and on the law applicable to a contract between a consumer and a professional (Article 4) apply. Special provisions on consumer contracts from Article 6(1) and (2) also do not apply to several types of consumer contracts, listed in Article 6(4).

266. It is also worth to mention that according to Article 11(4) the general rules on the law applicable to the form of contract do not apply to the form of consumer contracts. Instead, the form of consumer contracts is governed by the law of the country where the consumer has his habitual residence.

267. In the case of a consumer concluding the contract of carriage, it might be a doubtful which conflict-of-law rules should indicate the law applicable for such a contract – those on consumer contracts (Article 6) or those on contracts of carriage (Article 5). This issue is solved by the EU legislator, who in Article 6(4)(b) provides, that special conflict-of-law rules on consumer contracts do not, in principle, apply to contracts of carriage. Moreover, Recital 32 states that taking into account the particular nature of contracts of carriage, specific provisions should ensure an adequate level of protection of passengers. Therefore, Article 6 should not apply in the context of those particular contracts, but Article 5(1) or Article 5(2).

268. Polish domestic PILA contains provision which extends consumer protection on the cases which are not covered by the scope of Rome I Regulation. According to Article 30(1), irrespectively of the cases covered by the regulation, the parties' choice of law of a state that is not a member of the European Economic Area for a contract that has a close connection with the territory of at least one Member State, may not deprive the consumer of the protection afforded to him or her by provisions of Polish law that implement the EU directives.[310]

269. Article 30(2) PILA concerns several types of contracts concluded by consumers: timeshare, long-term holiday product, resale and exchange contracts. All those contracts fall within the scope of Directive 2008/122/EC.[311] According to Article 30(2) PILA, if the law applicable to such a contract is the law of a state that is not a member of the European Economic Area, the consumer may not be deprived of the protection afforded to him or her by provisions of Polish law implementing that directive, if any of the immovable properties are located in a Member State, or, in the case of a contract not directly related to immovable property, if the business entity pursues commercial or professional activities in a Member State or, by any means, directs such activities to a Member State, and the contract falls within the scope of these activities.

270. Both provisions serve to protect the consumer on the level of conflict-of-law rules. Article 30(1) applies only to the choice of law of a non-EEA country for a consumer contract which is closely connected with the territory of at least one Member State. Article 30(2) applies to each case of determination of the law applicable to timeshare contracts if the requirements set out in that provision are met.

271. The abovementioned regulations have been included in PILA in order to re-implement the provisions of EU directives. Before 2011, when PILA was

310. The following directives are listed in the provision: Council Directive 93/13/EEC (OJ L 95, 21.4.1993, pp. 29–34), Directive 97/7/EC (OJ L 144, 4.6.1997, pp. 19–27, no longer in force, repealed by Directive 2011/83/EU); Directive 1999/44/EC (OJ L 171, 7.7.1999, pp. 12–16); Directive 2002/65/EC (OJ L 271, 9.10.2002, pp. 16–24); Directive 2008/48/EC (OJ L 133, 22.5.2008, pp. 66–92).

311. OJ L 33, 3.2.2009, pp. 10–30.

adopted, these provisions were scattered over various domestic acts. For practical reasons, the national legislator decided to place them in one provision.[312]

IV. Employment Contract

272. The law applicable to individual employment contracts should be determined in accordance with Article 8 Rome I Regulation. Article 8(1) states that an individual employment contract is governed by the law chosen by the parties in accordance with the general rule of Article 3. Such a choice of law may not, however, have the result of depriving the employee of the protection afforded to him by provisions that cannot be derogated from by agreement under the law that, in the absence of choice, would have been applicable to the contract.

273. Pursuant to Article 8(2) if the parties of the employment contract did not choose the law applicable to it, the contract is governed by the law of the country in which or, failing that, from which the employee habitually carries out his work in performance of the contract. The country where the work is habitually carried out shall not be deemed to have changed if he is temporarily employed in another country. If the law applicable cannot be determined using those rules, the contract should be governed, according to Article 8(3), by the law of the country where the place of business through which the employee was engaged is situated. Recital 36 explains that work carried out in another country should be regarded as temporary if the employee is expected to resume working in the country of origin after carrying out his tasks abroad. The conclusion of a new contract of employment with the original employer or an employer belonging to the same group of companies as the original employer should not preclude the employee from being regarded as carrying out his work in another country temporarily.

274. Moreover, Article 8(4) contains the escape clause, according to which where it appears from the circumstances as a whole that the contract is more closely connected with a country other than that indicated by the conflict-of-law rules, the law of that other country shall apply.

275. Rome I Regulation provides for special conflict-of-law rules for individual employment contracts. These rules are designed to protect the weaker party of the employment contract, as underlined in Recital 23, in case of contracts concluded with parties regarded as being weaker, those parties should be protected by conflict-of-law rules that are more favoured to their interests than the general rules. Therefore, Article 8 provides for modified rules on choice of law applicable rules. It was assumed that the employer may influence the employee so that the employee, wishing to establish or maintain an employment relationship, may agree to choose the

312. B. Gnela in: J. Poczobut (ed.), *Prawo prywatne międzynarodowe. Komentarz*, Wolters Kluwer Polska, Warszawa 2017, pp. 520–521; M. Jagielska in: Pazdan, M. (ed.), *System Prawa Prywatnego. Tom 20 B. Prawo prywatne międzynarodowe*, Wydawnictwo C. H. Beck, Warszawa 2015, pp. 298–299.

law that would provide the most favourable regulations for the employer, but would put the employee at a disadvantage. Because of that, the choice of law for the employment contract is permissible, but it cannot deprive the employee of the protection that he would have been legally entitled to, had there been no choice of law.[313]

276. The conflict-of-law rules which indicate the law applicable to individual employment contracts in the absence of a choice of law are also modified compared to general rules. The concept of characteristic performance that is used in general conflict-of-law rules, for example, to indicate law applicable to sales contracts or service contracts, is not used in those provisions. Instead, the indication of the applicable law is based primarily on the connecting factor of the place of work carried out by the employee (*lex loci laboris*). In addition, there are rules that should be applied if the law applicable to the employment contract cannot be determined based on this connecting factor.

277. Recital 34 reminds also that the conflict-of-law rules included in the Regulation do not prejudice the application of the overriding mandatory provisions of the country to which a worker is posted in accordance with Directive 96/71/EC.[314]

V. Contracts of Carriage

A. *Carriage of Persons*

278. A contract of carriage of persons is an example of a contract concluded between the stronger (the carrier) and weaker (the passenger) party. According to Recital 23 of Rome I Regulation in the case of contracts concluded with parties regarded as being weaker, those parties should be protected by conflict-of-law rules that are more favourable to their interests than the general rules. Hence, the rules on contracts of carriage of persons differ from the general rules on contractual obligations and also from the rules on contracts of carriage of goods (*see* below).[315]

279. Law applicable to contracts of carriage of persons should be determined in accordance with Article 5(2). The provision provides for the limited choice of law, as the parties can choose only the law applicable from the listed options: the law of the country where the passenger has his habitual residence; or the law of the country where the carrier has his habitual residence; or the law of the country where the

313. W. Kurowski in: M. Pazdan (ed.), *System Prawa Prywatnego. Tom 20 B. Prawo prywatne międzynarodowe*, Wydawnictwo C. H. Beck, Warszawa 2015, p. 473.

314. Directive 96/71/EC of the European Parliament and of the Council of 16 Dec. 1996 concerning the posting of workers in the framework of the provision of services, OJ L 18, 21.1.1997, pp. 1–6.

315. M. Świerczyński in: M. Pazdan (ed.), *System Prawa Prywatnego. Tom 20 B. Prawo prywatne międzynarodowe*, Wydawnictwo C. H. Beck, Warszawa 2015, p. 259.

carrier has his place of central administration; or the law of the country where the place of departure is situated; or the law of the country where the place of destination is situated.

280. If the parties did not choose the law applicable, contract for the carriage of passengers should be governed by the law of the country where the passenger has his habitual residence, provided that either the place of departure or the place of destination is situated in that country. If these requirements are not met, the law of the country where the carrier has his habitual residence should apply. The Article 5(3) provides for an escape clause, according to which, where it is clear from all the circumstances of the case that the contract, in the absence of a choice of law, is manifestly more closely connected with a country other than that indicated by the conflict-of-law rules presented above, the law of that other country shall apply.

281. It should be noted the contract of carriage is often regulated by uniform law conventions. The Montreal Convention on international carriage by air (1999)[316] may serve as an example. Pursuant to its Article 1(1) this convention applies to all international carriage of persons, baggage or cargo performed by aircraft for reward. In general, the expression international carriage means any carriage in which, according to the agreement between the parties, the place of departure and the place of destination, whether or not there be a break in the carriage or a transshipment, are situated either within the territories of two contracting countries or within the territory of a single contracting country if there is an agreed stopping place within the territory of another State, even if that State is not a State Party (Article 1(2)). Hence, the law applicable designated by Rome I Regulation might be applied to contract of carriage of persons only to those matters that are not covered by uniform law conventions, Montreal Convention being one of them.[317]

B. Carriage of Goods

282. The parties of the contracts of carriage of goods are allowed to choose the law applicable in accordance with general rule of Article 3 Rome I Regulation. Therefore, unlike for the contracts of carriage of persons, the unlimited choice of law is permissible. Article 5(1) contains the conflict-of-law rules indicating the law applicable to contracts of carriage of goods in the absence of choice of law. According to this provision the contract should be governed by the law of the country of habitual residence of the carrier, provided that the place of receipt or the place of delivery or the habitual residence of the consignor is also situated in that country. If

316. Convention for the Unification of Certain Rules for International Carriage by Air (the Montreal Convention), OJ L 194, 18.7.2001, pp. 39–49 and Council Decision 2001/539/EC of 5 Apr. 2001 on the conclusion by the European Community of the Convention for the Unification of Certain Rules for International Carriage by Air (the Montreal Convention), OJ L 194, 18.7.2001, p. 38.

317. *See* A. Bělohlávek, *Law Applicable to International Carriage: EU Law and International Treaties*, Czech Yearbook of International Law 2015, pp. 27–60.

those requirements are not met, the law of the country where the place of delivery as agreed by the parties is situated is applicable.

283. The Article 5(3) provides for an escape clause, according to which, where it is clear from all the circumstances of the case that the contract, in the absence of a choice of law, is manifestly more closely connected with a country other than that indicated by the conflict-of-law rules presented above, the law of that other country shall apply.

284. Additionally, according to Recital 22, single-voyage charter parties and other contracts the main purpose of which is the carriage of goods should be treated as contracts for the carriage of goods. For the purposes of this Regulation, the term 'consignor' should refer to any person who enters into a contract of carriage with the carrier and the term 'the carrier' should refer to the party to the contract who undertakes to carry the goods, whether or not he performs the carriage himself.

285. It should be noted the contract of carriage is often regulated by uniform law conventions. The Convention on the Contract for the International Carriage of Goods by Road (CMR) (1956)[318] may serve as an example. Pursuant to its Article 1(1) this convention applies to every contract for the carriage of goods by road in vehicles for reward, when the place of taking over of the goods and the place designated for delivery, as specified in the contract, are situated in two different countries, of which at least one is a contracting country, irrespective of the place of residence and the nationality of the parties. Hence, the law applicable designated by Rome I Regulation might be applied to contract of carriage of goods only to those matters that are not covered by uniform law conventions, CMR Convention being one of them.[319]

VI. Insurance Contracts

286. In Rome I Regulation insurance contracts are divided in two groups. First, insurance contracts covering a large risk. The term 'large risk' (French *grand risque*, German *Großrisiko*) is defined in Article 5(d) of the First Council Directive 73/239/EEC of 24 July 1973 on the coordination of laws, regulations and administrative provisions relating to the taking-up and pursuit of the business of direct insurance other than life assurance.[320] Rome I Regulation applies to those contracts whether or not the risk covered is situated in a Member State. According to Article 7(2) Rome I Regulation, parties of the insurance contracts covering a large risk are allowed to choose the law applicable, according to the general rule stated in Article 3. If there is no choice of law, then Article 7(2) will apply, which states that insurance contracts of that type are governed by the law of the country where the insurer

318. Dz. U. z 1962 r. nr 49 poz. 238.
319. *See* A. Bělohlávek, *Law Applicable to International Carriage: EU Law and International Treaties*, Czech Yearbook of International Law 2015, pp. 27–60.
320. OJ L 228, 16.8.1973, pp. 3–19.

has his habitual residence. However, if it is clear from all the circumstances of the case that the contract is manifestly more closely connected with another country, the law of that other country shall apply.[321]

287. Second, all other insurance contracts than those covering a large risk. The conflict-of-law rules included in Rome I Regulation apply to them if they cover risks situated inside the territory of EU Member States. The regulations provide for the rules on determination where the risk is situated, making a reference to EU directives.

288. Article 7(3) concerns the choice of law for insurance contracts other than those covering a large risk and covering risks situated inside the territory of EU Member States. According to this provision such choice of law is limited, as the parties can choose only laws listed in this provision. In the absence of choice of law, the insurance contract is governed by the law of the Member State in which the risk is situated at the time of conclusion of the contract. If the contract covers risks situated in more than one EU Member State, the contract should be considered as constituting several contracts each relating to only one Member State.

289. Article 7 of Rome I Regulation does not apply to reinsurance contracts. The law applicable to reinsurance contracts should be determined in accordance with the general rules of the regulation (Article 3 and Article 4).[322]

290. In the case of a consumer concluding the insurance contract, it might be doubtful which conflict-of-law rules should indicate the law applicable for such a contract – those on consumer contracts (Article 6) or those on insurance contracts (Article 7). This issue is solved by the EU legislator, who in Recital 32 states that taking into account the particular nature of insurance contracts, specific provisions should ensure an adequate level of protection of policyholders. Therefore, Article 6 should not apply in the context of those particular contracts, but Article 7.

291. To the insurance contracts not covered by the provisions of the Rome I Regulation, according to Article 1(2)(j), Article 28(2) PILA instructs to apply the provisions of the Rome I Regulation which are appropriate for the given obligation. In other words, Polish legislator decided to apply provisions of Rome I Regulation *mutatis mutandis* to other types of insurance contracts. The authority applying the law should assess whether the general rules of the Regulation (Articles 3 and 4) or the rules on insurance contracts (Article 7) should apply to such an insurance contract.[323]

---

321. M. Kropka, *Kolizyjnoprawna regulacja umowy ubezpieczenia według rozporządzenia Rzym I*, PPPM 2011, t. 9, pp. 129–148.
322. M. Pilich, *Law Applicable to Insurance Contracts in the Light of the Rome I Regulation*, Studia Iuridica 2012, nr 54, p. 202.
323. M. Pazdan in: M. Pazdan (ed.), *Prawo prywatne międzynarodowe. Komentarz*, Wydawnictwo C. H. Beck, Warszawa 2018, pp. 308–309.

292. PILA also contains provisions on insurance contracts in case of compulsory insurance. According to Article 29(1) PILA this type of insurance is subject to Polish law, if Polish law provides for compulsory insurance. If the law of a Member State of the European Economic Area, which provides for compulsory insurance, determines its own law as applicable to the insurance contract, according to Article 29(2), this law applies.[324]

VII. IP Contracts

A. Licence Agreement

293. The law applicable to contracts concerning intellectual property rights, for example, licence agreements granting the right to exploit an intangible right, is determined in accordance with provisions of Rome I Regulation. The regulation does not contain any special conflict-of-law rules in that matter. According to the general rules, the parties can choose the law applicable to such contract (Article 3). In the absence of choice of law, the contract shall be governed by the law of the country where the party required to effect the characteristic performance of the contract has his habitual residence (Article 4(2)). Although, if it is clear from all the circumstances of the case that the contract is manifestly more closely connected with other country, the law of that other country shall apply (Article 4(3)). If the law applicable cannot be determined pursuant to those rules, the contract shall be governed by the law of the country with which it is most closely connected (Article 4(4)).[325]

B. Trademark Agreement

294. There is no special provision on trademark agreements in Rome I Regulation. The parties are allowed to choose the law applicable to the contract upon Article 3 Rome I Regulation. If they have not done so, the law applicable to the contract should be determined according to Article 4(2), which states that the contract shall be governed by the law of the country where the party required to effect the characteristic performance of the contract has his habitual residence.[326] In most cases this means the application of the law of the country where the licensor has his or her habitual residence.

---

324. M. Pazdan in: M. Pazdan (ed.), *Prawo prywatne międzynarodowe. Komentarz*, Wydawnictwo C. H. Beck, Warszawa 2018, pp. 309–312.
325. P. Grzybczyk in: M. Pazdan (ed.), *System Prawa Prywatnego. Tom 20 C. Prawo prywatne międzynarodowe,* Wydawnictwo C. H. Beck, Warszawa 2015, pp. 22–29; R. Sikorski, O prawie właściwym dla licencji praw autorskich, PPPM 2009, t. 4, pp. 117–133.
326. M. Załucki, *Prawo właściwe dla umów licencyjnych znaku towarowego (cz. I)*, Prawo i Podatki Unii Europejskiej w Praktyce 2007, nr 12, pp. 26–32; M. Załucki, *Prawo właściwe dla umów licencyjnych znaku towarowego (cz. II)*, Prawo i Podatki Unii Europejskiej w Praktyce 2008, nr 1, pp. 22–26.

C. Other

295. Rome I Regulation does not contain specific conflict-of-law rules regarding other IP contracts. Therefore, the general provision on choice of law (Article 3) and on the law applicable in the absence of choice of law (Article 4) will apply (*see* above).

VIII. Hybrid Contracts

A. Leasing

296. In Rome I Regulation there is no special conflict-of-law rule on leasing contracts. Therefore, the general rules on choice of law (Article 3) apply. In the absence of choice of law, pursuant to Article 4(2) hybrid contracts are governed by the law of the country where the party required to effect the characteristic performance of the contract has his or her habitual residence. In a typical leasing contract this would mean the law of the publisher. In a typical financial leasing contract this would mean the law of the financing company rather than the party to which the object is leased.[327]

B. Factoring

297. Rome I Regulation does not contain any special rules applying to factoring contracts. The general rules on choice of law (Article 3) apply. In the absence of choice of law, pursuant to Article 4(2) hybrid contracts are governed by the law of the country where the party required to effect the characteristic performance of the contract has his or her habitual residence. Usually it will lead to application of the law of the factoring company.[328]

298. It is also worth to mention that some countries, including EU Member States,[329] are party to UNIDROIT Convention on International Factoring (1988) done in Ottawa, which in Article 2(1)(b) states that the Convention applies whenever the receivables assigned pursuant to a factoring contract arise from a contract of sale of goods between a supplier and a debtor whose places of business are in different states and both the contract of sale of goods and the factoring contract are governed by the law of a contracting state. Therefore, even though Poland is not a

327. D. Wolski, *Prawo właściwe dla umowy mieszanej w oparciu o postanowienia rozporządzenia rzymskiego pierwszego oraz wcześniej obowiązujących regulacji*, PWPM 2010, vol. 8, p. 132. On the law applicable to leasing agreements under PILA 1965, *see* J. Poczobut, *Właściwość prawa dla umowy leasingu – zagadnienia węzłowe*, Rejent 2001, nr 7–8, pp. 216–244.
328. A. Wowerka, *Prawo właściwe dla transakcji faktoringowych*, PPPM 2009, t. 4, p. 156.
329. Belgium, France, Germany, Hungary, Italy, Latvia and also Nigeria, Russia and Ukraine.

party to this Convention, Polish courts have to apply it, if law indicated as applicable is the law of one of the contracting states.[330]

C. Franchise

299. Parties are allowed to choose law applicable to the franchise contract. If they do not make a choice of law, Article 4(1)(e) Rome I Regulation will apply. According to this provision a franchise contract is governed by the law of the country where the franchisee has his habitual residence. The habitual residence should be determined in accordance with Article 19 of the regulation.

300. The Regulation does not provide for a definition of a franchise, which should be interpreted autonomously. In the EU law it was defined by the CJEU in the *Pronuptia* case,[331] in which the Court described it as a system whereby the franchisor grants independent traders, for a fee, the right to establish themselves in other markets using its business name and the business methods that have made it successful.

D. Publishing Contract

301. There is no special conflict-of-law rule in Rome I Regulation devoted to publishing contracts. Therefore, the general rules on choice of law (Article 3) apply. In the absence of choice of law, pursuant to Article 4(2) hybrid contracts are governed by the law of the country where the party required to effect the characteristic performance of the contract has his or her habitual residence. In a typical publishing contract this would mean the law of the publisher.

E. Other

302. No comments.

IX. Negotiable Instruments

A. Bills of Exchange

303. According to Article 1(2)(d) Rome I Regulation obligations arising under bills of exchange are excluded from the scope of the regulation. Conflict-of-law rules on those obligations can be found in domestic legal act of Bill of Exchange

330. A. Wowerka, *Umowa faktoringu w świetle konwencji ottawskiej o faktoringu międzynarodowym*, PPPM 2009, t. 5, pp. 58–59.
331. Case 161/84 *Pronuptia de Paris GmbH v Pronuptia de Paris Irmgard Schillgallis*, Judgment of the Court of 28 Jan. 1986.

Law of 1936[332] (BEL). The provisions of this act are based on the provisions of Geneva Convention providing a Uniform Law for Bills of Exchange and Promissory Notes (1930).[333] Conflict-of-law rules on bills of exchange are included in Section XIV of the domestic act.[334]

304. Capacity to incur bill obligations is governed by the law indicated in Article 77 BEL. According to this provision, a person's capacity to incur bill obligations should be assessed according to his national law. If this law is recognized as the applicable law of another country, it should be applied. If applicable law does not grant a person such capacity, the person is nevertheless validly obliged if he has signed a bill of exchange in a country according to which law, he has capacity to do it. This solution does not apply to a Polish citizen who has incurred a bill obligation abroad.

305. Pursuant to Article 78 BEL the form of the bill of exchange declaration should be assessed according to the laws of the country in which the declaration was signed. However, if the bill of exchange declaration, invalid due to the provisions of this law, corresponds to the law of the country in which the declaration was signed, the validity of the declaration should not be affected by the fact that the form of the declaration was incorrect. Additionally, bills of exchange liabilities incurred abroad by a Polish citizen are valid in Poland in relation to another Polish citizen also if they were incurred in the form provided for in this law.

306. The effects of the obligation of the bill of exchange acceptor are determined, according to Article 79 BEL, by the law of the place of payment of the bill of exchange. The effects of the obligations of other persons, signed on the bill of exchange, are determined by the law of the country in which these persons signed this bill.

B. Cheques

307. According to Article 1(2)(d) Rome I Regulation obligations arising under cheques are excluded from the scope of the regulation. Conflict-of-law rules on those obligations can be found in domestic legal act of Cheque Law of 1936[335] (CL). The provisions of this act are based on the provisions of Geneva Convention

332. Dz. U. 1936 nr 37 poz. 282.
333. Dz. U. 1937 nr 26 poz. 175.
334. M. Czarnecki, L. Bagińska, *Prawo wekslowe i czekowe. Komentarz*, Wydawnictwo C. H. Beck, Warszawa 2018, pp. 544–561; M. Czepelak, in: M. Stec (ed.), Prawo instrumentów finansowych, Wydawnictwo C. H. Beck, Warszawa 2016, pp. 115–230; P. Machnikowski in: M. Pazdan (ed.), *System Prawa Prywatnego. Tom 20 B. Prawo prywatne międzynarodowe*, Wydawnictwo C. H. Beck, Warszawa 2015, pp.720–723; P. Machnikowski, *Międzynarodowe prawo wekslowe i czekowe*, Studia Prawa Prywatnego 2013, nr 3, pp. 17–29.
335. Dz. U. 1936 nr 37 poz. 283.

for the Settlement of Certain Conflicts of Laws in connection with Cheques (1931).[336] Conflict-of-law rules on bills of exchange are included in Section XIII of the domestic act.[337]

308. According to Article 62 CL, a person's capacity to incur cheque obligations should be assessed according to his national law. If the law of another country deems it to be applicable, it should be applied. Whoever is unable to incur cheque obligation under the applicable law is nevertheless legally obligated if he has signed a cheque in a country, which law grants him such capacity. This solution does not apply to a Polish citizen who has incurred a cheque obligation abroad.

309. Article 63 CL states that the law of the country of the place of payment of the cheque determines who the cheque may be issued to. If, under this law, a document is invalid as a cheque due to the person for whom it was issued, the obligations arising from the signatures on that document in other countries whose laws do not contain such a provision are nevertheless valid.

310. The form of the check declaration is assessed, pursuant to Article 64 CL, according to the laws of the country where the declaration was signed; however, it is sufficient to meet the form required by the law of the place of payment. However, if the cheque declaration, invalid due to the provisions of law applicable, corresponds to the law of the country in which the declaration was signed, the validity of the declaration is not affected by the fact that the form of the declaration was incorrect. Additionally, cheque liabilities incurred abroad by a Polish citizen are valid in Poland in relation to another Polish citizen also if they were contracted in the form provided for in this practice.

311. Pursuant to Article 65 CL the effects of cheque obligations shall be determined by the laws of the country in which the obligations were incurred.

C. Letters of Credit

312. Rome I Regulation does not provide for any special rules on law applicable to letters of credit, therefore its general provisions (Article 3 and Article 4) apply.

---

336. Dz. U. 1937 nr 26 poz. 181.
337. M. Czarnecki, L. Bagińska, *Prawo wekslowe i czekowe. Komentarz*, Wydawnictwo C. H. Beck, Warszawa 2018, pp. 859–872; M. Czepelak, in: M. Stec (ed.), Prawo instrumentów finansowych, Wydawnictwo C. H. Beck, Warszawa 2016, pp. 115–230; P. Machnikowski in: M. Pazdan (ed.), *System Prawa Prywatnego. Tom 20 B. Prawo prywatne międzynarodowe*, Wydawnictwo C. H. Beck, Warszawa 2015, pp.707–720; P. Machnikowski, *Międzynarodowe prawo wekslowe i czekowe*, Studia Prawa Prywatnego 2013, nr 3, pp. 17–29.

X. Agency Contracts

313. In the case of an agency contract, it is necessary to distinguish between two types of relationship that exist within this legal relationship. First, the internal relationship between the representative (agent) and the principal, for example, stipulations of the contract regarding remuneration, is governed by the law applicable determined by the provision of Rome I Regulation. Therefore, depending on the case, the conflict-of-law rules on employment contracts or contracts for the provision of services, will apply to indicate the law applicable to the agency contract.

314. Second, the authority of the representative (agent) to represent the principal. This issue is not covered by the Regulation, due to Article 1(2)(g) which states that the question whether an agent is able to bind a principal, or an organ to bind a company or other body corporate or unincorporated, in relation to a third party is excluded from the scope of the Regulation. Because of that, the law applicable to this issue is determined according to provisions of PILA (Article 23) (*see* Part I., Chapter 3, §5., II).

§3. Non-contractual Obligations

315. The main source of PIL rules with respect to non-contractual obligations in Poland is now the Rome II Regulation.[338] Here it should be explained that the Rome II Regulation is not analysed in detail in this monograph as being part of EU PIL it is already subject of comprehensive literature.[339] At the same time, one should bear in mind that, from the practical point of view, together with Hague Convention on Traffic Accidents (mentioned below), currently it is the most important piece of legislation in Poland concerning law applicable to non-contractual obligations.[340] Both instruments contain rules of universal application meaning that they are applied without any requirement of reciprocity and replace any domestic PIL rules to that respect (*see* Article 3 Rome II Regulation and Article 11 Hague Convention). Similarly, both instruments exclude *renvoi* (*see* Article 24 Rome II Regulation and the use of term 'internal law' in the Hague Convention[341]).

316. Rome II Regulation is applied in Poland starting from 11 January 2009 to non-contractual obligations in civil and commercial matters resulting from events giving rise to damage which occurred starting from that date (Articles 31 and

338. Regulation (EC) No 864/2007 of the European Parliament and of the Council of 11 Jul. 2007 on the law applicable to non-contractual obligations (Rome II), OJ L 199, 31.7.2007, pp. 40–49.

339. *See*, for example: U. Magnus, P. Mankowski, *European Commentaries on Private International Law. Volume III. Commentary. Rome II Regulation*, Otto Schmidt, Köln 2019.

340. For Polish literature, *see* A. Nowicka in: J. Poczobut ed. *Prawo prywatne międzynarodowe. Komentarz*, Wolters Kluwer, Warszawa 2017, pp. 570–601; M. Pazdan, ed. *Prawo prywatne międzynarodowe. Komentarz*, Wydawnictwo C. H. Beck, Warszawa 2018, pp. 885–1036; M. Czepelak, *Międzynarodowe prawo zobowiązań Unii Europejskiej*, LexisNexis, Warszawa 2012.

341. *See* Explanatory report written by E. Essén published in Acts and Documents of the Eleventh Session (1968), tome III, Traffic accidents, p. 206.

32).[342] This fact is reminded by Article 33 PILA, which stresses that law applicable to non-contractual obligations is determined in accordance with Rome II Regulation. PILA never contained its own rules on non-contractual obligations (with exceptions mentioned below) as it entered into force on 16 May 2011, once Rome II Regulation was already applied. Its predecessor PILA 1965 contained such rule in the Article 31.[343] It was the only Article devoted to non-contractual obligations in PILA 1965. It provided for the *lex loci delicti commissi* principle (Article 31 §1 PILA 1965), but also stated that if both parties are nationals of the same country and have there their domicile, the law of that country applies (Article 31 §2 PILA). Article 31 §3 PILA 1965 made clear that law applicable to non-contractual obligations governed the question whether a person with limited capacity assumes liability. Choice of applicable law was not provided for in PILA 1965.

317. Article 1(1) and 1(2) Rome II Regulation enumerates issues left outside of its scope, for example, the liability of the State for acts and omissions in the exercise of State authority (*acta iure imperii*) or non-contractual obligations arising out of violations of privacy and rights relating to personality, including defamation. The former issue is specifically regulated by Article 35 PILA, whereas the latter by Article 16 PILA (*see* Part II., Chapter 4, §1 for details).

318. Here it should also be noted that, in accordance with Article 28(1), Rome II Regulation does not prejudice the application of international conventions to which one or more Member States are parties at the time when the Regulation was adopted and which lay down conflict-of-law rules relating to non-contractual obligations. Poland is party to the (multilateral) Hague Convention on Traffic Accidents since 2002, and therefore, in Poland this Convention takes precedence before Rome II Regulation.[344] This is also reminded by Article 34 PILA.[345] The Hague Convention lays down rules on law applicable to civil non-contractual liability arising from traffic accidents. Article 28(1) Rome II Regulation equally applies to bilateral conventions with non-EU states. EU Member States are obliged to notify the list of such conventions to the European Commission. As a result Poland notified that it will continue to apply bilateral conventions, which contain rules on law applicable to non-contractual obligations, with former Yugoslavia (1960) (now applied in relations with Bosnia and Herzegovina, Serbia, Montenegro and North Macedonia), Korea (1986), Vietnam (1993), Ukraine (1993), Belarus (1993) and Russia

342. Case C-412/10 *Homawoo*, Judgment of the CJEU of 17 Nov. 2011.
343. T. Pajor, *Odpowiedzialność deliktowa w prawie prywatnym międzynarodowym*, Państwowe Wydawnictwo Naukowe, Warszawa 1989, pp. 140–282.
344. M. Krzymuski, *Wybór prawa właściwego dla pozaumownej odpowiedzialności cywilnej wynikającej z wypadków drogowych*, w: *Znad granicy ponad granicami. Księga dedykowana prof. Dieterowi Martiny*, red. M. Krzymuski, M. Margoński, Warszawa 2014, pp. 133–151. *See also*: Notifications under Article 29(1) of Regulation (EC) No 864/2007 on the law applicable to non-contractual obligations (Rome II), OJ C 343, 17.12.2010, pp. 7–11.
345. A. Nowicka in: J. Poczobut ed. *Prawo prywatne międzynarodowe. Komentarz*, Wolters Kluwer, Warszawa 2017, pp. 602–613.

(1996).[346] Inversely, in accordance with Article 28(2) Rome II Regulation takes precedence over bilateral conventions between EU Member States. This concerns also bilateral conventions concluded by Poland with other EU Member States, which contain applicable law rules with respect to non-contractual obligations (e.g., bilateral convention with former Yugoslavia (1960) in relations with Slovenia and Croatia or bilateral convention with Lithuania (1993)).

I. Party Autonomy

319. Rome II Regulation is divided into chapters. Chapter I deals with its scope, Chapter II is dedicated to torts/delicts, Chapter III to specific non-contractual obligations (like unjust enrichment), whereas Chapter IV to party autonomy. Chapter IV consist of only one provision, namely Article 14 (freedom of choice). Recital 31 explains that to respect the principle of party autonomy and to enhance legal certainty, the parties are allowed to make a choice as to the law applicable to a non-contractual obligation. At the same time, it underlines that protection should be given to weaker parties by imposing certain conditions on the choice. As a result, the rules on choice of applicable law are different with respect to situations where all parties are pursuing commercial activity and others. In the first instance, where all the parties are pursuing a commercial activity, parties may agree on the law applicable by an agreement freely negotiated, even before the event giving rise to the damage occurred (Article 14(1)(b)). In other cases, choice of applicable law is admissible only by an agreement entered into after the event giving rise to the damage occurred (Article 14(1)(a)). In both cases, the choice must be express or tacit (demonstrated with reasonable certainty by the circumstances of the case) and must not prejudice the rights of third parties. Recital 31 underlines that where establishing the existence of the agreement, the court has to respect the intentions of the parties.

320. When discussing party autonomy and admissibility of the choice of applicable law, one should bear in mind limitations provided for in Article 14(2), which concerns purely domestic cases and Article 14(3), which concerns intra-EU cases. These provisions are modelled just like Article 3(3) and (4) of the Rome I Regulation (*see* Part II, Chapter 2, §1. Contractual obligations, I. Party autonomy). A choice of applicable law in purely domestic cases (where all the elements relevant to the situation at the time when the event giving rise to the damage occurs are located in a country other than the country whose law has been chosen) or intra EU-cases (where such elements are located in one or more of the EU Member States and a non-EU state law is chosen), such a choice does not prejudice the application of provisions of the law which cannot be derogated from by an agreement of – respectively – that other country or EU law (where appropriate – as implemented in the Member State of the forum). These rules, which cannot be derogated by an agreement mean *ius congens* within the substantive law and should not be confused

346. *See also*: Notifications under Article 29(1) of Regulation (EC) No 864/2007 on the law applicable to non-contractual obligations (Rome II), OJ C 343, 17.12.2010, pp. 7–11.

with overriding mandatory provisions to which Article 9 Rome II refers. As a result, the application of Article 14(2) and (3) reduces a choice of applicable law to merely a material law reference (German *materiellrechtliche Verweisung*) of foreign law provisions into the applicable law designated by an objective connecting factor.[347]

321. In certain cases, the Regulation makes it clear that choice of applicable law is not admissible. This is the case, for example, of unfair competition where Article 6(4) states that the law applicable may not be derogated from by an agreement. Similar provision may be found in Article 8(3) with respect to infringement of intellectual property rights.

II. Objective Connection

322. Applicable law rules, which use objective connecting factors are located in Chapter II of the Rome II Regulation when it comes to torts and Chapter III when it comes to other specific non-contractual obligations. Chapter II consist of a general rule (Article 4) and specific rules for specific delicts/torts (Articles 5–9). Chapter III consists of specific rules only (Articles 10–12).

323. As Recital 14 explains the Regulation provides for a general rule but also for specific rules and, in certain provisions, for an escape clause which allows a departure from these rules where it is clear from all the circumstances of the case that the tort/delict is manifestly more closely connected with another country. This creates a flexible framework and enables the court seized to treat individual cases in an appropriate manner.

324. As mentioned above, the general rule that is set forth in Article 4(1) Rome II Regulation states that the law applicable to a non-contractual obligation arising out of a tort/delict is the law of the country in which the damage occurs (*lex loci damni*) irrespective of the country in which the event giving rise to the damage occurred and irrespective of the country or countries in which the indirect consequences of that event occur. Recital 17 explains that in cases of personal injury or damage to property, the country in which the damage occurs should be the country where the injury was sustained, or the property was damaged, respectively. Article 4(2) Rome II Regulation creates an exception to this general principle. It states that where the person claimed to be liable and the person sustaining damage both have their habitual residence in the same country at the time when the damage occurs, the law of that country applies. The definition of habitual residence with respect to natural persons acting in the course of their business activity and legal entities is to be found in Article 23 Rome II Regulation.

347. M. Czepelak, *Międzynarodowe prawo zobowiązań Unii Europejskiej*, LexisNexis, Warszawa 2012, pp. 145–150.

III. Law of Torts

A. *Lex Loci Delicti*

325. As underlined in Recital 15 Rome II Regulation, the principle of the *lex loci delicti commissi* used to be in the past the basic solution for non-contractual obligations in virtually all the EU Member States (which is also truth for PILA 1965 and, in general, bilateral agreements concluded by Poland), but the practical application of this principle, where the component factors of the case were spread over several countries, varied. This endangered certainty as to the law applicable. As a result, Rome II departs from this principle. Consequently, in general, the law applicable is determined based on where the damage occurs (*lex loci damni*), regardless of the country or countries in which the indirect consequences could occur. Accordingly, in cases of personal injury or damage to property, the country in which the damage occurs should be the country where the injury was sustained, or the property was damaged respectively (Recital 17). It is believed that a connection with the country where the direct damage occurred strikes a fair balance between the interests of the person claimed to be liable and the person sustaining the damage, and also reflects the modern approach to civil liability and the development of systems of strict liability (Recital 16). This is supposed to enhance the foreseeability of court decisions and ensure a reasonable balance between the interests of persons involved.

B. *Scope of Application*

326. Article 15 Rome II Regulation lists, in a non-exhaustive manner, issues governed by the law applicable. This includes, *inter alia*, the basis and extent of liability, including the determination of persons who may be held liable for acts performed by them the grounds for exemption from liability, any limitation of liability and any division of liability, the existence, the nature and the assessment of damage or the remedy claimed, within the limits of powers conferred on the court by its procedural law, the measures which a court may take to prevent or terminate injury or damage or to ensure the provision of compensation, the question whether a right to claim damages or a remedy may be transferred, including by inheritance, persons entitled to compensation for damage sustained personally, liability for the acts of another person and the manner in which an obligation may be extinguished and rules of prescription and limitation, including rules relating to the commencement, interruption and suspension of a period of prescription or limitation. Recital 12 underlines that the law applicable also governs the question of the capacity to incur liability.

C. *Damages (Compensation)*

327. Article 15(c) Rome II Regulation states that the law applicable governs the existence, the nature and the assessment of damage or the remedy claimed. This means that the question of compensation is also governed by the law applicable. At the same time, Recital 33 suggests that when quantifying damages for personal injury in cases in which the accident takes place in a state other than that of the habitual residence of the victim, the court should take into account all the relevant actual circumstances of the specific victim, including in particular the actual losses and costs of after-care and medical attention.

328. Rome II Regulation provides also for a classical public policy clause in Article 26. Recital 32 gives an example of the situation where this clause may come to play. It suggests that awarding non-compensatory exemplary or punitive damages of an excessive nature in accordance with applicable law designated by the Regulation, depending on the circumstances of the case and the legal order of the forum, might trigger the use of public policy clause.

D. Insurance and Social Security Law

329. When it comes to insurance, Article 18 Rome II Regulation deals with a question of a direct action against the insurer of the person liable. It provides that a person having suffered damage may bring a claim directly against the insurer of the person liable to provide compensation if the law applicable to the non-contractual obligation or the law applicable to the insurance contract so provides. The law applicable to an insurance contract is the one designated by the Article 7 Rome I Regulation. Rome II Regulation refers also to subrogation in Article 19, which might take place when an insurer covers the non-contractual obligation of a liable person. It states that where a person (the creditor) has a non-contractual claim upon another (the debtor), and a third person has a duty to satisfy the creditor, or has in fact satisfied the creditor in discharge of that duty, the law which governs the third person's duty to satisfy the creditor determines whether, and the extent to which, the third person is entitled to exercise against the debtor the rights which the creditor had against the debtor under the law governing their relationship. Social security law belongs to administrative matters, which are outside the scope of application of both – Rome I and Rome II Regulations.

IV. Unfair Competition

330. A separate provision of the Rome II Regulation is devoted to unfair competition and acts restricting free competition.[348] However, Recital 21 underlines that this rule is not an exception to the general *lex loci damni* principle, but rather a clarification of it. Article 6(1) states that the law applicable is the law of the country where competitive relations or the collective interests of consumers are, or are likely to be, affected. On the other hand, where an act of unfair competition affects exclusively the interests of a specific competitor, Article 4 (the general rule) applies

348. *See* E. Figura-Góralczyk, *Nieuczciwa konkurencja w prawie prywatnym międzynarodowym*, Wolters Kluwer, Warszawa 2017.

(Article 6(2)). The law applicable to obligation arising out of a restriction of competition is the law of the country where the market is, or is likely to be, affected (Article 6(3)(a)). In cases where the market is, or is likely to be, affected in more than one country, the claimant is able, in certain circumstances, to choose to base the claim on the law of the *forum* (Article 6(3)(b)). Recitals 22 and 23 explain that the notion of restrictions of competition encompasses infringements of both national and EU competition law and covers prohibitions on agreements between undertakings, decisions by associations of undertakings and concerted practices which have as their object or effect the prevention, restriction or distortion of competition, as well as prohibitions on the abuse of a dominant position. Choice of applicable law is not admissible.

V. Negotiorum Gestio

331. Article 11 Rome II Regulation provides for a separate rule with respect to *negotiorum gestio*. It states that if non-contractual liability resulting from an act performed without due authority in connection with the affairs of another person concerns a relationship existing between the parties (a contract or a delict) that is closely connected with that non-contractual obligation, it is governed by the law that governs that relationship (*lex cause* – Article 11(1)). Where the law applicable cannot be determined on that basis and the parties have their habitual residence in the same country when the event giving rise to the damage occurs, the law of that country applies (Article 11(2)). In other cases, it is the law of the country in which the act was performed (Article 11(3)). Also an escape clause is provided (Article 11(4)) stating that where it is clear from all the circumstances of the case that the obligation is manifestly more closely connected with a country other than that indicated in the above rules, the law of that other country applies. PILA 1965 never contained a specific rule with respect to *negotiorum gestio*, so the general rule of Article 31 PILA applied.[349]

VI. Unjust Enrichment

332. Article 10 Rome II Regulation provides for a separate rule with respect to unjust enrichment, which is construed similarly to the one on *negotiorum gestio*. If a non-contractual obligation arising out of unjust enrichment, including payment of amounts wrongly received, concerns a relationship existing between the parties, such as one arising out of a contract or a tort/delict, that is closely connected with that unjust enrichment, it shall be governed by the law that governs that relationship (*lex causae* – Article 10(1)). Where the law applicable cannot be determined on that basis and the parties have their habitual residence in the same country when the event giving rise to unjust enrichment occurs, the law of that country applies

349. T. Pajor, *Odpowiedzialność deliktowa w prawie prywatnym międzynarodowym*, Państwowe Wydawnictwo Naukowe, Warszawa 1989, p. 210.

(Article 10(2)). In other cases, it is the law of the country in which the unjust enrichment took place (Article 10(3)). Also, an escape clause is provided (Article 10(4)). As mentioned above, PILA does not provide for any rules concerning non-contractual obligations, apart from Article 35 (*acta iure imperii*). PILA 1965 never contained a specific rule with respect to unjust enrichment (or other specific situations), so the general rule of Article 31 PILA 1965 applied.[350]

VII. *Culpa in Contrahendo*

333. Article 12 Rome II Regulation provides for a separate rule with respect to *culpa in contrahendo*, which is construed similarly to the one on *negotiorum gestio* and unjust enrichment. *Culpa in contrahendo* for the purposes of the Regulation, as explained in Recital 30, is an autonomous concept and should not necessarily be interpreted within the meaning of national law. It should include the violation of the duty of disclosure and the breakdown of contractual negotiations. This provision covers only non-contractual obligations presenting a direct link with the dealings prior to the conclusion of a contract. It applies regardless of whether the contract was actually concluded or not. The law applicable to *culpa in contrahendo* is the law that applies/would have been applicable to the contract (Article 12(1)). Hence, the applicable law should be ascertained based on Rome I Regulation. If the law applicable cannot be determined on that basis, it is the law of the country in which the damage occurs or, where the parties have their habitual residence in the same country at the time when the event giving rise to the damage occurs, the law of that country. Also, an escape clause is provided (Article 12(2)(c)). PILA 1965 never contained a specific rule with respect to *culpa in contrahendo*.

VIII. Other

334. Recital 19 Rome II Regulation states that the general rule not always allows a reasonable balance to be struck between the interests at stake. That is why Rome II Regulation contains separate rules for specific delicts. This include, apart from unfair competition dealt with above, product liability (Article 5), environmental damage (Article 7), infringement of intellectual property rights (Article 8) and industrial action (Article 9). As mentioned above, the issues left outside the material scope of Rome II Regulation might be regulated by rules contained in bilateral conventions and, if no bilateral convention is in place or does not cover non-contractual obligations, by PILA. However, PILA specifically addresses only the question of *acta iure imperii*. In accordance with Article 35 PILA, non-contractual obligations resulting from acts or omissions of bodies executing public powers in a given country is governed by the law of that country.[351]

---

350. P. Mostowik, *Bezpodstawne wzbogacenie w prawie prywatnym międzynarodowym*, LexisNexis, Warszawa 2006.

351. A. Nowicka in: J. Poczobut ed. *Prawo prywatne międzynarodowe. Komentarz*, Wolters Kluwer, Warszawa 2017, pp. 613–622.

Chapter 3. Property

§1. *Lex Rei Sitae*

335. Property is regulated in Chapter 9 PILA called 'Ownership and other rights *in rem*. Possession'. It consists of Articles 41–45. Article 41(1) states that ownership and other rights in rem are governed the law of the country, where their object is situated (*lex rei sitae*). Pursuant to Article 41(2) acquisition and loss of the ownership, as well as acquisition, loss and change in the content or priority of other rights in rem are governed by the law of the country, where the object of these rights was situated at the time that the event resulting in these legal consequences occurred. Articles 41–44 apply also to possession (Article 45 PILA). Similar rules were contained in PILA's predecessor, namely Article 24 PILA 1965.

336. The above rules apply equally to movable and immovable property. The notion of 'rights in rem' used in Article 41 PILA might rise doubts as different rights might be considered as rights in rem in different states. Similarly, the distinction between obligations and rights in rem is not necessarily clear. It is underlined that the most characteristic feature of rights in rem is their *erga omnes* effect. However, it is a law of a given country that attaches *erga omnes* effect to a given right. As a result, *lex rei sitae* should decide whether a given right is in fact a right in rem and if so, might be consequently applied as law applicable.[352] *Lex rei sitae* decides also whether a given asset should be classified as movable or immovable property.[353]

337. Localizing an immovable property should not, in general, be problematic. This is not always truth when it comes to movable property and rights, which may also be object of the right in rem. A movable property is 'located' for the purpose of *lex rei sitae* rule, where it is located physically (*situs naturalis*). If a right being object of the rights in rem relates to a tangible property it is perceived to be located where the tangible object is located. For example, a mortgage over a claim, which is secured by a mortgage over an immovable property is 'located' where an immovable property is located. In lack of this relation to tangible property, the right should be perceived as being 'located' in a country, which law is applicable to this right (*lex causae*).[354] Rights in rem over a document incorporating a right are located in a country where the document is located (*lex cartae*).

338. As Article 41(2) PILA states literally, *lex rei sitae* governs acquisition and loss of the ownership, as well as acquisition, change of the content, priority and extinction of rights in rem. The *lex rei sitae* answers also, *inter alia*, the question whether certain 'assets' might be subject of a right in rem (e.g., human organs) and

352. J. Górecki in: M. Pazdan (ed.), *Prawo prywatne międzynarodowe. Komentarz*, Wydawnictwo C. H. Beck, Warszawa 2018, p. 379.
353. M. Tomaszewski, in: J. Poczobut (ed.), *Prawo prywatne międzynarodowe. Komentarz*, Wolters Kluwer, Warszawa 2017, p. 689.
354. J. Górecki in: M. Pazdan (ed.), *Prawo prywatne międzynarodowe. Komentarz*, Wydawnictwo C. H. Beck, Warszawa 2018, p. 383.

whether an accessory part of an asset might constitute a separate object of rights in rem. *Lex rei sitae* covers also following issues: what requirements must be fulfilled for a right in rem to be created, transferred or terminated (e.g., whether the possession of an object of a right in rem is necessary for the right to be transferred), whether a given right in rem is transferable or constitutes so-called *res extra commercium*, what are the legal titles based on which a right in rem might be transferred (e.g., a contract or an acquisitive prescription), at what point in time the transfer takes place. Similarly, *lex rei sitae* decides which rights in rem might be created by operation of law and how certain legal events (e.g., abandoning of an asset) influence rights in rem.[355]

339. Here it should be explained that in Poland (in its substantive law), in general, a contract obliging to transfer a right in rem (from example, a sale contract) has so-called dual effect, meaning that it simultaneously transfers this right to the acquirer. It may happen, under certain circumstance (e.g., if parties decide so), that in order to transfer a right in rem a contract separate from the obliging contract must be concluded.[356] In some countries, such dual effect is not known, and therefore, two separate contracts are always concluded. In others, no such distinction exists and consequently a single contract suffices to transfer a right in rem. Hence, it is suggested that *lex rei sitae* principle governs these contracts, which only transfer rights in rem, whereas law applicable to contractual obligation (designated in accordance with Rome I Regulation) governs the obliging contract. *Lex rei sitae* governs also in rem effects of an obliging contract, which based on the law applicable to it has dual effect. *Lex rei sitae* decides whether in rem effect is conditional upon additional requirements (e.g., entering the right into a register or transferring the possession of an asset).[357] It is debated in Poland whether an obliging contract governed by substantive law, which do not know the dual effect, but requires two separate contracts to be concluded, will anyway produce the dual effect, as long as the dual effect is provided for by *lex rei sitae*.[358] Substantive validity of an obliging contract (also the one having a dual effect) is governed by the law applicable to this contract and not *lex rei sitae*, whereas substantive validity of the contract, which solely transfers right in rem is governed by *lex rei sitae*.[359]

355. J. Górecki in: M. Pazdan (ed.), *Prawo prywatne międzynarodowe. Komentarz*, Wydawnictwo C. H. Beck, Warszawa 2018, pp. 383–391.
356. P. Machnikowski, J. Balcarczyk, M. Drela, *Contract Law in Poland*, Wolters Kluwer, Alphen aan der Rijn 2014, p. 41.
357. J. Górecki in: M. Pazdan (ed.), *Prawo prywatne międzynarodowe. Komentarz*, Wydawnictwo C. H. Beck, Warszawa 2018, pp. 385–386.
358. For positive answer, *see* J. Górecki in: M. Pazdan (ed.), *Prawo prywatne międzynarodowe. Komentarz*, Wydawnictwo C. H. Beck, Warszawa 2018, p. 386; whereas for negative answer, *see* M. Tomaszewski, in: J. Poczobut (ed.), *Prawo prywatne międzynarodowe. Komentarz*, Wolters Kluwer, Warszawa 2017, p. 694.
359. J. Górecki in: M. Pazdan (ed.), *Prawo prywatne międzynarodowe. Komentarz*, Wydawnictwo C. H. Beck, Warszawa 2018, pp. 386–387.

340. It must be noted that rules on ownership and rights in rem concerning immovable property providing for *lex rei sitae* principle are also contained in some of bilateral agreements concluded by Poland. As mentioned before bilateral agreements take precedence before PILA.

§2. MOVEABLE PROPERTY

I. Collateral

341. A pledge, where a movable property or other rights constitute collateral against the debt is a right in rem and, therefore, governed by *lex rei sitae.*

342. When it comes to moveable property, which may be moved across borders, the issue of change of the applicable law appears. Article 41(2) PILA remedies this by stating that acquisition, loss, change in the content or priority of the rights in rem is governed by *lex rei sitae* applicable at the moment that these legal consequences took place. It may however happen that a given right in rem created under 'the old' *lex rei sitae* simply does not exist in the 'new' *lex rei sitae* (due to *numerus clausus* of rights in rem rule). It is currently advocated that this issue should be resolved by adaptation, which means treating a given right in rem created under 'the old' *lex rei sitae* as its closest equivalent in 'the new' *lex rei sitae.*[360]

II. Goods in Transit

343. In accordance with Article 43 PILA rights in rem in movables in transit are governed by the law of the country from which they were dispatched (*lex loci expeditionis*). However, if the circumstances of the case indicate that these rights are more closely connected with another country, the law of that other country applies. In PILA 1965 there was no separate provision concerning goods in transit.

III. Cultural Property

344. Claims for return of cultural objects are regulated in Poland by the EU Directive,[361] which was implemented into domestic law, namely the Act on the restitution of national cultural objects.[362] The latter contains rule on PIL. In accordance with its Article 8, the ownership of a national cultural object returned to

360. J. Górecki in: M. Pazdan (ed.), *Prawo prywatne międzynarodowe. Komentarz*, Wydawnictwo C. H. Beck, Warszawa 2018, pp. 392–393; I. Karasek, *Kolizyjnoprawna problematyka nieposesoryjnych zabezpieczeń rzeczowych ustanowionych pod rządem praw obcych*, Transformacje Prawa Prywatnego 2006, v. 2, p. 19.
361. Directive 2014/60/EU of the European Parliament and of the Council of 15 May 2014 on the return of cultural objects unlawfully removed from the territory of a Member State and amending Regulation (EU) No 1024/2012 (Recast), OJ L 159, 28.5.2014, pp. 1–10.
362. Act of 25 May 2017 on the restitution of national cultural property, Dz. U. 2017 poz. 1086.

Poland, as well as acquisition and loss of the ownership of this object is governed by Polish law no matter if at the moment of the event resulting in acquisition or loss of ownership this object was located at the territory of Poland.

345. International conventions also apply, for example, UNESCO Convention (1970)[363] and Hague Convention (1954).[364] Poland is not yet a party to UNIDROIT Convention (1995).[365] When it comes to export of cultural goods restriction provided for in the EU Regulation[366] and in the Act on the Protection and Care of Monuments[367] apply.

IV. Other

346. Pursuant to Article 42 PILA, rights in rem with respect to certain transport vehicles (aircrafts, vessels and rail vehicles) are governed by the law of the country, in which the vehicle is entered into the register, and in case there is no register or no entry into the register, the law of the country of the home port, home station or other similar place. There are also specific rules in place which constitute *lex specialis* to Article 42 PILA. In accordance with Article 355(2) Maritime Code,[368] rights in rem in a vessel entered into national register are governed by the law of the country of this register. Pursuant to Article 11(2) Aviation Law,[369] rights in rem in aircrafts created in accordance with foreign law, in which an aircraft was registered at the time of their creation and entered into the register in that state, are recognized also in Poland, if they were entered into register in Poland.

§3. Immoveable Property

I. Mortgage

347. Mortgage is understood in Poland as a right in rem, which may have as its object an immovable property, certain other rights in rem (e.g., perpetual usufruct) and a claim secured with a mortgage. Mortgage is governed by *lex rei sitae* (Article 41(1) PILA).

---

363. Convention of 14 Nov. 1970 on the Means of Prohibiting and Preventing the Illicit Import, Export and Transfer of Ownership of Cultural Property, 1970, Dz. U. z 1974 r. nr 20 poz. 106.
364. Hague Convention of 14 May 1954 for the Protection of Cultural Property in the Event of Armed Conflict, Dz. U. z 1957 r. nr 46 poz. 212.
365. UNIDROIT Convention on Stolen or Illegally Exported Cultural Objects signed in Rome on 24 Jun. 1995.
366. Council Regulation (EC) No 116/2009 of 18 Dec. 2008 on the export of cultural goods (Codified version), OJ L 39, 10.2.2009, pp. 1–7.
367. Act of 23 Jul. 2003 on the protection and care of monuments (*Ustawa o ochronie zabytków i opiece nad zabytkami*), Dz. U. 2020 poz. 282.
368. Dz. U. 2018 poz. 2175.
369. Dz. U. 2019 poz. 1580.

II. Immissions

348. There is no provision concerning immissions in PILA. On one hand, it was suggested that immissions are covered by *lex rei sitae* principle,[370] on the other that it could be treated as delict and, therefore, rules concerning non-contractual obligations should apply.[371]

III. Easements

349. Easements are rights in rem which are governed by *lex rei sitae* pursuant to Article 41(1) PILA.

§4. Securities

350. Pursuant to Article 31 PILA obligations resulting from a security, other than a bill of exchange or cheque, is governed by the law of the country, in which this security was issued. Whereas, in accordance with Article 1(2)(d) Rome I Regulation, obligations arising under bills of exchange, cheques and promissory notes and other negotiable instruments to the extent that the obligations under such other negotiable instruments arise out of their negotiable character are outside of its scope. Recital 9 explains that the above covers bills of lading to the extent that the obligations under the bill of lading arise out of its negotiable character. Hence, it was suggested that obligations, which do not arise out of the negotiable character of an instrument are covered by Rome I Regulation. For example, obligations resulting from the loan agreement, which is secured by such an instrument are governed by the law applicable to the contract designated in accordance with Rome II Regulation, whereas Article 31 PILA covers relations between the issuer and each holder of the security.[372] Specific applicable law rules concerning bills of exchange and cheques (including legal capacity, their material and formal validity) are provided for, respectively, in Articles 77–79 Bill of Exchange Law and 62–68 Cheque Law. When it comes to dematerialized securities which are entered to the account held within a settlement system a separate PIL rule is provided for in Article 44 PILA. It states that rights resulting from an entry of the security to the account held within a settlement system is governed by the law of the country in which the account is held.

---

370. J. Górecki in: M. Pazdan (ed.), *Prawo prywatne międzynarodowe. Komentarz*, Wydawnictwo C. H. Beck, Warszawa 2018, p. 390.
371. J. Górecki, *Prawa rzeczowe i posiadanie w projekcie ustawy o prawie prywatnym międzynarodowym*, PWPM 2009, pp. 19–20.
372. A. Wiśniewski in: J. Poczobut (ed.), Prawo prywatne międzynarodowe. Komentarz, Wolters Kluwer, Warszawa 2017, pp. 543–558; P. Machnikowski in: M. Pazdan (ed.), *Prawo prywatne międzynarodowe. Komentarz*, Wydawnictwo C. H. Beck, Warszawa 2018, pp. 322–327.

§5. TRUST

351. Both, Rome I and Rome II Regulations provide that the constitution of trusts and the relationship between settlors, trustees and beneficiaries are excluded from their scope of application. Similarly, Succession Regulation states that the creation, administration and dissolution of trusts is excluded from the scope of the EU Succession Regulation. The concept of trust does not exist in substantive law in Poland. Hence, there is no PIL rule in domestic law specifically devoted to trusts. It is suggested that, in certain circumstances, trusts are covered by Article 67 PILA which provides that a legal relationship, to which rules contained in domestic, international and EU PIL does not designate law applicable, is governed by the law of the country with which it is most closely connected. In such case, rules included in the Hague Convention on Trusts (1985)[373] might serve as guidance, even though Poland is not party to this convention.[374]

§6. EXPROPRIATION

352. Lex rei sitae (Article 41(1) PILA) governs events which have legal consequences with respect to ownership and other rights in rem, for example acquisition of property as a result of acquisitive prescription or confusion of goods, as well as acts of state power, including expropriation.[375]

373. Convention of 1 Jul. 1985 on the Law Applicable to Trusts and on their Recognition.
374. M. Zachariasiewicz in: M. Pazdan (ed.), *Prawo prywatne międzynarodowe. Komentarz*, Wydawnictwo C. H. Beck, Warszawa 2018, pp. 547–559.
375. M. Tomaszewski, in: J. Poczobut (ed.), *Prawo prywatne międzynarodowe. Komentarz*, Wolters Kluwer, Warszawa 2017, p. 695.

Chapter 4. Intangible Property Rights

§1. Rights of Personality

I. Applicable Law

353. Article 16 PILA refers to rights of personality of individuals. The law applicable to rights of personality is the national law of the individual (Article 16(1)). PILA provides for a separate rule designating the law under which the protection of rights of personality may be claimed (*see below*), which leads to doubts as to relation between the two provisions.[376] Same rules are applied accordingly to the protection of rights of personality of legal entities (Article 20). Hence, the 'national law' of the legal entity should be ascertained in accordance with Article 17(1) and 17(2).

II. Remedies

354. In accordance with Article 1(2)(g) Rome II Regulation non-contractual obligations arising out of violations of privacy and rights relating to personality, including defamation are excluded from its scope. Pursuant to Article 16(2) PILA, an individual, whose rights of personality are endangered by infringement or have been infringed may claim protection under the law of the state, on the territory of which an event causing this endangerment or infringement occurred or the law of the state, on the territory of which the consequences of this endangerment or infringement occurred. Pursuant to Article16(3) PILA if the infringement of the rights of personality of an individual was effected in mass media, the right of reply, to issue a corrected version or other equivalent measure is governed by the law of the country in which the broadcaster or publisher has its seat or habitual residence. Mass media encompasses newspapers, television, radio, and internet.[377]

§2. Intellectual Property

I. Creation

355. Chapter 10 'Intellectual Property' of PILA refers to all intellectual property rights, namely copyright, related rights, the sui generis right for the protection of databases and industrial property rights, including patents, trademarks and industrial designs.[378] It consists of two articles (Article 46 and Article 47). Pursuant to

376. *See* E. Figura-Góralczyk, P. Mostowik in: M. Pazdan (ed.), *Prawo prywatne międzynarodowe. Komentarz*, C. H. Beck, Warszawa 2018, pp. 74–85.
377. M. Pilich in: J. Poczobut (ed.), *Prawo prywatne międzynarodowe. Komentarz*, Wolters Kluwer, Warszawa 2017, p. 324.
378. A. Nowicka in: J. Poczobut (ed.), *Prawo prywatne międzynarodowe. Komentarz*, Wolters Kluwer, Warszawa 2017, pp. 725–726.

Article 46(1) the creation, content and extinction of the intellectual property right is governed by the law of the country where the property is being exploited (l*ex loci protectionis*).[379]

II. Protection

356. Article 46(3) states that protection of intellectual property is governed by the law of the country for which protection is claimed (*lex loci protectionis*). The scope of application of this provision is limited by Rome II Regulation, which covers non-contractual obligations arising from an infringement of an intellectual property rights[380] (*see below*).

III. Ownership and Transfer

357. Contractual obligations regarding intellectual property rights are covered by Rome I Regulation. Pursuant to its Article 3(1) a contract is governed by the law chosen by the parties. If there is no choice of applicable law made by the parties, it provides that, for example, a sale contract is governed by the law of the country of the habitual residence of the seller (Article 4(1)(a)) and a contract not covered by Article 4(1), for example, a license contract, is governed by the law of the country where the party required to effect the so-called characteristic performance has his habitual residence (Article 4(2)).

358. The question who is the initial owner of the intellectual property rights (Article 46(1) PILA)[381] and its transfer is governed by *lex loci protectionis*. Article 46(2) PILA makes it clear that *lex loci protectionis* applies to the disposition of intellectual property rights and to ascertainment of their priority. Hence, a contractual obligation resulting from, for example, a sale contract having as its object a patent is governed by the law designated by Rome I Regulation (the law of the country of the habitual residence of the seller), whereas the transfer of the patent to the buyer is governed by the law designated by Article 26(2) PILA (*lex loci protectionis*).[382]

359. Pursuant to Article 47 PILA rights of the employee towards the employer with respect to intellectual property related to the activity within the employment contact are governed by the law applicable to that employment (which in turn is covered by Rome I Regulation).

379. A. Nowicka in: J. Poczobut (ed.), *Prawo prywatne międzynarodowe. Komentarz*, Wolters Kluwer, Warszawa 2017, pp. 729.
380. A. Nowicka in: J. Poczobut (ed.), *Prawo prywatne międzynarodowe. Komentarz*, Wolters Kluwer, Warszawa 2017, pp. 751–752.
381. A. Nowicka in: J. Poczobut (ed.), *Prawo prywatne międzynarodowe. Komentarz*, Wolters Kluwer, Warszawa 2017, p. 730.
382. A. Nowicka in: J. Poczobut (ed.), *Prawo prywatne międzynarodowe. Komentarz*, Wolters Kluwer, Warszawa 2017 p. 748.

IV. Infringement

360. Rome II Regulation covers non-contractual obligation arising from an infringement of an intellectual property rights. Pursuant to Article 8 Rome II Regulation it is governed be the law of the country for which protection is claimed (*lex loci protectionis*). Recital 26 Rome II Regulation explains that intellectual property rights means, for instance, copyright, related rights, the sui generis right for the protection of databases and industrial property rights. Choice of applicable law is excluded (Article 8(3)).

361. Pursuant to Article 8(2) Rome II in the case of a non-contractual obligation arising from an infringement of a unitary EU intellectual property right (e.g., an EU trademark or EU design), the law applicable for any question that is not governed by the relevant EU instrument is the law of the country in which the act of infringement was committed (*lex loci delicti*).

362. It should be mentioned that protection of intellectual property rights is subject of numerous international conventions[383] to which Poland is party to, and therefore, might limit the scope of application of the above-mentioned provisions.

383. For example, Paris Act 1971 concerning Berne Convention for the protection of literary and artistic works (Dz. U. z 1990 r. nr 82 poz. 474), Paris Convention for the protection of industrial property as revised at Stockholm on July 14, 1967 (Dz. U. z 1975 r. nr 9 poz. 51), or Universal Copyright Convention as revised at Paris on 24 Jul. 1971 (Dz. U. z 1978 r. nr 8 poz. 28).

Chapter 5. Family Law

§1. State Law – Religious Law

363. The dominant religion in Poland is Catholicism. Belonging to the Catholic Church is declared by over 85% of Poles. Nevertheless, Poland is formally a secular state. According to Article 10(1) of 1989 Act on guarantees of freedom of conscience and religion 'The Republic of Poland is a secular state, neutral in matters of religion and belief'.[384] Such provision is, however, not included in the 1997 Constitution of the Republic of Poland,[385] which in Article 25(1) states only that public authorities in Poland should be impartial in matters of personal conviction, whether religious or philosophical, or in relation to outlooks on life, and shall ensure their freedom of expression within public life.

364. In 1993 Poland signed the Concordat[386] with the Holy See, which came into force in 1998.[387] This agreement primarily determines the position of the Catholic Church in Poland and regulates a number of issues related to church activities and matters of faith, for example, the principles of religious education, the influence of state authorities on the appointment of episcopal positions, the issues of Church property. The Concordat and provide the basis for religious marriage with civil law consequences, which requires a special form and additional statement made by the spouses during the religious celebration. This rule is stated in Article 1(3) Family and Guardianship Code of 1964 (FGC).[388] Such recognition in civil law applies not only to religious marriages concluded in accordance with Catholic canon law, but also marriages concluded according to the rules of other religions, because Article 25 of Constitution grants equal rights to churches and other religious organizations.

365. Polish PIL allows to treat as applicable law only legal norms which are part of the legal system of a particular state.[389] Therefore conflict-of-law rules cannot indicate religious law, for example, sharia or canon law, as a law applicable, unless it is perceived as a state law.

§2. Marriage

I. Engagement

366. In Polish substantive family law, the promise of marriage, *id est* engagement, is not regulated. There is also no conflict-of-law rule indicating the law

384. Dz. U. 1989 nr 29 poz. 155.
385. Dz. U. 1997 nr 78 poz. 483.
386. Dz. U. 1998 nr 51 poz. 318.
387. Previous Concordat, signed in 1925, was in force till 1945.
388. Act of 25 Feb. 1964 – Family and Guardianship Code, Dz. U. 1964 nr 9 poz. 59.
389. J. Poczobut in: J. Poczobut (ed.), Prawo prywatne międzynarodowe. Komentarz, Wolters Kluwer, Warszawa 2017, p. 135.

applicable to an engagement. In such a case, the law applicable to the capacity to form an engagement, the effects of engagement and the effects of breaking it off may be designated in various ways.

367. First, it is possible to apply Article 67 PILA (referring to matters not covered by any previous rules) and thus apply to the engagement the law which the relationship is most closely connected with. Second, it is also possible to apply directly conflict-of-law rules determining the law applicable to a marriage – Articles 48–49 PILA.[390] First solution seems to have the advantage, as there is no formal legal basis for Articles 48 and 49 being applied directly to the engagement, while such a basis is provided by Article 67 PILA. Nevertheless, it should be noted that in most cases both solutions will lead to the same effect, *id est* applying to the engagement the same law that would be applied to the marriage. This is because most often the engagement will be most closely connected with the law that will also be applicable to the marriage itself.

368. The consequences of breaking off engagement should be assessed in accordance with the law applicable to the engagement, and therefore in the light of the national law of the fiancé and fiancée. Thus, the provisions of this law will decide whether the consequences of breaking off an engagement fall within the terms of the contractual statute or the tort statute.[391]

II. Heterosexual Marriage

369. In PILA law applicable to marriage is regulated by Article 48 and Article 49. Traditionally, since PILA 1926, Polish PIL distinguishes between substantial and formal premises of entering into marriage.[392]

A. Substance

370. Article 48 PILA deals with the ability to conclude marriage. This term is understood as substantial premises of entering into marriage. Those premises refer

390. W. Popiołek in: M. Pazdan (ed.), Prawo prywatne międzynarodowe. Komentarz, Wolters Kluwer, Warszawa 2018, p. 437; also *see*, with regard to PILA 1965, M. Sośniak in: M. Sośniak, B. Walaszek, E. Wierzbowski (eds), Międzynarodowe prawo rodzinne, Wydawnictwo PAN, Wrocław-Warszawa-Kraków 1969, p. 23.

391. E. Kamarad, *Zawarcie małżeństwa jako zagadnienie prawa rodzinnego, prawa prywatnego międzynarodowego i prawa konsularnego*, Wydawnictwo Uniwersytetu Jagiellońskiego, Kraków 2019, pp. 160–166.

392. K. Pietrzykowski in: J. Poczobut (ed.), Prawo prywatne międzynarodowe. Komentarz, Wolters Kluwer, Warszawa 2017; W. Popiołek in: M. Pazdan (ed.), System Prawa Prywatnego. Tom 20 C. Prawo prywatne międzynarodowe, Wydawnictwo C. H. Beck, Warszawa 2015. *See also*, with regard to PILA 1965: M. Sośniak in: M. Sośniak, B. Walaszek, E. Wierzbowski (eds), Międzynarodowe prawo rodzinne, Wydawnictwo PAN, Wrocław-Warszawa-Kraków 1969. K. Pietrzykowski, *Zawarcie małżeństwa i przesłanki jego ważności w prawie prywatnym międzynarodowym*, Warszawa 1985.

to persons' intention to conclude marriage, determining their capacity to do it, as well as to the expression of their will to marry. In other words, all the requirements that must be fulfilled in order to conclude a valid marriage, that are not related to the course of the wedding ceremony, are covered by the Article 48 PILA. Therefore, all the prohibitions or obstacles to enter into marriage fall into scope of this provision.[393] According to the Article 48 PILA, the ability to conclude marriage shall be determined for each of the parties by their respective national laws at the time of concluding the marriage.

371. If the spouse is a stateless person or a refugee, his or her ability to conclude marriage is governed by *lex domicili* according to Article 3 PILA or, in the absence of domicile, by the law of the country in which the spouse is habitually resident. In the case of spouse's multiple nationality reference should be made to Article 2(1) and (2) PILA.

372. One should also be aware of the possible use of the public policy clause (Article 7 PILA) (*see* Part I. Chapter 3, §7) and provisions on *renvoi* (Article 5(1) PILA).

373. The issue of the law applicable to the ability to conclude marriage is regulated in numerous bilateral international agreements signed by Poland. Most often they indicate as the applicable law the national law of the spouse. In some conventions, which take precedence over PILA, *lex loci celebrationis matrimonii* (e.g., bilateral agreements between Poland and Russia and between Poland and Finland) is complementary to this rule.

374. Poland is also a party to the Convention on Consent to Marriage, Minimum Age for Marriage and Registration of Marriages (1962).[394] Poland was also a party to the Hague Convention relating to the settlement of the conflict of the laws concerning marriage (1902),[395] but it was denounced in 1970.[396]

B. Form

375. Article 49 PILA indicates the law applicable to the form of the marriage. Formal requirements include those that concern the way of carrying out the marriage ceremony, including: participation of a competent state authority and witnesses, required documents, the possibility of concluding a marriage by proxy, announcing the marriage to the public and drawing up a marriage certificate.

393. W. Popiołek in: M. Pazdan (ed.), System Prawa Prywatnego. Tom 20 C. Prawo prywatne międzynarodowe, Wydawnictwo C. H. Beck, Warszawa 2015, p. 42.
394. Dz. U. 1965 nr 9 poz. 53.
395. Convention du 12 juin 1902 pour régler les conflits de lois en matière de mariage.
396. Dz. U. 1929 nr 80 poz. 594, Dz. U. 1970 nr 26 poz. 214.

376. According to Article 49 PILA the formal validity of a marriage is governed by the law of the state in which it is concluded (*lex loci celebrationis matrimonii*). If a marriage is concluded outside Poland, it suffices to comply with formal requirements provided for by the law of nationality of both spouses, or by the law of the place of their common domicile or habitual residence as of the day when the marriage is concluded.

III. Same-Sex Marriage

A. Substance

377. According to Polish family law, marriage can be concluded only by a man and a woman (Article 1 FGC[397]). Therefore, there is no provision concerning same-sex marriage, either in Polish substantive law or in PIL. If the law applicable to marriage (*see above*) allows marriage to be contracted with a person of the same sex, the possibility of contracting a marriage before a Polish civil registrar will be blocked by invoking the public order clause (Article 7 PILA). The principle of the different sex of spouses is treated as a fundamental principle of the Polish legal order.[398]

378. In the case of same-sex marriage concluded abroad, under foreign law, there is the question of its recognition and granting it legal effects of some sort, for example, in connection with inheritance or maintenance. The views of Polish doctrine are divergent: there is a view that granting such effects should also be blocked by invoking the public policy clause and the view that the public policy clause should not be applied in such cases.[399] Nevertheless, if necessity to assess the validity of same-sex marriage concluded abroad is a preliminary question in another case, it may be argued that it should be done in the light of the applicable law determined by the conflict-of-law rules on the ability to conclude a marriage (Article 48 PILA) and on the formal validity of marriage (Article 49 PILA).[400] There is no Polish jurisprudence yet in this matter.

397. Dz. U. 1964 nr 9 poz. 59.
398. M. Zachariasiewicz, *Klauzula porządku publicznego jako instrument ochrony materialnoprawnych interesów i wartości fori*, Wydawnictwo C. H. Beck, Warszawa 2018, pp. 298–311; K. Pietrzykowski, *Zawarcie małżeństwa i przesłanki jego ważności w prawie prywatnym międzynarodowym*, Warszawa 1985, p. 48.
399. *See* W. Popiołek in: M. Pazdan (ed.), System Prawa Prywatnego. Tom 20 C. Prawo prywatne międzynarodowe, Wydawnictwo C. H. Beck, Warszawa 2015, p. 58.
400. *See* M. A. Zachariasiewicz, *Nowa ustawa o prawie prywatnym międzynarodowym a małżeństwa i związki osób tej samej płci*, PPPM 2012, t. 11, pp. 71–113; E. Kamarad, *Zawarcie małżeństwa jako zagadnienie prawa rodzinnego, prawa prywatnego międzynarodowego i prawa konsularnego*, Wydawnictwo Uniwersytetu Jagiellońskiego, Kraków 2019, pp. 149–150.

B. Form

379. With respect to law applicable to the formal validity of same-sex marriages please compare comments above (Part II., Chapter 5, §2, III., A).

IV. Personal Effects of Marriage

380. Pursuant to Article 51(1) PILA the personal relations between spouses are governed by the law of the state of which both spouses are currently nationals. If one or both spouses have a multiple nationality Article 2(3) PILA applies. It states that in order to establish the applicable law, when it is required that given persons are citizens of the same state, it suffices that the law of this state treats these persons as its citizens. If spouses are not nationals of the same state, according to Article 51(2) PILA the law of the state in which both spouses are domiciled governs the personal relations between them, and if spouses are not domiciled in the same state – the law of the state, in which both spouses have their habitual residence. If the spouses do not have their habitual residence in the same state, the law of the state with which both spouses are otherwise most closely connected applies.

381. Personal relations between spouses within the meaning of Article 51 cover the personal rights and obligations of spouses, such as: the obligation to live together (*id est* to maintain a spiritual, physical and economic relationship with each other), the obligation to reside together and the obligation of mutual assistance.[401]

V. Dissolution

382. In Polish law, a marriage may be dissolved in two ways: by annulment of marriage or by divorce. Annulment of marriage may be made in a court judgment for reasons such as: failure to reach the required age, total incapacitation, mental illness, bigamy, kinship or affinity, adoption or defects in a declaration of intent when submitting a declaration of entering into marriage. As long as a marriage contracted in breach of the prohibition is not annulled, it is treated as valid and enjoys full legal protection. The court's decision to annul the marriage has *ex nunc* effect. The provisions on divorce apply *mutatis mutandis* to the effects of marriage annulment with regard to the relationship between the spouses and their common children and joint property. If those marital obstacles have ceased (e.g., the appropriate age has been reached), the marriage is validated. As a result, a marriage contracted despite the existence of this obstacle cannot be annulled.

383. Polish law does not know the marriage nullity *ex lege*. However, the concept of non-existent marriage is known (*matrimonium non existens*). A marriage is considered non-existent if the conditions listed in Article 1(1) and (2) FGC are not

401. K. Pietrzykowski in: J. Poczobut (ed.), Prawo prywatne międzynarodowe. Komentarz, Wolters Kluwer, Warszawa 2017.

met. Those conditions are: gender difference of the spouses, simultaneous declaration of intent of entering into marriage and participation of the competent state body authorized to solemnize the marriage.

A. Annulment

384. According to the Article 50 PILA the consequences of the lack of ability to conclude a marriage or of a failure to comply with formal requirements of marriage are determined by the law specified in Article 48 and Article 49, respectively. Therefore, the consequences of the lack of ability to conclude a marriage are governed, for each of the parties, by his or her national law and the consequences of a failure to comply with formal requirements of marriage are governed by *lex loci celebrationis matrimonii*.

385. The scope of Article 50 is broad, as it covers all types of effects of a malfunctioning marriage known to various legal systems, including in particular: marriage nullity *ex lege*, non-existent marriage (*matrimonium non existens*), marriage annulment and mutability of marriage.[402]

386. For the application of the conflict-of-law rule of Article 50 PILA it is essential that the grounds for marriage annulment exist at the time the marriage was celebrated. If the reasons for it arise during the marriage, it would be the basis for the termination of marriage and the applicable law should be determined based on Article 54 PILA. If, on the other hand, a specific circumstance, existing at the time the marriage was celebrated, is treated by foreign law as the basis for a request for divorce, the application of Article 50 or of Article 54 must be determined with taking into account all the circumstances of the case.[403]

B. Divorce

387. The Divorce Regulation[404] does not apply to Poland, since Poland has not taken part in enhanced cooperation within which the Regulation was adopted.[405] Therefore law applicable to divorce has to be designated by national conflict-of-law rules included in PILA 2011 or bilateral agreement, including those with the EU Member States.

---

402. W. Popiołek in: M. Pazdan (ed.), System Prawa Prywatnego. Tom 20 C. Prawo prywatne międzynarodowe, Wydawnictwo C. H. Beck, Warszawa 2015, pp. 74–77.
403. *See* A. Mączyński, *Rozwód w prawie prywatnym międzynarodowym*, Wydawnictwo Prawnicze, Warszawa 1983, pp. 62–65; K. Pietrzykowski, *Zawarcie małżeństwa i przesłanki jego ważności w prawie prywatnym międzynarodowym*, Warszawa 1985, p. 113.
404. Council Regulation (EU) No 1259/2010 of 20 Dec. 2010 implementing enhanced cooperation in the area of the law applicable to divorce and legal separation, OJ L 343, 29.12.2010, pp. 10–16.
405. On possibility to join the enhance cooperation in this matter by Poland, *see* P. Mostowik, *Kwestia przystąpienia przez Polskę do rozporządzenia unijnego Rzym III*, EPS 2016, nr 10, pp. 36–43.

388. According to Article 54(1) PILA the termination of marriage is governed by the law of the state of which both spouses are nationals at the time when the termination of marriage is requested. In the case of multiple nationality of one or both spouses, the rules of Article 3(2) PILA apply (*see* Part I., Chapter 2, §4., II).

389. Article 54(2) PILA states that in the absence of a common law of nationality, the law of the state in which both spouses are domiciled at the time when the termination of marriage is requested applies, and if spouses are not domiciled in the same state at that time – the law of the state in which both spouses had their last habitual residence applies, as long as one of them has still his or her habitual residence there. Article 54(3) provides with an escape clause, which states that if the circumstanced do not allow the applicable law to be determined pursuant to Article 53(1) and (2), the termination of marriage is governed by Polish law.

390. Law applicable to divorce governs the reasons for the dissolution of the marriage by divorce and the circumstances excluding the divorce (negative grounds for divorce). This law also determines the how long spouses must be separated in order to be able to file for divorce.[406]

391. In is possible to apply provisions on *renvoi* (Article 5(1) PILA) and to invoke the public policy clause (Article 7 PILA), especially when the law designated as applicable does not guarantee the spouses equal rights with regard to the request for divorce.[407] Conflict-of-law rules indicating law applicable to divorce can be also found in bilateral agreements signed by Poland.[408]

C. Other

392. Separation has been an institution of Polish family law since 1999, when the FGC was amended.[409] Even before this change in substantive law, the law applicable to separation was determined on the basis of Article 18 PILA 1965, which indicated the law applicable to divorce.[410] In 1999, PILA 1965 was amended and the scope of Article 18 was changed, in order to include also separation. In PILA 2011, the law applicable to separation is covered by Article 53(4), which provides that Article 53(1), (2) and (3) *mutatis mutandis* apply to a separation.

---

406. A. Mączyński, *Rozwód w prawie prywatnym międzynarodowym*, Wydawnictwo Prawnicze, Warszawa 1983, pp. 57–60; A. Kozioł in: M. Pazdan (ed.), System Prawa Prywatnego. Tom 20 C. Prawo prywatne międzynarodowe, Wydawnictwo C. H. Beck, Warszawa 2015.
407. *See* Decision of Court of Appeal in Katowice of 20 Aug. 2009, I ACa 410/09, mentioned in Part I Chapter 3, §7.
408. *See* K. Pietrzykowski in: J. Poczobut (ed.), Prawo prywatne międzynarodowe. Komentarz, Wolters Kluwer, Warszawa 2017, pp. 833–834.
409. Dz. U. 1999 nr 52 poz. 532.
410. W. Popiołek, *Separacja w prawie prywatnym międzynarodowym* in: M. Pazdan (ed.), Valeat aequitas, Wydawnictwo Uniwersytetu Śląskiego, Katowice 2000, pp. 351–361.

§3. MATRIMONIAL PROPERTY

393. The Matrimonial Property Matters Regulation[411] is not applied in Poland.[412] Because of that, the law applicable to matrimonial property has to be indicated by provisions of PILA 2011.

394. According to Article 51(1) PILA the matrimonial property relations are governed, as well as the personal relations between spouses, by the law of the state of which both spouses are currently nationals. If one or both spouses have a multiple nationality Article 2(3) PILA applies. It states that in order to establish the applicable law, when it is required that given persons are citizens of the same state, it suffices that the law of this state treats these persons as its citizens.

395. Article 51(2) PILA states that in the absence of the common law of nationality, the law of the state in which both spouses are domiciled applies, and if spouses are not domiciled in the same state – the law of the state, in which both spouses have their habitual residence. If the spouses do not have their habitual residence in the same state, the law of the state with which both spouses are otherwise most closely connected applies.

396. Article 52(1) PILA allows spouses to choose law applicable to their matrimonial property relations (*see below* 'Choice of Law Agreement'). In the absence of a choice of law, the matrimonial property agreement is governed by the law applicable to the spouses' personal relationship and the matrimonial property regime, as of the day when the agreement was concluded.

397. The form of matrimonial property agreement, in the absence of choice of law, is governed by the law applicable indicated by the Article 25 PILA. This provision states that the form of a judicial act is governed by the law applicable to that judicial act, therefore law applicable to matrimonial property relations (Article 51). However, it suffices to satisfy the formal requirements provided in the law of the state in which the judicial act has been made.[413]

398. Law indicated as applicable to the matrimonial property relations governs, among others, the type of property regime between the spouses and the impact of

---

411. Council Regulation (EU) 2016/1103 of 24 Jun. 2016 implementing enhanced cooperation in the area of jurisdiction, applicable law and the recognition and enforcement of decisions in matters of matrimonial property regimes, OJ L 183, 8.7.2016, pp. 1–29.

412. Nevertheless, the regulation is analysed by Polish doctrine, *see* M. Sokołowski, *Stosowanie rozporządzenia nr 2016/1103 przez polskie sądy – nowe majątkowe prawo małżeńskie Unii Europejskiej a sytuacja obywateli polskich*, EPS 2017, nr 11, pp. 4–12; M. Sokołowski, *Intercyza europejska jako metoda kształtowania małżeńskich ustrojów majątkowych*, Wydawnictwo C. H. Beck, Warszawa 2018.

413. K. Pietrzykowski in: J. Poczobut (ed.), Prawo prywatne międzynarodowe. Komentarz, Wolters Kluwer, Warszawa 2017, p. 828.

matrimonial property agreements on that regime. It also covers the issue of the obligation to satisfy the needs of the family and the spouses' liability for debts incurred for this purpose.[414]

399. PILA contains also special rule aimed at protecting the good faith of third parties entering into relations with a spouse or spouses. According to Article 53(1) if, at the time when an obligation was created, the spouse and the third-party creditor had their habitual residence in the same state, the law of that state determines the effectiveness of the matrimonial property regime against a third party, unless at the time when the obligation was created, the third party was aware of the character and content of the regime, or could have learnt of it, if he or she had exercised due care, or if requirements as too the publicity and registration under the law applicable to the matrimonial property regime, or – in the case of the property rights relating to immovable property – in the law of the state where the immovable property is located, were satisfied.[415]

400. Conflict-of-law rules indicating law applicable to matrimonial property regime can be found also in numerous bilateral treaties signed by Poland.[416] They usually use cascade of connecting factors to indicate law applicable (*see* Part I., Chapter 2, §6).

I. Choice of Law Agreement

401. As mentioned above, Article 52(1) PILA allows spouses to choose law applicable to their matrimonial property relations. However, this choice is limited, as the spouses are free to choose the law of nationality of one of the spouses, or the law where one of the spouses is domiciled or has habitual residence. The choice can be made before the marriage is concluded or during the marriage.[417] Such choice has to be made in the form of a matrimonial property agreement. It suffices to comply with the formal requirements established for the matrimonial property agreements in the chosen law, or in the law of the state in which the choice was made.

402. Pursuant to Article 52(2) PILA the matrimonial property agreement is governed by the law chosen by the spouses in accordance with Article 52(1). To the form of choice of law for the matrimonial property regime the same rule from Article 52(3) PILA applies. Therefore, in making the choice of law for the matrimonial property agreement, it suffices to comply with the formal requirements established for the matrimonial property agreements in the chosen law, or in the law of the state in which the choice was made.

---

414. K. Pietrzykowski in: J. Poczobut (ed.), Prawo prywatne międzynarodowe. Komentarz, Wolters Kluwer, Warszawa 2017, p. 820.
415. A. Sapota, *Wybór prawa w międzynarodowym prawie rodzinnym*, Wydawnictwo C. H. Beck, Warszawa 2016, pp. 155–160.
416. M. Pazdan, *Prawo prywatne międzynarodowe*, LexisNexis, Warszawa 2012, p. 232.
417. P. Twardoch in: M. Pazdan (ed.), System Prawa Prywatnego. Tom 20 A. Prawo prywatne międzynarodowe, Wydawnictwo C. H. Beck, Warszawa 2014, p. 476.

II. Relationship to Succession Law

403. According to Polish substantive law upon the conclusion of the marriage, by virtue of the law, marital community of property is established between the spouses and covers their property (Article 31 FGC[418]). The statutory community of property of spouses is a special type of joint ownership. During the marriage – or until the community of property is abolished – each item belonging to the community of property of the spouses belongs to both of them at the same time. When the statutory joint property is in force, neither of the spouses may claim the division of the community of property. The spouses may extend, limit or exclude the marital community of property by a matrimonial property agreement. The agreement should be concluded in the form of a notarial deed. It can also be concluded before entering into marriage (Article 47 FGC).

404. The marital community of property expires upon the termination of a marriage after the death of one of the spouses. In this case, joint property in fractional parts will be created in the place of the community. Only at this point can it be said that each spouse has half of the marital property. In the case of inheritance, this means that half of the joint property is inherited after the death of one of the spouses – the remainder remains with the other spouse.

405. If the inheritance includes the testator's share of the property covered by matrimonial property regime, the division of the inheritance might require prior or simultaneous liquidation of this regime. The law applicable in the proceeding on liquidation of the matrimonial property regime should be indicated by the conflict-of-law rules on matrimonial property regime (PILA 2011, Articles 51–54), since the Matrimonial Property Matters Regulation[419] does not bind Poland.[420] While the law applicable in the proceeding on division of the inheritance should be determined by the conflict-of-law rules on succession, therefore based on the provisions of the Succession Regulation[421] on succession. According to Article 1(2) (d) of the Regulation questions relating to matrimonial property regimes are excluded from its scope. In practice, however, such delimitation of the scope of application of conflict-of-law rules on matrimonial property regime and succession is not easy in every case (*see* Judgment of the CJEU in the case *Mahnkopf*[422]).

418. Act of 25 Feb. 1964 – Family and Guardianship Code, Dz. U. 1964 nr 9 poz. 59.
419. Council Regulation (EU) 2016/1103 of 24 Jun. 2016 implementing enhanced cooperation in the area of jurisdiction, applicable law and the recognition and enforcement of decisions in matters of matrimonial property regimes, OJ L 183, 8.7.2016, pp. 1–29.
420. Criticism of this Regulation, *see* P. Mostowik, *O uzasadnionych powodach nieprzystąpienia Polski do rozporządzeń UE Nr 2016/1103 i 2016/1104 dotyczących wewnętrznych i zewnętrznych relacji małżonków i rejestrowanych partnerów* in: J. Gołaczyński, W. Popiołek (eds), Kolizyjne i procesowe aspekty prawa rodzinnego, Wydawnictwo C. H. Beck, Warszawa 2018, pp. 105–115.
421. Regulation (EU) No 650/2012 of the European Parliament and of the Council of 4 Jul. 2012 on jurisdiction, applicable law, recognition and enforcement of decisions and acceptance and enforcement of authentic instruments in matters of succession and on the creation of a European Certificate of Succession, OJ 2012 L 201, pp. 107–134.
422. Case C-558/16 *Mahnkopf*, Judgment of 1 Mar. 2018.

§4. REGISTERED PARTNERSHIP: PARTNERSHIP/CIVIL UNIONS

I. Conclusion, Personal Effect, Dissolution and Property

406. Registered partnerships or civil unions are not regulated by Polish substantive law. Polish PIL also does not provide for a separate norm indicating the law applicable to a registered partnership. It is possible for registered partnerships to be included in the scope of the conflict-of-law rules governing marriage and apply them *mutatis mutandis*, therefore Articles 48 and 49 PILA to concluding registered partnership, Article 51 PILA to personal effects of registered partnership, Article 52 to property of the partners and Article 54 to dissolution of registered partnership.[423] However, such solution raises some doubts as, despite many similarities between marriage and partnership, there are nevertheless significant differences, especially in the case of those partnerships, which are designed as a relationship of rather contractual nature.[424]

407. Another solution might be to designate as applicable the law most closely connected with the registered partnership. This solution is possible under the PILA, which in Article 67 states that if there is no specific conflict-of-law rules, the law most closely connected with the relationship applies.[425] It seems that most often it will be the law of the state where partnership has been registered (*lex loci registrationis*).[426] It is also possible to apply the law of the common habitual residence of the partners, especially to issues related to their property.[427] There is no Polish jurisprudence in this matter yet.

408. In accordance with Article 67 PILA it is worth to mention that the Property Consequences of Registered Partnerships Regulation[428] is not applicable in Poland, due to the fact that Poland has not taken part in enhanced cooperation within which this Regulation was adopted.[429]

---

423. A. Kozioł in: M. Pazdan (ed.), System Prawa Prywatnego. Tom 20 C. Prawo prywatne międzynarodowe, Wydawnictwo C. H. Beck, Warszawa 2015, pp. 515–519, 527–529.
424. P. Twardoch in: M. Pazdan (ed.), System Prawa Prywatnego. Tom 20 C. Prawo prywatne międzynarodowe, Wydawnictwo C. H. Beck, Warszawa 2015, pp. 508–509.
425. E. Kamarad, *Zawarcie małżeństwa jako zagadnienie prawa rodzinnego, prawa prywatnego międzynarodowego i prawa konsularnego*, Wydawnictwo Uniwersytetu Jagiellońskiego, Kraków 2019, pp. 151–153.
426. M. Pilich, *Związki quasi-małżeńskie w polskim prawie prywatnym międzynarodowym*, PiP 2011, z. 2, pp. 84–94.
427. P. Mostowik, *Kwestie kompetencji Unii Europejskiej oraz warunków pomocniczości i proporcjonalności prawodawstwa unijnego na tle projektów rozporządzeń o jurysdykcji, prawie właściwym i skuteczności zagranicznych orzeczeń w majątkowych sprawach małżeńskich i partnerskich*, Zeszyty Prawnicze 2011, nr 3(31), pp. 9–41.
428. Council Regulation (EU) 2016/1104 of 24 Jun. 2016 implementing enhanced cooperation in the area of jurisdiction, applicable law and the recognition and enforcement of decisions in matters of the property consequences of registered partnerships, OJ L 183, 8.7.2016, pp. 30–56.
429. Criticism of this Regulation, *see* P. Mostowik, *O uzasadnionych powodach nieprzystąpienia Polski do rozporządzeń UE Nr 2016/1103 i 2016/1104 dotyczących wewnętrznych i zewnętrznych relacji małżonków i rejestrowanych partnerów* in: J. Gołaczyński, W. Popiołek (eds), Kolizyjne i procesowe aspekty prawa rodzinnego, Wydawnictwo C. H. Beck, Warszawa 2018, pp. 105–115.

§5. EXTRA-MARITAL COHABITATION

I. Personal Effect, Dissolution and Property

409. In Poland cohabitation is not a legal concept. The doctrine defines it as the actual relationship between a man and a woman who are not married. Usually the term cohabitation only includes factual relationships between persons of different sexes.[430] However, it cannot be excluded that actual same-sex relationships are also covered by this concept.[431]

410. Regarding the law applicable to cohabitation, it should be noted that cohabitation arises when a relationship is formed between the partners and there is no intention of getting married. There are no legal consequences with the creation of a cohabitation itself, so there is no question which law should apply to this situation. The establishment of a cohabitation does not fall within the scope of the conflict-of-law rules indicating the law applicable to the marriage (Article 48 and Article 49 PILA).

411. However, the law may give certain effects to cohabitation, and what law will apply to these effects depends on the particular situation. If, for example, the question arises whether a given person can inherit from a partner with whom he or she was in an informal relationship, this issue is governed by the law applicable to succession.

412. As in the case of registered partnerships, Polish PIL does not contain separate conflict-of-law rules indicating the law applicable to extra-marital cohabitation. Therefore, to some issues, for example personal effects of cohabitation, it is possible to apply by analogy the conflict-of-law rules applicable to marriage (*see* above) or, on the basis of Article 67 PILA, the law most closely connected with the relationship, which in this case would probably be the law of the common habitual residence of cohabitees.

413. Another question is what law should be applicable to determine if the partners of extra-marital cohabitation were actually in an informal relationship. Under Polish PIL, cohabitation might be classified as a type of incidental question of the main case. The consequence of this approach is the inclusion of cohabitation within the scope of application of the *lex causae* (*id est* law applicable to succession, ownership or maintenance obligation), depending on the main case.[432]

---

430. Judgment of Supreme Court of 31 Mar. 1988, I KR 50/88. *See also*: K. Pietrzykowski in: K. Pietrzykowski (ed.), Kodeks rodzinny i opiekuńczy. Komentarz, Warszawa 2018. p. 96.
431. M. Nazar in: T. Smyczyński (ed.), *System prawa prywatnego. Tom 11. Prawo rodzinne i opiekuńcze*, Wydawnictwo C. H. Beck, Warszawa 2014, pp. 983–986.
432. E. Kamarad, *Zawarcie małżeństwa jako zagadnienie prawa rodzinnego, prawa prywatnego międzynarodowego i prawa konsularnego*, Wydawnictwo Uniwersytetu Jagiellońskiego, Kraków 2019, pp. 151–160.

§6. MAINTENANCE LAW

414. PILA does not contain conflict-of-law rules on the law applicable to maintenance obligations. Article 63 only states that the law applicable to maintenance obligations is determined by the Maintenance Regulation.[433] According to Article 15 of this Regulation conflict-of-law rules on maintenance obligations are found in the Hague Protocol (2007).[434]

415. Pursuant to Article 69 of the Regulation it does not affect the application of bilateral or multilateral conventions and agreements to which one or more Member States are party and which concern matters governed by the Regulation. However, the Regulation, in relations between Member States, takes precedence over those conventions and agreements which concern matters governed by the Regulation.

416. Poland is a party to Convention on the Recovery Abroad of Maintenance (1956),[435] to Hague Convention on the Recognition and Enforcement of Decisions Relating to Maintenance Obligations (1973),[436] to Hague Convention on the Law Applicable to Maintenance Obligations (1973)[437] and to Hague Convention on the International Recovery of Child Support and Other Forms of Family Maintenance (2007).[438]

I. Spousal Maintenance

417. Conflict-of-law rules on law applicable to the maintenance obligations between spouses or ex-spouses are part of the Hague Protocol (2007).[439] Pursuant to Article 8 it is allowed to make a limited choice of law.[440] In the absence of choice of law, the general rule on applicable law from Article 3 applies. According to this provision the law applicable to the maintenance obligation is the law of the state of the habitual residence of the creditor.

418. In Article 5 a special rule with respect to spouses and ex-spouses can be found. According to it in the case of a maintenance obligation between spouses, ex-spouses or parties to a marriage which has been annulled, the general rule from

433. Council Regulation (EC) No 4/2009 of 18 Dec. 2008 on jurisdiction, applicable law, recognition and enforcement of decisions and cooperation in matters relating to maintenance obligations, OJ L 7, 10.1.2009, pp. 1–79.
434. The text of the Protocol is an annex to 2009/941/EC: Council Decision of 30 Nov. 2009 on the conclusion by the European Community of the Hague Protocol of 23 Nov. 2007 on the Law Applicable to Maintenance Obligations, OJ L 331, 16.12.2009, pp. 17–23.
435. Dz. U. 1961 nr 17 poz. 87.
436. Dz. U. 2000 nr 2 poz. 13.
437. Dz. U. 2000 nr 39 poz. 444.
438. Convention of 23 Nov. 2007 on the International Recovery of Child Support and Other Forms of Family Maintenance, OJ L 192, 22.7.2011, pp. 39–50.
439. OJ L 331, 16.12.2009, pp. 17–23.
440. A. Sapota, *Wybór prawa w międzynarodowym prawie rodzinnym*, Wydawnictwo C. H. Beck, Warszawa 2016, pp. 168–169.

Article 3 does not apply if one of the parties objects and the law of another state, in particular the state of their last common habitual residence, has a closer connection with the marriage. In such a case the law of that other State shall apply.[441]

II. Partnership Maintenance

419. As already mentioned, (*see* Part II. Chapter 5, §4), in the Polish substantive law there is no institution of registered partnership. There are also no conflict-of-law rules relating directly to registered partnerships. Nevertheless, there may be a need to indicate the law applicable to the maintenance obligation between partners who concluded a registered partnership in another country and under foreign law.

420. According to Recital 11 of the Maintenance Regulation[442] its provisions cover all maintenance obligations arising from a family relationship, parentage, marriage or affinity, in order to guarantee equal treatment of all maintenance creditors. Therefore, it seems that the scope of this Regulation might also include the issue of law applicable to the maintenance obligation between partners in registered partnerships.[443] The law applicable to this issue should be thus determined according to the Hague Protocol (2007) to which Maintenance Regulation refers in regard to law applicable (Article 15). Hence, maintenance obligations between partners in registered partnership, in accordance with Article 3 of the Hague Protocol (2007), are governed by the law of the state of the habitual residence of the creditor.

III. Maintenance of Cohabitees

421. As it was mentioned above in regard to registered partnerships, Maintenance Regulation[444] covers all maintenance obligations arising from a family relationship, parentage, marriage or affinity. However, it is questionable whether the cohabitation, as an informal relationship, can be treated as 'family relationship' for this matter. If not, then maintenance of cohabitees will not fall within the material scope of the Hague Protocol (2007).[445] Another way to indicate the law applicable would be by refereeing to Article 67 PILA, which states that the law applicable is the law most closely connected with the relationship.

---

441. A. Juryk, *Alimenty w prawie prywatnym międzynarodowym*, LexisNexis, Warszawa 2015, pp. 273–288.
442. Council Regulation (EC) No 4/2009 of 18 Dec. 2008 on jurisdiction, applicable law, recognition and enforcement of decisions and cooperation in matters relating to maintenance obligations, OJ L 7, 10.1.2009, pp. 1–79.
443. A. Juryk, *Alimenty w prawie prywatnym międzynarodowym*, LexisNexis, Warszawa 2015, pp. 270–271; A. Kozioł in: M. Pazdan (ed.), System Prawa Prywatnego. Tom 20 C. Prawo prywatne międzynarodowe, Wydawnictwo C. H. Beck, Warszawa 2015, pp. 520–525.
444. Council Regulation (EC) No 4/2009 of 18 Dec. 2008 on jurisdiction, applicable law, recognition and enforcement of decisions and cooperation in matters relating to maintenance obligations, OJ L 7, 10.1.2009, pp. 1–79.
445. OJ L 331, 16.12.2009, pp. 17–23.

§7. Child Law

I. Determination of Parenthood

422. Article 55 (1) PILA covers all means of determination of parenthood, except acknowledgement of a child.[446] Therefore, it applies to establishing or denying both fatherhood and motherhood. It does not matter whether the child was born to parents who are legally married to each other or is a child born out of wedlock.[447] Article 55(1) contains a general rule on determination of parenthood, according to which the determination and challenge of the child's filiation is governed by the child's law of nationality as of the time of his or her birth. Article 55(2) PILA adds on that if the child's law of nationality as of the time of his or her birth does not provide for the judicial determination of fatherhood, the judicial determination of fatherhood is subject to the child's law of nationality as of the time when filiation is determined. If this law also does not provide for a judicial determination of fatherhood, then the public order clause would have to be applied, causing the refusal of application of the foreign law and the application of the law that allows such determination.[448]

423. The applicable law governs in particular the presumption of paternity of a child born in marriage, including its nature and conditions, as well as the admissibility of an action to determine the fatherhood of a child born in marriage and the main effect of the presumption of paternity, which is, *inter alia*, the kinship relationship between the child and the mother's husband. The applicable law also governs denial of parenthood. In this context, the law applicable determines substantive law premises, time limits, the circle of persons entitled to bring an action for denial of parenthood, the participants in a proceeding and the effects of denial of parenthood.[449]

424. Article 55(3) concerns acknowledgement of a child. Pursuant to this provision the declaration of acknowledgement is governed by the child's law of nationality as of the time of acknowledgment. If that law does not provide for the declaration of acknowledgement, the child's law of nationality as of the time of birth applies, as long as that law provides for acknowledgement. Similar to determination of the parenthood, it is possible to apply public policy clause if the law indicated as applicable does not provide for the acknowledgement of a child.

---

446. Also *see*, with regard to PILA 1965: E. Skrzydło-Tefelska, *Uznanie dziecka w prawie prywatnym międzynarodowym*, Zakład Narodowy im. Ossolińskich, Wrocław 1990, pp. 74–77.
447. M. Pazdan in: M. Pazdan (ed.), Prawo prywatne międzynarodowe, Wolters Kluwer Polska, Warszawa 2017.p. 510.
448. M. Pazdan, *Prawo prywatne międzynarodowe*, LexisNexis, Warszawa 2012, p. 241.
449. P. Mostowik in: J. Poczobut (ed.), Prawo prywatne międzynarodowe. Komentarz, Wolters Kluwer, Warszawa 2017, pp. 855–858.

425. If the child has a multiple nationality Article 2(1) and (2) PILA applies and if he or she is a stateless person or a refuge the law of his or hers domicile or habitual residence will be applied, according to Article 3(1). It is also possible to apply *renvoi* (Article 5(1) PILA).

426. The declaration of acknowledgement of an unborn but already conceived child (*nasciturus*), according to Article 55(4) PILA is subject to the mother's law of nationality as of the time of acknowledgement.

427. The phrase 'the time of acknowledgement' used in Article 55(1) and Article 55(4) means the moment of submitting the declaration of acknowledgement by the person acknowledging the child.[450]

428. Applicable law indicated by Article 55(3) or (4) governs in particular the legal nature of the acknowledgement, the requirement of the mother's consent, the requirement of a consent of the statutory representative of the child or the child himself, the content of the declaration of acknowledgement and the grounds for annulment and revocation of the acknowledgement.[451]

II. Custody and Contact

429. Article 56(1) PILA informs that the law applicable to parental authority and access to children is determined in accordance with the Hague Convention on Parental Responsibility and Protection of Children (1996).[452] Poland is a party to this Convention since 2010.

430. According to Article 1(2) of this Convention the term 'parental responsibility' includes parental authority, or any analogous relationship of authority determining the rights, powers and responsibilities of parents, guardians or other legal representatives in relation to the person or the property of the child. Provisions of the Convention apply to children from the moment of their birth until they reach the age of 18 years.

431. Article 15(1) provides for the general rule on the law applicable, stating that in exercising their jurisdiction the authorities of the contracting state apply their own law (*lex fori*). However, there are a few exceptions to this rule. According to Article 15(2) when the protection of the child or the property of the child requires it, the law of another state, with which the situation has a substantial connection, may be exceptionally applied or taken into consideration. Couple provisions indicate also as applicable the law of the state of the habitual residence of the child: for

450. M. Pazdan in: M. Pazdan (ed.), Prawo prywatne międzynarodowe, Wolters Kluwer Polska, Warszawa 2017, p. 512.
451. P. Mostowik in: J. Poczobut (ed.), Prawo prywatne międzynarodowe. Komentarz, Wolters Kluwer, Warszawa 2017, pp. 858–860.
452. Dz. U. 2010 nr 172 poz. 1158.

the attribution or extinction of parental responsibility by operation of law, without the intervention of a judicial or administrative authority (Article 16(1)), for the attribution or extinction of parental responsibility by an agreement or a unilateral act, without intervention of a judicial or administrative authority (Article 16(2)) and for the exercise of parental responsibility (Article 17(1)).[453]

432. The provisions of the Hague Convention (1996) concern also issues related to the change of applicable law resulting from the change of child's habitual residence (Article 15(3), Article 16(3) and (4)). However, there is no provision on the consequences of the change of child's habitual residence to a place in a non-contracting state. That is the reason why PILA contains a special provision on that. According to Article 56(2)PILA if the habitual residence of a child is transferred to a state that is not a party to the Hague Convention (1996), the law of that state determines, from the time of the transfer, the condition under which measures adopted in the state of previous habitual residence may be made use of.

433. Conflict-of-law rules on legal relations between parents and a child can also be found in bilateral agreements signed by Poland. Usually the law applicable to those relations is the national law of the child.[454]

III. Guardianship

434. Pursuant to Article 59(1) PILA the law applicable to guardianship and curatorship is determined in accordance with the Hague Convention on Parental Responsibility and Protection of Children (1996).[455] According to Article 1(2) od the Hague Convention (1996) the term 'parental responsibility' includes parental authority, or any analogous relationship of authority determining the rights, powers and responsibilities of parents, guardians or other legal representatives in relation to the person or the property of the child. Provisions of the Hague Convention (1996) apply to children from the moment of their birth until they reach the age of 18 years.[456]

435. Article 3 of the Hague Convention (1996) specifies what measures may be taken to protect the child or child's property. Those measures may deal in particular with guardianship, curatorship and analogous institutions. The law applicable to those measures are determined by the same conflict-of-law rules, as those indicating the law applicable to custody and contact (*see* above).

436. Article 59(2) PILA mirrors Article 56(2), stating that if the habitual residence of a child is transferred to a state that is not a party to the Hague Convention

453. P. Mostowik, *Władza rodzicielska i opieka nad dzieckiem w prawie prywatnym międzynarodowym*, Wydawnictwo JAK, Kraków 2015, pp. 167–177.
454. M. Pazdan, *Prawo prywatne międzynarodowe*, LexisNexis, Warszawa 2012, pp. 251–253.
455. Dz. U. 2010 nr 172 poz. 1158.
456. P. Mostowik, *Władza rodzicielska i opieka nad dzieckiem w prawie prywatnym międzynarodowym*, Wydawnictwo JAK, Kraków 2015, pp. 151–152.

(1996), the law of that state determines, from the moment of transfer, the condition under which measures adopted in the state of previous habitual residence may be made use of.

IV. Adoption

437. Pursuant to Article 57(1) PILA adoption is governed by the law of nationality of the adoptive parent. According to Article 58 PILA adoption cannot, however, take place without satisfying the requirements of the national law of the person who is to be adopted relating to his or her consent, the consent of his or her legal representative, the permission from the relevant public authority, and the limits to adoption relating to the transfer of the domicile to another state. [457]

438. Such restriction of adoption due to the upcoming change of the child's place of residence in Poland to the place of residence abroad is provided for, for example, in Article 114^2 FGC.[458] This provision would apply when a foreigner would adopt a child who has Polish citizenship.

439. Article 58 PILA applies only to the restrictions listed therein. These restrictions are to be met if they are abided by the law of nationality of the adoptive parent or the law of nationality of the person who is to be adopted. Thus, for adoption the cumulative applicability of two legal systems is provided.[459] Other restrictions, for example, concerning the adoptive age, will have to be met if they are required by the applicable law indicated by Article 57 (1), *id est* by the law of nationality of the adoptive parent.

440. Article 3 PILA will apply if the adopter or adoptee is a stateless person or a refugee. It is also possible to apply *renvoi* (Article 5(1) PILA).

441. The PILA also regulates joint adoption by spouses. Article 57(2) PILA states that adoption by a married couple is subject to their common law of nationality. In the absence of the common law of nationality, the law of the state in which both spouses are domiciled applies, and if spouses are not domiciled in the same state – the law of the state in which both spouses have their habitual residence. If the spouses do not have their habitual residence in the same state, the law of a state with which both spouses are otherwise most closely connected applies.[460] It is worth

457. B. Gnela, *Prawo właściwe dla przysposobienia według nowej ustawy Prawo prywatne międzynarodowe* in: J. Poczobut (ed.) Współczesne wyzwania prawa prywatnego międzynarodowego, Wolters Kluwer Polska, Warszawa 2013 pp. 85–112; B. Gnela, in: M. Pazdan (ed.), System Prawa Prywatnego. Tom 20 C. Prawo prywatne międzynarodowe, Wydawnictwo C. H. Beck, Warszawa 2015, pp. 357–492.

458. Act of 25 Feb. 1964 – Family and Guardianship Code, Dz. U. 1964 nr 9 poz. 59.

459. M. Pazdan, *Prawo prywatne międzynarodowe*, LexisNexis, Warszawa 2012, pp. 253–254.

460. B. Gnela in: J. Poczobut (ed.), Prawo prywatne międzynarodowe. Komentarz, Wolters Kluwer, Warszawa 2017, pp. 893–899.

to mention that according to Article 2(3) PILA the spouses will have common law of nationality also if one of them has multiple nationality.

442. The applicable law indicated by the Article 57 and Article 58 governs the admissibility of an adoption, its type, method of adoption, its dissolution and the content of the adoption relationship.

443. Poland is a party to European Convention on the Adoption of Children (1967)[461] and to Hague Convention on Protection of Children and Co-operation in Respect of Intercountry Adoption (1993).[462]

444. Provisions regarding the law applicable to adoption are also included in bilateral conventions signed by Poland. Most often they provide for the same conflict-of-law rules as those presented above.

V. Artificial Insemination, Surrogacy

445. In Polish substantive law artificial insemination is regulated in the 2015 Act on the treatment of infertility,[463] which does not include any conflict-of-law rules. There are no directly applicable rules in PILA, either. Surrogacy is regulated neither in substantive law, nor PILA.

446. Most provisions in PILA concerning parenthood are in general applicable in the case of artificial insemination and surrogacy. In cases concerning those matters Polish courts would most likely apply *lex fori*.

447. So far, Polish courts have dealt with cross-border cases related to artificial insemination and surrogacy in the context of registering children born out of surrogacy arrangements in Polish civil register, transcription of their foreign birth certificates and granting them Polish citizenship. The decisions of the courts in these cases were contradictory.[464]

VI. Child Support

448. Law applicable to the maintenance obligations of parents towards their children and of persons, other than parents, towards persons who have not attained

461. ETS No.058, Dz. U. 1999 nr 99 poz. 1157.
462. Dz. U. 2000 nr 39 poz. 448. *See* A. Wysocka-Bar, *Umowy międzynarodowe dotyczące przysposobienia dzieci*, Metryka 2018, t. 8, nr 1, pp. 69–76 and nr 2, pp. 65–75.
463. Dz. U. 2015 poz. 1087.
464. *See* for example: Judgment of Supreme Administrative Court of 17 Dec. 2014 r., II OSK 1298/13; Judgment of Supreme Administrative Court of 6 May 2015, II OSK 2372/13 and II OSK 2419/13; Judgment of Supreme Administrative Court of 29 Aug. 2018, II OSK 2129/16; Resolution of the Supreme Administrative Court of 2 Dec. 2019, II OPS 1/19.

the age of 21 are part of the Hague Protocol (2007).[465] The Protocol covers maintenance obligations arising from parentage and other family relationships. It does not matter whether it is a natural or legal relationship (e.g., adoptive parentage). The lineage and degree of kinship are also irrelevant, neither is the marital or extramarital origin of the child.[466]

449. Pursuant to Article 3 of the Protocol maintenance in those cases is governed by the law of the state of the habitual residence of the creditor. However, Article 4 states that if the creditor is unable, by virtue of that law, to obtain maintenance, the law of the *forum* applies. *Lex fori* applies also if the child has seized the court of the state of the habitual residence of the debtor. However, if the law of that state does not allow the child to obtain maintenance from the debtor, the law of the state of the habitual residence of the creditor applies. And if the creditor is unable, by virtue of *lex fori* or the law of the state of the habitual residence of the creditor, to obtain maintenance from the debtor, the law of the state of their common nationality, if there is one, applies.

VII. Child Abduction

450. Poland is a party to the Hague Convention on Child Abduction (1980).[467] According to Article 1 of the Hague Convention (1980), it objects are: to secure the prompt return of children wrongfully removed to or retained in any contracting state; and to ensure that rights of custody and of access under the law of one contracting state are effectively respected in the other contracting states. The Article 3 explains that the removal or the retention of a child is to be considered wrongful where it is in breach of rights of custody attributed to a person, an institution or any other body, either jointly or alone, under the law of the State in which the child was habitually resident immediately before the removal or retention; and at the time of removal or retention those rights were actually exercised, either jointly or alone, or would have been so exercised but for the removal or retention.

451. The Hague Convention (1980) has been ratified by all Member States of the EU and it continues to apply to cases of child abduction between Member States. The Hague Convention (1980) has, however, been supplemented by certain provisions of the Brussels II *bis* Regulation,[468] that are applicable in such cases. Therefore, as regards the functioning of the Hague Convention (1980) in relations between the Member States, the provisions of the Regulation Brussels II *bis* prevail over the principles of the Hague Convention (1980) in child abduction cases.

465. OJ L 331, 16.12.2009, pp. 17–23.
466. A. Juryk, *Alimenty w prawie prywatnym międzynarodowym*, LexisNexis, Warszawa 2015, pp. 204–205.
467. Dz. U. 1995 nr 108 poz. 528.
468. Council Regulation (EC) No 2201/2003 of 27 Nov. 2003 concerning jurisdiction and the recognition and enforcement of judgments in matrimonial matters and the matters of parental responsibility, repealing Regulation (EC) No 1347/2000, OJ L 338, 23.12.2003, pp. 1–29.

452. In the event of the abduction of a child from one Member State ('home Member State') to another Member State ('requested Member State'), the Regulation Brussels II *bis* ensures that the jurisdiction of the courts of the home Member State to decide on the right to custody is maintained, irrespective of the abduction. After an application for the return of the child has been submitted to a court of the requested Member State, that court will apply the Hague Convention (1980) as amended by the Regulation. If the court of the requested Member State decides not to return the child on the grounds set out in Article 13 of the Convention, it must immediately forward a copy of his decision to the court having jurisdiction in the home Member State, which may then, at the request of a party, examine the question of custody of the child, if this issue has not yet been raised before him. If the court of the home Member State decides on return the child, this decision should be directly recognized and enforceable in the requested Member State without the need for an *exequatur* procedure.

453. In Polish national law there is the Act of 26 January 2018 on the exercise of official powers in family matters in the field of law based on European Union law and international agreements.[469] The Act defines the rules and procedure of the Polish central authority, Polish courts and other Polish authorities in family matters under European Union law and international agreements, as well as proceedings before the Polish central authority in matters covered by Hague Convention (1980) and the Regulation Brussels II *bis*. According to Article 3(1) of the Act, the Polish central authority performing the tasks provided for in the Hague Convention (1980) or the Regulation Brussels II *bis* is the Minister of Justice.

§8. PROTECTION OF ADULTS

454. Poland is not party to the Hague Convention on the International Protection of Adults (2000), thus national conflict-of-law rules apply to protection of adults.

455. Pursuant to Article 60(1) PILA establishing a guardianship, curatorship or other protective measures for an adult is governed by that person's national law. If the Polish court decides on those measures with respect to a foreigner who is domiciled or has his or her habitual residence in Poland, according to Article 60(2), Polish law applies. Pursuant to Article 60(3) PILA exercising the measures referred to in Article 60(1) is subject to the law of the state in which the person affected by these measures has his or her habitual residence.

469. Dz. U. 2018 poz. 416.

456. Therefore, the establishment of a protective measure has been subjected to the national law of the adult and the enforcement of this measure has been subjected to the law of his or her habitual residence. The repeal of a protection measure should rather be governed by the national law of the adult and not by the law of the state of habitual residence.[470]

457. Moreover, Article 60(4) PILA states that in cases referred to in Article 1107(2) and (3) CPC, Polish law applies. First of those cases is when Polish court issues the order in terms of care and guardianship as to the located in Poland property of a foreigner, who has a domicile or a place of habitual residence abroad, if it proves necessary in the interest of that foreigner. Second one – when Polish court issues an interim measures in terms of care and guardianship in other cases, if the case has a sufficient connection with the Polish legal order or if there is an urgent need to grant protection to a foreigner, who has a domicile or a place of habitual residence abroad, but is staying in Poland.[471]

---

470. A. Juryk, *The Protection of Adults in Private International Law*, Silesian Journal of Legal Studies 2016, vol. 8, pp. 27–43.

471. A. Kozioł, P. Twardoch in: M. Pazdan (ed.), System Prawa Prywatnego. Tom 20 C. Prawo prywatne międzynarodowe, Wydawnictwo C. H. Beck, Warszawa 2015, pp. 531–532.

Chapter 6. Succession Law

§1. *Lex Successionis*

458. The main source of PIL rules with respect to successions in Poland is now the Succession Regulation[472] and the Hague Convention on Form of Wills (1961).[473] Succession Regulation is not analysed in detail in this monograph as being part of EU PIL it already has its place in legal literature.[474] Same thing may be said about the (multilateral) Hague Convention on Form of Wills,[475] which is in force in Poland since 1969.[476]

459. The EU Succession Regulation is applied in Poland starting from 17 August 2015 to the succession cases of persons deceased as of that day (Article 83(1) and 84). It defines succession as succession to the estate of a deceased person and covers all forms of transfer of assets, rights and obligations by reason of death, whether by way of a voluntary transfer under a disposition of property upon death or a transfer through intestate succession (Article 3(1)(a)). Article 1(2) enumerates the issues left outside of its scope, for example the formal validity of dispositions of property upon death made orally and property rights, interests and assets created or transferred otherwise than by succession (for instance pension plans and insurance contracts). The law applicable to succession (*lex successionis*) is the law of the habitual residence of the deceased at the time of death, subject to the operation of the closer connection clause (Article 21). The testator has the competence to designate *lex successionis*. This autonomy is limited to the national law of the deceased at the time of making the choice or at the time of death (Article 22).[477]

460. In accordance with Article 75(1) multilateral and bilateral agreements to which third states are parties take precedence before Succession Regulation. Hence, EU Member States which are parties to the Hague Convention on Form of Wills

472. Regulation (EU) No 650/2012 of the European Parliament and of the Council of 4 July 2012 on jurisdiction, applicable law, recognition and enforcement of decisions and acceptance and enforcement of authentic instruments in matters of succession and on the creation of a European Certificate of Succession, OJ 2012 L 201, p. 107.

473. Convention of 5 Oct. 1961 on the Conflicts of Laws Relating to the Form of Testamentary Dispositions, Dz. U. 1969 r. nr 34 poz. 284.

474. *See* for example: C. Pamboukis, *EU Succession Regulation No 650/2012. A Commentary*, C. H. Beck: München 2017; A. Bonomi, P. Wautelet, *Le droit européen des successions commentaire du Règlement (UE) no 650/2012 du 4 juillet 2012*, Bruylant: Bruxelles 2016.

475. *See* for example: A. von Overbeck, *Divers aspects de l'unification du droit international privé, spécialement en matière de successions*, Recueil des Cours de l'Académie de droit international de La Haye 1961, pp. 593–622.

476. A. Mączyński, *Dziedziczenie testamentowe w prawie prywatnym międzynarodowym. Ustawowe i konwencyjne unormowanie problematyki formy*, Zeszyty Naukowe Uniwersytetu Jagiellońskiego. Prace prawnicze 1976, vol. 75; E. Kamarad, *Prawo właściwe dla czynności prawnych mortis causa – uwagi de lege lata i de lege ferenda*, PPPM 2011, vol. 9, pp. 55–91.

477. A. Wysocka-Bar, *Prawo właściwe dla dziedziczenia według unijnego rozporządzenia dotyczącego spraw spadkowych*, KPP 2012, nr 4, pp. 899–948; A. Wysocka, *How can a valid professio iuris be made under the EU Succession Regulation?*, Nederland Internationaal Privaatrecht 2012, vol. 4, pp. 569–575.

(1961), including Poland, continue to apply it instead of Article 27 of the Succession Regulation with regard to the formal validity of wills and joint wills. Article 75(1) Succession Regulation equally applies to bilateral conventions with non-EU states. As a result, Poland continues to apply bilateral conventions with third states, which contain rules on international succession law. Inversely, in accordance with Article 75(2) Succession Regulation takes precedence over bilateral conventions between EU Member States. This concerns also bilateral conventions concluded by Poland with other EU Member States, which contain international succession law rules (e.g., bilateral convention with Austria of 1963).

461. It might be pointed that the Succession Regulation replaced in Poland rules of Articles 64–66 contained in Chapter 16 PILA.[478] These rules were repealed as of 17 August 2015 (but are still applicable to succession cases of persons who died before 17 August 2015). In accordance with Article 64(2) PILA succession is governed by the national law of the deceased at the time of death. Under Article 64(1)PILA, the testator was granted a competence to designate as *lex successionis* one of the following laws: national law, law of the domicile or habitual residence – at the time of making the disposition or at the time of death. The validity of a disposition of property upon death was governed by the national law of the deceased at the time of making the disposition (Article 65). Article 66(1) PILA informed about the applicability of the Hague Convention on Form of Wills (1961), whereas Article 66(2) PILA extended Convention's application on other dispositions of property upon death (e.g., agreements as to succession). Currently, Chapter 16 PILA consists only of Article 66a, which reminds about applicability of the Succession Regulation. In PILA 1965 international succession law was regulated in Chapter XI.[479] In accordance with Article 34 PILA 1965 succession was governed by the national law of the deceased at the time of death. No choice of applicable law was allowed. Article 35 stated that validity of dispositions of property upon death is governed by the national law of the deceased at the time of making the disposition. However, it was enough to abide by the requirements as to the form provided for in the law of the country where the disposition was made. Article 35 was soon partly replaced by the provisions of the Hague Convention on Form of Wills once it entered into force in Poland in 1969, as it contains rules of universal application.

§2. Scope of Application

462. Article 23 Succession Regulation lists, in a non-exhaustive manner, issues governed by *lex successionis*. This includes, *inter alia*, the determination of the beneficiaries and their respective shares, determination of other succession rights,

478. On international succession law in PILA, *see*, for example: J. Pazdan in: J. Poczobut (ed.) Prawo prywatne międzynarodowe. Komentarz, Wolters Kluwer, Warszawa 2017, pp. 982–992; A. Wysocka-Bar, *Prawo właściwe dla dziedziczenia w polskim prawie prywatnym międzynarodowym z 2011 r.* in: M. Margoński, M. Krzymuski (eds), Znad granicy ponad granicami. Prace z okazji 70 urodzin Profesora Dietera Martiny, C. H. Beck, Warszawa 2014, pp. 405–422.

479. M. Pazdan, *Dziedziczenie ustawowe w prawie prywatnym międzynarodowym. Metody regulacji właściwości prawa*, Prace Naukowe Uniwersytetu Śląskiego w Katowicach 1973, nr 45.

including the succession rights of the surviving spouse or partner, the capacity to inherit, disinheritance and disqualification by conduct, the powers of the executors of the wills and other administrators of the estate, the disposable part of the estate, the reserved shares and other restrictions on the disposal of property upon death and the sharing-out of the estate. Recital 9 explains that *lex successionis* should cover all civil-law aspects of succession to the estate of a deceased person. *Lex successionis* governs succession as a whole, meaning that it applies to all the assets of the estate, irrespective of where the assets are located.

463. The Succession Regulation contains separate rules relating the validity of the dispositions of property upon death. It also contains specific rules concerning commorientes (*id est* persons whose successions are governed by different laws, who died in circumstances in which it is uncertain in what order their deaths occurred – Article 32) and estate without claimant (Article 33). Article 30 exceptionally allows for application of *lex rei sitae* if the law of the state in which certain immovable property, certain enterprises or other special categories of assets are located contains special rules which, for economic, family or social considerations, impose restrictions concerning or affecting the succession in respect of those assets and those special rules, under the law of that state, should be applied irrespective of the *lex successionis*.

§3. Testamentary Disposition

I. Legal Capacity

464. Article 1(2)(b) of the Succession Regulation excludes the legal capacity of natural persons from its scope. The exclusion does not cover every aspect of this capacity. Article 26(1)(a) states that the capacity of the person making the disposition of property upon death to make such a disposition is governed by the law applicable to substantive validity of dispositions of property upon death. Namely the law chosen by the testator or (if no choice was made) the law indicated by Articles 24–25. Where a person has the capacity to make a disposition of property upon death under the law applicable pursuant to Articles 24–25, a subsequent change of the law applicable does not affect capacity to modify or revoke such a disposition. Similarly, the law indicated in Articles 24–25 governs the particular causes which bar the person making the disposition from disposing in favour of certain persons or which bar a person from receiving succession property from the person making the disposition (Article 26(1)(b)). Capacity to inherit is governed by *lex successionis* (Article 23(2)(c)). Capacity in general, as excluded from the scope of the Succession Regulation, is governed by the law indicated by Article 11 PILA.

II. Choice of Law

465. As mentioned above, the Succession Regulation provides that the testator may choose as *lex successionis* the national law at the time of death or at the time of making the choice.[480] Pursuant to Article 24(2) this law may also be chosen to govern a disposition of property upon death (other than agreements as to succession) as regards its admissibility and substantive validity. Similarly, pursuant to Article 25(3) parties may chose law applicable to govern their agreement as to succession, as regards its admissibility, its substantive validity and its binding effects between the parties, including the conditions for its dissolution. The chosen law may be the law which the person (or one of the persons) whose estate is involved could have chosen in accordance with Article 22 (*id est* national law at the time of making the choice or at the time of death). There is no choice of applicable law when it comes to formal validity of a disposition of property upon death.

III. Compulsory Portion

466. In accordance with Article 23(2)(h) of the EU Succession Regulation, *lex successionis* governs the disposable part of the estate, the reserved shares and other restrictions on the disposal of property upon death as well as claims which persons close to the deceased may have against the estate or the heirs. Recital 38 explains that the autonomy to designate *lex successions* is limited in order to ensure a connection between the deceased and the law chosen and to avoid a law being chosen with the intention of frustrating the legitimate expectations of persons entitled to a reserved share. Recital 54 explains that provisions providing for a reserved share of the estate greater than that provided for in *lex successionis* may not be regarded as constituting special rules allowing for the application of *lex rei sitae* (to which Article 30 refers to).[481]

IV. Interpretation

467. Pursuant to Article 26(1)(d) of the Succession Regulation, the interpretation of the disposition of property upon death pertains to its substantive validity. Hence, it is governed by the law chosen or (if no choice was made) by the law indicated by Articles 24–25.

---

480. A. Wysocka-Bar, *Wybór prawa w międzynarodowym prawie spadkowym*, LexisNexis, Warszawa 2013.
481. A. Wysocka-Bar, *EU Succession Regulation: Choice of applicable law and protection of family members* in: K. Boele-Woelki, The Future of Family Property in Europe, Intersentia Antwerp 2011, pp. 383–405.

V. Last Will

A. Formal Validity

468. In the EU Member States, which – like Poland – are parties to the Hague Convention on Form of Wills (1961)[482] formal validity is still governed by this Convention (Article 75(1)). The Convention is based on the *favor validitatis* principle. Pursuant to Article 1 of this Convention, a will is formally valid as long as it abides by the formal requirements of at least one of numerous laws listed in this provision (e.g., of the place where the testator made it, or of a nationality possessed by the testator, either at the time when he made the disposition, or at the time of his death, or of a place in which the testator had his domicile either at the time when he made the disposition, or at the time of his death, etc.).

B. Substantive Validity

469. The law applicable to substantive validity of the disposition of property upon death (other than an agreement as to succession) is governed by the law chosen by the testator or, if no choice was made, by the so-called hypothetical *lex successionis*. The hypothetical *lex successionis* is the law which would have been applicable if the testator had died on the day on which the disposition was made (Article 24(1) Succession Regulation), so in other words the law of habitual residence at the time of making the disposition. Pursuant to Article 24(3), the hypothetical *lex successionis* applies, as appropriate, to the modification or revocation of a disposition of property upon death (other than an agreement as to succession). If the testator has chosen applicable law, the modification or revocation is governed by the chosen law.

470. Article 26 enumerates elements which pertain to substantive validity of dispositions of property upon death. This includes, *inter alia*, the capacity of the person making the disposition of property upon death to make such a disposition, the admissibility of representation for the purposes of making a disposition of property upon death, the interpretation of the disposition, as well as fraud, duress, mistake and any other questions relating to the consent or intention of the person making the disposition.

VI. Legacy

471. The Succession Regulation also covers legacies. Article 23(2)(e) mentions the transfer to the legatees of the assets forming part of the estate and conditions and effects of the acceptance or waiver of a legacy as exemplary matters governed by the *lex successionis*. Recital 47 explains that *lex successionis* should determine

482. Hague Convention of 5 Oct. 1961 on the Conflicts of Laws Relating to the Form of Testamentary Dispositions, Dz. U. 1969 nr 34 poz. 284.

who the beneficiaries are in any given succession and that under most laws, the term 'beneficiaries' covers both heirs and legatees although the legal position of legatees is not the same under all laws. Under some laws, the legatee may receive a direct share in the estate whereas under other laws the legatee may acquire only a claim against the heirs. Both types of legacies currently exist in Polish substantive succession law.

472. The question of the effectiveness of a legacy by vindication (*legatum per vindicationem*) made under Polish law being *lex successionis* in case an immovable property subject to this legacy is located in another EU Member State, the substantive law of which provides only for legacy by damnation (*legatum per damnationem*) was subject of the Judgment of the CJEU in *Kubicka*[483] case (C-218/16).[484]

A. *Formal Validity*

473. Please refer to section V.A above and section VII.A below.

B. *Substantive Validity*

474. Please refer to section V.B above and section VII.B below.

VII. Testamentary Contract

A. *Formal Validity*

475. The Succession Regulation, in Article 3(1)(d), names agreements as to successions as one of the dispositions of property upon death. Agreement as to succession is defined as an agreement, including an agreement resulting from mutual wills, which, with or without consideration, creates, modifies or terminates rights to the future estate or estates of one or more persons party to the agreement (Article 3(1)(b)).

476. The Hague Convention on Form of Wills (1961) does not apply to agreements as to succession. Hence, its formal validity is governed by the law applicable designated by Article 27 of the Succession Regulation.[485] It states that an agreement as to succession made in writing is valid as regards form if its form complies

483. Case C-218/16 *Kubicka*, Judgment of the Court (Second Chamber) of 12 Oct. 2017.
484. P. Tereszkiewicz, A. Wysocka-Bar, *Legacy by Vindication Under the EU Succession Regulation No. 650/2012 Following the Kubicka Judgment of the ECJ*, European Review of Private Law 2019, vol. 4, pp. 875–894.
485. A. Wysocka-Bar, *Prawo właściwe dla formy rozrządzeń na wypadek śmierci według rozporządzenia spadkowego* w: red. M. Pazdan, J. Górecki, *Nowe europejskie prawo spadkowe*, Wolters Kluwer, Warszawa 2015, pp. 130–143.

with one of the following laws: of the state in which the agreement as to succession was concluded, of a state whose nationality at least one of the persons whose succession is concerned by an agreement as to succession possessed, either at the time when the agreement was concluded, or at the time of death, of a state in which at least one of the persons whose succession is concerned by an agreement as to succession had his domicile, either at the time when the agreement was concluded, or at the time of death, of the State in which at least one of the persons whose succession is concerned by an agreement as to succession had his habitual residence, either at the time when the agreement was concluded, or at the time of death or in so far as immovable property is concerned, of the state in which that property is located. The provision was clearly influenced by the *favor validitatis* principle of the Hague Convention (1961).

477. Article 24(3) lists matters which pertain to formal validity of a disposition of property upon death. It covers any provision of law which limits the permitted forms of dispositions of property upon death by reference to the age, nationality or other personal conditions of the persons whose succession is concerned by an agreement as to succession, as well as qualifications to be possessed by any witnesses required for the validity of a disposition of property upon death.

B. *Substantive Validity*

478. Article 25 of the Succession Regulation refers to substantive validity of the agreements as to succession. As mentioned above, matters pertaining to substantive validity are listed in Article 26. An agreement as to succession regarding the succession of one person is governed (if no choice of applicable law was made), as regards its admissibility, its substantive validity and its binding effects between the parties, including the conditions for its dissolution, by the hypothetical *lex successionis*. In other words, it is governed by the law which would have been applicable to the succession of that person if this person had died on the day on which the agreement was concluded (Article 25(1)).

479. An agreement as to succession regarding the succession of several persons is admissible only if it is admissible under the law chosen by the parties or, in case no choice of law was made, under all hypothetical *lex successionis* of all the persons involved cumulatively. An admissible agreement as to succession is governed (if no choice of law was made), as regards its substantive validity and its binding effects between the parties, including the conditions for its dissolution, by the law, from among all hypothetical *lex successionis* of persons involved, with which it has the closest connection.

§4. Inheritance and Liability

480. Article 23(1)(g) of the Succession Regulation makes it clear that *lex successionis* governs the liability for the debts under the succession. Article 28 provides that a declaration designed to limit the liability of the person making this declaration, shall be valid as to form where it meets the requirements of *lex successionis* or the law of the state in which the person making the declaration has habitual residence.

Part III. Annex: International Civil Procedure

Chapter 1. Sources of International Civil Procedure

481. As already explained in Part I., Chapter 1. Sources of PIL, PIL rules in Poland are contained in domestic law, international agreements, both multilateral and bilateral, as well as EU regulations. The same is truth with respect to international civil procedure, meaning rules on jurisdiction, procedural matters with respect to cross-border cases and rules on recognition and enforcement of foreign judgments.

482. In domestic law rules on international civil procedure are contained in Part IV 'Provisions on international civil procedure' CPC. This part of CPC is divided into five books as follows: Book 1 – Jurisdiction, Book 1a – Jurisdictional and enforcement immunity, Book 2 – Procedure, Book 3 – Recognition and Declaration of Enforceability and Book 4 – Recognition and Declaration of Enforceability of Certain Judgments of courts of the Member States of the European Union, as well as settlements and authentic instruments originating from these States. Rules contained in CPC are of a vast material scope in comparison to rules of international agreements and EU instruments, which may refer to a limited subject matter (e.g., matrimonial and parental responsibility matters).

483. In the EU law rules on international civil procedure are contained in numerous regulations, which concern jurisdiction (*see* Chapter 4. International Jurisdiction, §1 Statutory Forums), service of documents (*see* Chapter 4. International Jurisdiction, §4. International Service), taking of evidence (Chapter 4. International Jurisdiction, §5. Rules of Evidence), recognition and enforcement of judgments (*see* Chapter 5. Recognition and Enforcement of Foreign Decisions). These regulations are listed in more details in the respective chapters.

484. As explained in Part I., Chapter 1. Sources of PIL rules on international civil procedure are also contained in multilateral agreements to which Poland is party to (e.g., Lugano II Convention (2007),[486] Hague Convention on Choice of Court (2005)[487]) and bilateral agreements (*see* the list of Bilateral Agreements under Table of International Treaties).

485. The above creates obviously complicated mosaic of legal sources. Hence, finding an applicable piece of legislation must be done on case-by-case basis. The following rules establish relation between different instruments. In general, EU instruments take precedence over (to the extent of their material scope) rules contained in bilateral agreements between Poland and other EU Member States, as well as rules contained in Part IV CPC 'Provisions on international civil procedure'. Multilateral international agreements (like 2007 Lugano II Convention and 2005 Hague Convention on Choice of Court) take precedence before CPC. Their relations with EU instruments are more nuanced. Bilateral conventions with non-EU states, in general, take precedence before EU regulations and CPC. Hence, CPC is an instrument of the 'last resort'. It applies only if no EU or international law instrument is applicable to a given case.

486. As noted above, EU instruments and multilateral agreements are already subject to voluminous literature, and therefore, will only be mentioned or shortly summarized. Similarly, the existence of bilateral convention will be signalled. These conventions will not be analysed in detail due to their number and variety of their scope, as well as solutions provided therein.

486. Convention on jurisdiction and the recognition and enforcement of judgments in civil and commercial matters done at Lugano on 30 Oct. 2007, OJ L 339, 21.12.2007, pp. 3–41.
487. Convention of 30 Jun. 2005 on Choice of Court Agreements, OJ L 133, 29.5.2009, pp. 1–13.

Chapter 2. The Principle of *Lex Fori*

487. With respect to procedure, in general, only domestic rules are applied in accordance with *lex fori processualis* principle.[488] Procedural rules of CPC apply equally to purely domestic and international cases, taking into account particularities included in Part IV 'International Civil Procedure' CPC, for example with respect to capacity to be a party to the proceeding held in Poland (*see below* Chapter 4. International Jurisdiction, §3. Procedural Requirements). The *lex fori processualis* principle is sometimes literally stated in CPC, for example in Article 1135[1] CPC, which provides that an application of a foreign court concerning taking of evidence or service of documents in Poland is executed in accordance with Polish law.

488. It may happen that it is doubtful where to draw a line between material law questions which should be dealt with in accordance with applicable law and procedural law questions which are subject to *lex fori processualis*. A classic example is the rule on prescription. In continental Europe, including Poland, these rules are perceived as material law rules, whereas in *common law* jurisdictions they are treated as matters pertaining to procedure. In EU Regulations it is clearly stated that rules on prescription are governed by the law applicable to contractual and non-contractual obligations (*see* Article 12(1)(d) Rome I Regulation[489] and Article 15(h) Rome II Regulation[490]). Similar rule is included in Article 11(e) Hague Protocol.[491] In accordance with Article 26 PILA (which is applied to those matters that are not covered by EU instruments), prescription is governed by the law applicable to the claim (*lex causae*). The same applies to other institutions related to the lapse of time (Article 27 PILA). Hence, prescription is governed by the law applicable designated by a conflict-of-law rule, even if in this law it may be perceived as a matter of procedure.[492] Other doubtful matters include legal presumptions and the burden of proof.[493] This question is dealt with Article 6(2) PILA. If law applicable to a given legal relationship (*lex causae*) provides for presumptions or particular rules on burden of proof with respect to this legal relationship, these rules are applied. Similar solution may be found in EU instruments. For example, Article 18 Rome I Regulation provides that the law governing a contractual obligation apply to the extent that, in matters of contractual obligations, it contains rules which raise presumptions of law or determine the burden of proof.

---

488. P. Rodziewicz, *Stwierdzenie treści oraz zastosowanie prawa obcego w sądowym postępowaniu cywilnym*, Wydawnictwo C. H. Beck, Warszawa 2015, p. 201.
489. OJ L 177, 4.7.2008, pp. 6–16.
490. OJ L 199, 31.7.2007, pp. 40–49.
491. OJ L 331, 16.12.2009, pp. 17–23.
492. P. Rodziewicz, *Stwierdzenie treści oraz zastosowanie prawa obcego w sądowym postępowaniu cywilnym*, Wydawnictwo C. H. Beck, Warszawa 2015, p. 204.
493. P. Rodziewicz, *Stwierdzenie treści oraz zastosowanie prawa obcego w sądowym postępowaniu cywilnym*, Wydawnictwo C. H. Beck, Warszawa 2015, pp. 204–205.

Chapter 3. National Jurisdiction

489. If Polish courts have jurisdiction to hear a cross-border case (*see below* Chapter 4. International jurisdiction §1. Statutory Forums and §2. Choice of Forum Agreement) the next question that needs to be answered is which court precisely in Poland has competence to deal with it. CPC provides for rules concerning material competence. For example, Article 16 §1 CPC provides for the general competence of district courts for cases dealt with in contentious proceedings, unless a certain type of proceeding is reserved for provincial court. The competence of provincial courts encompasses, *inter alia*, claims with respect to property rights, where the value at stake exceeds PLN 75,000, with exceptions (e.g., maintenance claims are dealt with by district courts irrespective the value at stake). Similarly, CPC provides for rules on territorial competence. These rules are scattered in different parts of the CPC depending on the type of case. For example, a claim related to the execution of a contract may be brought to the court at the place, where the defendant is domiciled (in accordance with general rule of Article 27 CPC) or alternatively, at the place of the characteristic performance (Article 34 §1 CPC).

490. Please note that there are no separate rules on territorial competence provided for cross-border cases. Instead, the above rules apply. As might be imagined the application of rules on territorial competence to cross-border cases might be problematic. Often, the CPC itself resolves the problem. For example, when it comes to the sharing of the succession a court at the place of last habitual residence of the deceased is competent. If it is not possible to establish the last habitual residence of the deceased in Poland, the court at the place where the estate is located is competent. In the absence of the above grounds of competence, the district court competent for city centre of Warsaw may hear the case (Article 627 CPC). In extreme cases when CPC does not give the answer itself, it might be necessary to apply to the Supreme Court for the decision on which court is competent (Article 45 §1 CPC).

Chapter 4. International Jurisdiction

§1. Statutory Forums

491. Jurisdiction with respect to civil and commercial matters is regulated by the Brussels I *bis* Regulation.[494] It applies from 10 January 2015 to legal proceedings instituted starting from that date (Article 66(1) and 81). Certain matters are excluded from its material scope, for example legal capacity of natural persons, matrimonial property matters, bankruptcy, arbitration, maintenance obligations, successions (Article 1(2)). It applies when a defendant is domiciled in an EU Member States, including Poland (Article 4(1)). If a defendant is domiciled outside EU, jurisdiction, in general, is assessed based on domestic law, namely CPC (Article 6(1)). This rule is however subject to important limitations, as Brussels I *bis* applies anyway, no matter the domicile of defendant, in case of consumer contracts (Article 18(1)), employment contracts (Article 21(2)), exclusive jurisdiction (Article 24) and prorogation agreements (Article 25).

492. The general solution, contained in Article 4 Brussels I *bis* Regulation, provides for *actor sequitur forum rei* principle, based on which a defendant domiciled in Poland, irrespective of the nationality, may be sued in Poland. Articles 62 and 63 explain the term 'domicile'. Additionally, Brussels I *bis* provides for alternative jurisdiction in Articles 7, 8 and 9. For example, a defendant domiciled in a Member State (other than Poland) may be sued in Poland in matters relating to contract, if the place of performance of the obligation in question is located in Poland (Article 7(1)(a) or in matters relating to delict, if the harmful event occurred in Poland (Article 7(2)). Brussels I *bis* provides also for exclusive jurisdiction in Article 24. Based on this Article, courts in Poland have exclusive jurisdiction, for example, in proceedings which have as their object rights in rem in immovable property or tenancies of immovable property located in Poland. When it comes to certain contracts (namely, insurance contracts, consumer contracts and employment) special rules of jurisdiction are provided for in Brussels I *bis* Regulation. Brussels I *bis* Regulation provides for prorogation agreements, which will be explained right below (*see* §2. Choice of Forum Agreement).

493. Jurisdiction with respect to matrimonial matters (divorce, legal separation and marriage annulment) and parental responsibility matters is regulated by Brussels II *bis* Regulation.[495] It applies to proceedings instituted starting from 1 March 2004 (Articles 64 and 72). Certain matters are excluded from its material scope, for example the establishment or contesting of a parent-child relationship, decisions on adoption, the name and forenames of the child, maintenance obligations and successions (Article 1(3)).

494. The general rules concerning jurisdiction in matrimonial matters are set in Article 3. In accordance with this provision Polish courts are competent if the

494. OJ L 351, 20.12.2012, pp. 1–32.
495. OJ L 338, 23.12.2003, pp. 1–29.

spouses are habitually resident in Poland or they were last habitually resident in Poland, insofar as one of them still resides in Poland or the respondent is habitually resident in Poland or in the event of a joint application, either of the spouses is habitually resident in Poland or the applicant is habitually resident in Poland if the applicant resided in Poland for at least a year immediately before the application was made, or the applicant is habitually resident in Poland if the applicant resided there for at least six months immediately before the application was made and is either a Polish national or both spouses have Polish nationality. Brussels II *bis* provides for specific rules when it comes to counterclaim (Article 4) and conversion of separation into divorce (Article 5). Article 6 Brussels I *bis* underlines that a spouse, who is habitually resident in one of EU Member States or is a national of one of EU Member States may be sued in another EU Member State only based on the above rules. Hence, it will be not possible to sue a national of an EU Member State in matrimonial matter based on CPC if it would not be possible based on Brussels II *bis*. Inversely, in accordance with Article 7 Brussels I *bis*, Polish court may ascertain jurisdiction in matrimonial matter based on its own law (namely, in Poland this means rules provided for in CPC) only if no EU Member State has jurisdiction pursuant to Articles 3, 4 and 5 Brussels II *bis* Regulations. Such jurisdictional rules concerning matrimonial matters are included in CPC.

495. In parental responsibility matters the general rule is included in Article 8 Brussels II *bis* Regulation. Pursuant to this provision Polish court has jurisdiction if a child is habitually resident in Poland at the time the court is seized. Specific jurisdictional rules, including rules for intra-EU child abduction cases, are provided for in Article 9–13 Brussels II *bis* Regulation. Article 15 Brussels II *bis* provides for a mechanism of the transfer of jurisdiction between EU Member States in order to submit a case to a court better placed to it. Pursuant to Article 14 Brussels II *bis* Regulation, when none of EU Member State has jurisdiction pursuant to Articles 8–13, Polish courts may ascertain jurisdiction based on their own law (in Poland this means jurisdictional rules in parental responsibility matters contained in the Hague Convention on parental responsibility and child protection (1996)[496] and in CPC). Poland is party to this convention since 2010. The relation between Brussels II *bis* and the Hague Convention (1996) is explained in Articles 61 and 62 Brussels I *bis* Regulation. In accordance with these provisions, Brussels I *bis* Regulation prevails when the child concerned has habitual residence within the EU. If the child has habitual residence outside the EU, in a third state, which is party to the Hague Convention (1996), the Convention applies.

496. Jurisdiction with respect to maintenance obligations arising from a family relationship, parentage, marriage or affinity is regulated by the Maintenance Regulation.[497] It applies to proceedings instituted from 18 June 2018 (Articles 75(1) and 76 Maintenance Regulation). Pursuant to the general rule provided for in Article 3,

496. Convention of 19 Oct. 1996 on Jurisdiction, Applicable Law, Recognition, Enforcement and Co-operation in Respect of Parental Responsibility and Measures for the Protection of Children, Dz. U. 1995 nr 108 poz. 528.
497. OJ L 7, 10.1.2009, pp. 1–79.

maintenance claim may be heard in Poland if the maintenance debtor or the maintenance creditor is habitually resident in Poland, as well as in cases when Polish court has jurisdiction in other matter, to which maintenance is an ancillary one (namely, in proceedings concerning the status of a person, for example divorce or establishment of paternity or in proceedings concerning parental responsibility. To some degree choice of court is possible (Articles 4 and 5 Maintenance Regulation). Article 6 provides for jurisdiction of the courts of an EU Member State of the common nationality if certain conditions are met, whereas Article 7 concerns *forum necessitatis*. As opposed to Brussels I *bis* and Brussels II *bis* Regulations, in Maintenance Regulation no residual jurisdiction, meaning jurisdiction derived from domestic rules, is possible.

497. Jurisdiction with respect to succession matters is regulated in Succession Regulation.[498] It applies to succession of persons who has died starting from 17 August 2015 (Articles 83 and 84). Polish courts have jurisdiction in a succession matter if the deceased was habitually resident in Poland at the time of death (Article 4). In case of the deceased, who was habitually resident in a non-EU state at the time of death, Polish courts have jurisdiction if assets are located in Poland insofar as the deceased had Polish nationality at the time of death or, failing that, the deceased had his previous habitual residence in Poland, provided that, at the time the court is seized, a period of not more than five years has elapsed since that habitual residence changed (Article 10(1)). In certain cases, Polish court might have jurisdiction only based on the location of assets in Poland (Article 10(2)). Article 11 Succession Regulation provides also for *forum necessitatis*. If the deceased has chosen his national law as applicable to succession, it is possible to transfer jurisdiction to the EU Member State of that law in accordance with mechanisms set forth in Articles 5–9. The jurisdiction established under the Succession Regulation, in general (with exception set in Article 10(2)), covers movable and immovable property (the latter at least as long as it is located within the EU). If a person died before 17 August 2015, but the succession proceeding (e.g., sharing of the estate) was initiated after that day, the rules provided for in CPC apply. Pursuant to Articles 1107^1 and 1110^2 CPC such proceeding concerning immovable property located in Poland fall within the exclusive jurisdiction of Polish courts. When it comes to movables, Polish courts have jurisdiction if, for example, the deceased, at the time of death, had Polish nationality or had the domicile or habitual residence in Poland, as well as if the estate or important part thereof is located in Poland (Article 1108 CPC).[499]

498. The above regulations are the only ones which contain rules on jurisdiction that are applied in Poland. This is because Poland does not apply the 'twin' EU regulations on matrimonial property relations[500] and property relations of registered partnerships.[501] Hence, jurisdiction of Polish courts in these matters is assessed

498. OJ 2012 L 201, pp. 107–134.
499. A. Wysocka-Bar, *Jurysdykcja krajowa sądów polskich a kolizyjna jednolitość spadku*, PWPM 2016, t. 14, pp. 90–109.
500. OJ L 183, 8.7.2016, pp. 1–29.
501. OJ L 183, 8.7.2016, pp. 30–56.

based on bilateral conventions (with both EU and non-EU states) or, if no such bilateral convention applies, based on rules provided for in CPC. Similarly, jurisdiction of Polish courts in all other matters, which are not covered by the EU instruments, may result from multilateral and bilateral agreements, as well as CPC.

499. In CPC, jurisdictional rules are divided into two groups depending on the type of proceeding, in which a given case will be dealt with, namely contentious or non-contentions proceedings. Title III of the Book 1 'Jurisdiction' of Part IV CPC provides for jurisdictional rules concerning cases dealt with in contentious proceedings, whereas Title IV of the Book 1 'Jurisdiction' of the Part IV CPC provide for such rules concerning cases dealt with in non-contentious proceeding. Both titles however contain similar rules when it comes to cases concerning immovable property located in Poland (Articles 1103^8, 1107^1, 1110^2 CPC). In such cases Polish jurisdiction is exclusive if this immovable property is located in Poland. *A contrario* it seems that Polish courts do not have jurisdiction in cases concerning immovable property located abroad.[502] Please note that the above rules apply only in cases when the jurisdiction is assessed based on the CPC. It does not apply to, for example succession cases, which fall within the scope of the Succession Regulation.

500. When it comes to matrimonial property matters dealt with in contentious proceeding (e.g., when one of the spouses applies for changing the existing community of property regime into separation of property regime), Polish courts have jurisdiction if, for example, both spouses have habitual residence in Poland or both spouses have Polish nationality (Article 1103^1 CPC, which is in fact modelled on Article 3 Brussels II *bis* Regulation) and, in case of immovable property owned by the spouses, when it is located in Poland. In case of matters dealt with in non-contentious proceeding (e.g., when spouses apply for sharing of the common estate once the community regimes ceased to exist) Polish courts have jurisdiction if, for example, one of the spouses has Polish nationality or domicile in Poland, as well as if the common estate or important part thereof is located in Poland (Article 1106^2 CPC) and, when it comes to immovable property owned by the spouses, it is located in Poland.

501. Other matters, in which no EU instrument is applicable, and therefore, CPC (and to the obviously lesser extent) bilateral agreements come into play, include establishment of paternity. In such cases Polish courts have jurisdiction if, for example, the child has habitual residence in Poland (Article 1103^2 CPC), but also if the defendant is domiciled or habitually resident in Poland in accordance with *actor sequitur forum rei* general rule provided for in Article 1103 CPC.

502. Application for a presumption of death and for a declaration of the death is dealt with by Polish court if the missing person is Polish national or had the last domicile or habitual residence in Poland (Article 1106 CPC). Polish courts have

---

502. K. Weitz in T. Ereciński, *Kodeks postępowania cywilnego. Komentarz. Tom VI. Międzynarodowe postępowanie cywilne. Sąd polubowny (arbitrażowy)*,, Wolters Kluwer, Warszawa 2017, p. 128.

jurisdiction in matters concerning incapacitation of a natural person, if the person, who is supposed to be incapacitated, is a Polish national or has the domicile or habitual residence in Poland (Article 1106^1 CPC). In adoption cases Polish courts have jurisdiction if the person, adoptee has Polish nationality or has domicile or habitual residence in Poland, as well as in cases when the person, who wants to adopt has Polish nationality and has domicile or habitual residence in Poland (Article 1106^4 CPC).

§2. Choice of Forum Agreement

503. Prorogation agreements in favour of an EU Member State's courts, including Polish courts, are in general admissible in accordance with Article 25 Brussels I *bis* Regulation, irrespective of the domicile of the parties, with important modifications concerning insurance, consumer and employment contracts (Articles 15, 19 and 23 – respectively). Prorogation agreement may concern any dispute which has arisen, or which may arise in connection with a particular legal relationship. Article 25(1) *in fine* Brussels I *bis* sets formal requirements for such agreements (it may be in writing, which include communication by electronic means or evidenced in writing, but also in a form which accords with practices established between the parties or in international trade or commerce, under certain circumstances in a form which accords with a usage). Article 25(5) Brussels I *bis* Regulation provide for separability principle, meaning that a prorogation clause included in the main contract for the purpose of its validity should be treated as an agreement independent of the main contract. Article 26(1) Brussels I *bis* Regulation provides also for submission, meaning that the court of an EU Member State becomes competent if a defendant enters an appearance (e.g., files an answer to the application filed by the claimant) before this court. The jurisdiction of the court seized will not exist of the defendant enters appearance to contest the jurisdiction. Certain modifications concern insurance, consumer and employment contracts (Article 26(2)). In these cases, before assuming jurisdiction, the court must ensure that the defendant is informed of his right to contest the jurisdiction and of the consequences of entering (or not entering) an appearance.

504. It should be noted here that Poland, just like other EU Member States, is bound by the Hague Convention on Choice of Court Agreements (2005)[503] since 1 October 2015. This Convention binds Mexico, Montenegro, Singapore, Denmark (which is an EU Member State, but the one that is outside the judicial cooperation in civil matters) and the UK (which left EU on 1 February 2020). This Convention applies in international cases to exclusive choice of court agreements concluded in civil or commercial matters (Article 1(1)). Some exceptions exist, for example the

503. Council Decision of 26 Feb. 2009 on the signing on behalf of the European Community of the Convention on Choice of Court Agreements OJ L 133, 29.5.2009, pp. 1–13 and Council Decision of 4 Dec. 2014 on the approval, on behalf of the European Union, of the Hague Convention of 30 Jun. 2005 on Choice of Court Agreements OJ L 353, 10.12.2014, pp. 5–8.

carriage of passengers and goods is outside the scope of the Convention. The agreement is 'exclusive' meaning that jurisdiction lies with the courts of one state to the exclusion of the jurisdiction of courts of other states. The general idea of the Convention is that the court designated in the prorogation agreement decides the dispute (Article 5), whereas courts in all other states should decline it (Article 6). The relation between this Convention and Brussels I *bis* Regulation (as both instruments apply to prorogation agreements in civil and commercial matters) is explained in Article 26(6) of the Convention. The Convention is applied if at least one party to the agreement is resident in a non-EU contracting state (e.g., one party is resident in Sweden, the other in Montenegro and they choose the jurisdiction of Polish courts). Brussels I *bis* Regulation is applied if none of the parties is resident in a non-EU contracting state. For example, Brussels I *bis* Regulation applies if one party is resident in Russia, the other in Brazil (both countries are non-contracting states). Another example may include one party resident in Russia and the other one in Czech Republic (hence, one party is resident in the EU). The last example may include one party resident in Portugal, the other in Czech Republic (therefore both residents in the EU).

505. To a much narrower extent than in Brussels I *bis* party autonomy finds its place also in Article 12 Brussels II *bis* Regulation (parental responsibility matters dealt with matrimonial matter), Article 4 Maintenance Regulation (except maintenance obligation towards a child under the age of 18) and Article 5 Succession Regulation.

506. CPC (which is applied in all the matters not covered by the EU instruments and international agreements) distinguishes between prorogation agreements in favour of Polish courts (Article 1104 §1 CPC) and derogation agreements – agreements in favour of foreign courts in cases, which normally fall within the jurisdiction of Polish courts (1105 CPC). It also provides for submission, even if a derogation agreement is in place (Article 1104 §2 CPC). Such agreements (and submission) are admissible in cases which are decided in contentious proceedings and concern property rights. In certain instances, they are admissible in cases which are decided in non-contentious proceedings, for example sharing of the common estate of the spouses or division of property held in common (Article 1110^1 CPC). Derogation agreement cannot relate to cases, in which jurisdiction of Polish courts is exclusive. Both kinds of agreements have to be in writing or equivalent, for example in the form of e-mail correspondence (Article 1105^1 CPC).

§3. Procedural Requirements

507. Book II 'Procedure' of the Part IV CPC provides for certain specific rules relating to 'international' cases. In accordance with Article 1117 CPC the capacity of a foreigner to be a party to the judicial proceeding held in Poland is governed by the law applicable to legal capacity (which in turn is determined in accordance with

Article 11 PILA or some of bilateral agreements). A foreigner, who lacks this capacity pursuant to the applicable law, may nevertheless act in a judicial proceeding, if competent under Polish law.

508. Article 1119 CPC requires a foreigner, who initiates a proceeding in Poland, on the request of the defendant, to pay a deposit to cover prospective costs (*cautio judicatum solvi*). The above rules do not apply to claimants who have their domicile, habitual residence or a seat in Poland or other EU Member State. The deposit is supposed to cover compensation that the winning party may claim from the losing one. Some exemptions from this requirement are provided for in Article 1120 CPC and include, *inter alia*, cases when a claimant has sufficient assets in Poland or is entitled to or already obtained an exemption from judicial costs. Formalities concerning the deposit are regulated in Articles 1119–1128 CPC.

509. A foreigner might be exempted from judicial costs, including court fees and other expenses, in accordance with separate rules (Article 1129 CPC). The term 'separate rules' seems to cover general rules on the exemption from judicial costs, which are contained in Articles 94–118 Act on Judicial Costs in Civil Cases[504] (which are equally applicable to 'domestic' parties) and in laws[505] implementing in Poland the EU Legal Aid Directive,[506] which apply only to claimants having domicile or habitual residence in an EU Member State.

510. Also, EU regulations (e.g., Maintenance Regulation), multilateral conventions (e.g., Hague Child Abduction Convention (1980)) and bilateral agreements (e.g., bilateral agreement with Ukraine 1993) contain rules concerning the possibility of exemption from judicial costs.

§4. International Service

511. Poland applies EU Service Regulation.[507] Pursuant to its Article 1, it applies in civil and commercial matters where a judicial or extrajudicial document has to be transmitted from one EU Member State to another for service there. Poland is also party to the Hague Convention on the Service Abroad (1965)[508] since 1996. Some bilateral agreements to which Poland is party to contain rules on service of

504. Act of 28 Jul. 2005 on judicial costs in civil cases, Dz. U. 2020 poz. 755.
505. Act of 17 Dec. 2004 on the law of assistance in proceedings in civil cases conducted in the Member States of the European Union and on the law of assistance for the purpose of amicable settlement of a dispute prior to the initiation of such proceedings, Dz. U. 2005 nr 10 poz. 67.
506. Council Directive 2002/8/EC of 27 Jan. 2003 to improve access to justice in cross-border disputes by establishing minimum common rules relating to legal aid for such disputes, OJ L 26, 31.1.2003, pp. 41–47.
507. Regulation (EC) No 1393/2007 of the European Parliament and of the Council of 13 November 2007 on the service in the Member States of judicial and extrajudicial documents in civil or commercial matters (service of documents), and repealing Council Regulation (EC) No 1348/2000, OJ L *324, 10.12.2007, pp. 79–120.*
508. Hague Convention of 15 Nov. 1965 on the Service Abroad of Judicial and Extrajudicial Documents in Civil or Commercial Matters, Dz. U. 2000 nr 87 poz. 968.

documents. Also, CPC regulates this issue in case EU Service Regulation is not applicable and no international agreement is in place (Articles 1130–1135^{5}).

512. Pursuant to Article 1135^{5} CPC a party with no domicile, habitual residence or seat in Poland or in any other EU Member State, who does not have legal representative resident in Poland, is obliged to designate a representative for the purpose of service of documents in Poland. If such representative is not designated, any court documents addressed to this party are left in the court's files and are deemed to be properly served. This provision before amendment applied equally to EU residents, and therefore, was subject to an interesting case concerning EU Service Regulation before CJEU (*see Alder* case, C-325/11[509]).

§5. Rules of Evidence

513. Poland applies EU Evidence Regulation.[510] This Regulation applies in civil and commercial matters where the court of an EU Member State, in accordance with the provisions of the law of that State, requests the competent court of another EU Member State to take evidence or to take evidence directly in another EU Member State. Poland is also party to the Hague Convention on the Taking of Evidence Abroad (1970)[511] since 1996. Some bilateral agreements to which Poland is party to contain rules on taking of evidence. Also, CPC regulates this issue in case EU Evidence Regulation is not applicable and no international agreement is in place (Articles 1153^{13}–1153^{25} CPC).

§6. Temporary Relief

514. In general, a court dealing with the case on the merits may order provisional measures, which are listed and regulated under Part II CPC (which is equally applicable to purely domestic and cross-border cases).[512] Hence, provisional measures are governed by *lex fori processualis*. Another question is whether a court not dealing with the merits of the case may order such measures. For example, Article 35 Brussels I *bis* Regulation (which is applicable only to civil and commercial matters) stipulates that one may apply to the courts of an EU Member State for such provisional, including protective, measures as may be available under the law of

509. Case C-325/11 *Alder*, Judgment of the Court (First Chamber) of 19 Dec. 2012.
510. Council Regulation (EC) No 1206/2001 of 28 May 2001 on cooperation between the courts of the Member States in the taking of evidence in civil or commercial matters, OJ L 174, 27.6.2001, pp. 1–24.
511. Hague Convention of 18 Mar. 1970 on the Taking of Evidence Abroad in Civil or Commercial Matters, Dz. U. 2000 nr 50 poz. 582.
512. K. Weitz in T. Ereciński, *Kodeks postępowania cywilnego. Komentarz. Tom VI. Międzynarodowe postępowanie cywilne. Sąd polubowny (arbitrażowy)*, Wolters Kluwer, Warszawa 2017, p. 308.

that EU Member State, even if the courts of another EU Member State have jurisdiction as to the substance of the matter. Similar provisions may be found in Article 30 Brussels II *bis* Regulation, Article 14 Maintenance Regulation and Article 19 Succession Regulation.

515. In accordance with Article 1110^3 §1 CPC grounds of jurisdiction existing in CPC are applied also when it comes to provisional measures to be awarded by a court in Poland. Such jurisdiction exists also if provisional measure might be enforced in Poland or have effects in Poland. Hence, Article 1110^3 CPC indicates when courts in Poland are competent to grant a provisional measure irrespective whether the main proceeding is already pending and whether it will be commenced in Poland or abroad.[513] When it comes to the enforcement of the provisional measure, courts in Poland are competent if the enforcement is sought in Poland. For example, if an immoveable property, which is supposed to be secured with a mortgage, is located in Poland, a court in Poland is competent to proceed with such provisional measure as long as all the requirements provided for in Part II CPC are met.

516. Because conditions for the grant of provisional measures and the efficiency of their implementation vary considerably in procedural law of the EU Member States, EU legislator introduced a special unified measure in the form of a European Account Preservation Order (EAPO).[514] It applies to pecuniary claims in civil and commercial matters in cross-border cases. It allows a creditor to freeze funds held by the debtor in a bank account in another EU Member State (except Denmark and the UK). The EAPO is available in cases, where the account is held in an EU Member State other than where the creditor is domiciled, or the court seized with the claim is based. EAPO may be issued by the court which has jurisdiction in the main proceeding (e.g., based on Brussels I *bis* Regulation). EAPO is an alternative to national procedures and does not replace them.

---

513. K. Weitz in T. Ereciński, *Kodeks postępowania cywilnego. Komentarz. Tom VI. Międzynarodowe postępowanie cywilne. Sąd polubowny (arbitrażowy)*, Wolters Kluwer, Warszawa 2017, p. 306.
514. Regulation (EU) No 655/2014 of the European Parliament and of the Council of 15 May 2014 establishing a European Account Preservation Order procedure to facilitate cross-border debt recovery in civil and commercial matters, OJ L 189, 27.6.2014, pp. 59–92.

Chapter 5. Recognition and Enforcement of Foreign Decisions

517. It should be noted that a foreign judgment (but also court settlement and authentic instrument) might be in Poland subject to different rules on recognition and enforcement contained in different sources of law. The application of a given set of rules depends on two factors – the country of origin of the judgment and its subject matter (e.g., commercial matter, as opposed to family matter).

518. The rules on recognition and enforcement in one EU Member State (e.g., Poland) of a judgment (but also court settlement and authentic instrument) issued in another EU Member State are provided for in those regulations: Brussels I *bis* Regulation (Articles 36–60), which refer to civil and commercial matters; Brussels II *bis* Regulation (Article 21–48), which concerns divorce, legal separation, marriage annulment and parental responsibility matters; Maintenance Regulation (Articles 16–43) and Succession Regulation (Articles 39–55). Those rules differ quite extensively among these instruments, concerning the need of declaration of enforceability (*exequatur*) and grounds for refusal of recognition and enforcement.[515] In general, the EU 'system' does not allow for reviewing the substance of the judgment or jurisdiction of the court of origin (with certain exceptions provided for in Article 45(1)(e)(i) and (ii) in Brussels I bis Regulation). Simplified rules on enforcement are provided for judgments concerning pecuniary claims issued in one of the three special, non-mandatory, partially unified on EU level procedures. This concerns the European enforcement order for uncontested claims (EEO),[516] the European order for payment procedure (EOP)[517] and the European Small Claims Procedure.[518] Similarly, simplified recognition and enforcement rules are provided for other measures (EAPO and a protection measure in civil matter[519]) which are issued in one EU Member State and are supposed to produce effects in another (*see above* §6. Temporary Relief). Protection measure in civil matter means any decision imposing certain obligations on the person causing the risk, for example a prohibition on entering the place where the protected person resides. There are additional provisions in CPC relating to procedural aspects of the application in Poland of some of the above-mentioned EU instrument (Articles 1153^{13}–1153^{25} CPC). Those EU instrument take precedence over bilateral agreement concluded by Poland with other EU Member States.

---

515. A. Frąckowiak Adamska, *Uznawanie i wykonywanie orzeczeń w sprawach cywilnych w Unii Europejskiej*, Wolters Kluwer, Warszawa 2017.
516. Regulation (EC) No 805/2004 of the European Parliament and of the Council of 21 Apr. 2004 creating a European Enforcement Order for uncontested claims, OJ L 143, 30.4.2004, pp. 15–39.
517. Regulation (EC) No 1896/2006 of the European Parliament and of the Council of 12 Dec. 2006 creating a European order for payment procedure, OJ L 399, 30.12.2006, pp. 1–32.
518. Regulation (EC) No 861/2007 of the European Parliament and of the Council of 11 Jul. 2007 establishing a European Small Claims Procedure, OJ L 199, 31.7.2007, pp. 1–22.
519. Regulation (EU) No 606/2013 of the European Parliament and of the Council of 12 Jun. 2013 on mutual recognition of protection measures in civil matters, OJ L 181, 29.6.2013, pp. 4–12.

519. A judgment issued in one of the EU Member States, which concerns a matter, which is not covered by any of the EU instruments (e.g., a judgment establishing paternity) or is covered by an instrument which is not applied in Poland (e.g., a judgment concerning the division of common property of the spouses), may be subject to recognition and enforcement in accordance with an international agreement, including bilateral or, in lack of any international agreement to that respect, in accordance with the 'last resort' instrument, which is CPC. Similarly, a judgment issued in a non-EU state may be subjected to international agreement, including bilateral and, in lack of an agreement, to CPC.

520. If a judgment is not covered by the scope of application of any EU instrument or multilateral or bilateral agreement, it may still be recognized and enforced in Poland, as rules to that respect are contained also in CPC (Articles 1145–1152 CPC). In accordance with Article 1145 CPC a foreign judgment (and also other decision of a foreign authority) issued in a civil matter is recognized in Poland by virtue of law (*ex lege, de plano*), unless there exists one of the grounds specified in Article 1146. A person who seeks recognition is obliged to present an official copy of the judgment and a document certifying that it is final (unless the content of the judgment makes it obvious) and, in general, a certified translation of the above documents (Article 1147 §1 CPC). If a judgment was issued in a proceeding, in which the defendant have not disputed the merits of the case, additionally a document (together with its certified translation) confirming that the document instituting this proceeding was properly served on the defendant must be presented (Article 1147 §1 CPC). Any person who has a legal interest in it may apply to Polish court for a judgment whether a foreign judgment is or is not recognized in Poland (Article 1148 §1 CPC). Such application is dealt with by a provincial court indicated in Article 1148^1 §1 CPC. A judgment issued as a result of the application may be appealed and, subsequently, also appealed in cassation to the Supreme Court (Article 1148^1 §3 CPC).

521. In accordance with Articles 1150 and 1151 CPC a foreign judgment (and also other decision of a foreign authority) in a civil matter may be enforced in Poland if it is enforceable in the country of origin and obtained a declaration of enforceability (*exequatur*) in Poland. *Exequatur* may not be issued if there exists any of the grounds specified in Article 1146.

522. *Exequatur* is issued on the application of the creditor. The application should be supplemented by the documents listed in Article 1147 CPC and a document indicating that the judgment is enforceable in the country of origin (unless the content of the judgment makes it obvious). It is issued by a provincial court indicated in Article 1151^1 CPC. *Exequatur* judgment may be appealed and subsequently appealed in cassation to the Supreme Court. Enforcement proceeding may be initiated once the *exequatur* judgment becomes final (Article 1151^2 §1 CPC).

523. A judgment may neither be recognized nor enforced if at least one ground for refusal exists. A judgment, which is not final in the country of origin or was issued in a case falling within the exclusive jurisdiction of Polish courts will not be effective in Poland (Article 1146 §1(1) and (2) CPC). Recognition and enforcement should be refused in a situation, in which a defendant, who have not defended on the merits, was not properly served in due time to enable the defence (Article 1146 §1(3) CPC or a party to the proceeding was deprived of the possibility of defence (Article 1146 §1(4) CPC). Further grounds for refusal include *lis pendens* where a proceeding is pending in Poland (Article 1146 §1(4)) CPC or res iudicata, meaning that a there already is a final Polish Judgment or a foreign Judgment recognized in Poland on the same matter. Also, a classical public policy clause is provided for in Article 1146 §1(7) CPC (*see* Part I Chapter 3, §7).

524. Once a foreign judgment is equipped with declaration of enforceability it constitutes in Poland an execution title (1150 §1 CPC), based on which the creditor may initiate the execution proceeding in accordance with *lex fori processualis*, namely Part III 'Execution Proceeding' CPC.

Chapter 6. International Insolvency Law

525. International insolvency is regulated in the EU Member States by the Insolvency Regulation.[520] It provides for rules on jurisdiction, law applicable, as well as recognition and enforcement of judgments. The Regulation applies to insolvency proceedings opened from 26 June 2017, whereas proceeding opened before that date are still governed by its EU predecessor.[521] The Insolvency Regulation does not apply to insurance undertakings, credit institutions, investment firms and other similar firms, as well as collective investment undertakings, which are covered by separate EU legislation.

526. In general, the jurisdiction to initiate insolvency proceeding lies with the courts of an EU Member States based on the COMI (centre of main interests) principle. COMI is understood as the place where the debtor conducts the administration of its interests on a regular basis and which is ascertainable by third parties (Article 3(1) Insolvency Regulation).

527. In general, the applicable law is the law of the Member State of the opening of proceedings (*lex concursus* – Article 7(1)). Questions that are governed by the law applicable are included in a non-exhaustive list contained in Article 7(2) Insolvency Regulation. The law applicable determines, for example, the debtors against which insolvency proceedings may be brought on account of their capacity, the assets which form part of the insolvency estate or the effects of insolvency proceedings on current contracts to which the debtor is party. Certain specific questions might be governed by a different applicable law, for example, in accordance with Article 11(1) Insolvency Regulation the effects of insolvency proceedings on a contract conferring the right to acquire or make use of immoveable property is governed solely by *lex rei sitae*. Insolvency Regulation, in principle, does not regulate the proceeding itself, as reminded by Article 7(2), which explains that it is the law applicable that determines the conduct and the closure of the insolvency proceeding. The insolvency proceeding is regulated in Poland by the Bankruptcy Law 2003.[522]

528. An effective judgment opening insolvency proceedings in one of the EU Member States is recognized within the whole EU, except Denmark (Article 19(1)). Similarly, other judgments should also be recognized and enforced in other EU Member States, subject to public policy clause (Articles 32–33 Insolvency Regulation).

529. Concerning other legal sources, it should be explained that Poland is not party to any multilateral or bilateral convention concerning international insolvency

520. Regulation (EU) 2015/848 of the European Parliament and of the Council of 20 May 2015 on insolvency proceedings (recast) (OJ L 141, 5.6.2015, pp. 19–72).
521. Council Regulation (EC) No 1346/2000 of 29 May 2000 on insolvency proceedings, OJ L 160, 30.6.2000, pp. 1–18.
522. Dz. U. 2020 poz. 1228.

proceeding. At the level of domestic law, international insolvency is governed by Bankruptcy Law 2003 in its Part II and several sections of Part III (considering the reorganization and winding up of credit institutions and insurance undertakings in EU and the European Free Trade Association (EFTA). It should be remembered that this piece of legislation may be applied only to cases, which fall outside the scope of the Insolvency Regulation (e.g., to an insolvency proceeding opened in a non-EU state or concerning debtor, who does not have its centre of main interests in the EU, as well as to the proceedings not listed in Annex A to the Regulation, and therefore, not covered by its provisions). Bankruptcy Law 2003 provides for rules on jurisdiction, recognition and enforcement of judgments concerning foreign insolvency proceedings, ancillary insolvency proceeding which might be initiated in Poland, as well as rules on cooperation with foreign courts and foreign insolvency practitioners.

Chapter 7. International Arbitration

530. EU PIL does not regulate arbitration in the EU Member States. Brussels I *bis* excludes arbitration from its scope (Article 1(2)(d)). Similarly does Rome I Regulations in Article 1(2)(e). So, international arbitration is regulated by domestic law and international agreements, which take precedence before domestic law. In particular it should be mentioned that Poland is party to New York Convention (1958) [523] and Geneva Convention (1961).[524]

531. In Polish domestic law arbitration, including international, is regulated in Part V 'Arbitration proceeding' of CPC. These provisions were inspired by UNCITRAL Model Law (1985).[525] In general, these rules are applicable if the place of arbitration is located in Poland (Article 1154). Article 1157 CPC lists disputes, which may be subject to arbitration proceeding (e.g., disputes concerning maintenance are excluded).

532. In order to subject a given dispute to arbitration, an arbitration agreement has to be concluded, indicating the object of this dispute or legal relationship, from which the dispute arose or might arise (1161 §1 CPC). Article 1162 CPC establishes formal requirements for an arbitration agreement. Here it should be mentioned that Chapter 8 PILA deals with arbitration agreement from PIL perspective. Article 39(1) PILA provides that arbitration agreement is governed by the law chosen by the parties. If no choice was made, in accordance with Article 39(2) PILA, arbitration agreement is governed by the law of the country of the agreed place of arbitration. If parties failed to agree on the place of arbitration, arbitration agreement is governed by the law applicable to the legal relationship to which the dispute relates to. However, it is sufficient that the arbitration agreement is valid under the law of the country in which the proceeding takes place or where the arbitral tribunal issued an award. The form of arbitration agreement is governed by the law of the place of arbitration. It is sufficient however if it conforms with the form provided for in the law applicable to arbitration agreement (*lex causae* – Article 40 PILA).

533. Article 1165 §1 CPC obliges the court seized with a claim covered by the arbitration agreement to decline to hear the case, if one of the parties requests so, unless it finds that the arbitration agreement is, *inter alia*, null and void or the arbitration tribunal already decided on its lack of competence. Article 1180 §1 provides for *competence-competence* and separability principles. Article 1194 §1 CPC states that an arbitral tribunal resolves the dispute in accordance with the law applicable

523. United Nations Convention on the Recognition and Enforcement of Foreign Arbitral Awards singed in New York on 10 Jun. 1958, Dz. U. z 1962 r. nr 9 poz. 41 and 42.

524. European Convention on International Commercial Arbitration done at Geneva on 21 Apr. 1961, Dz. U. 1964 nr 40 poz. 270 and 271.

525. UNCITRAL Model Law on international commercial arbitration 1985, with amendments as adopted in 2006, available at official UNICITRAL website: https://www.uncitral.org/.

to a given relationship or, if the parties have expressly authorized it to do so, in accordance with general principles of the law or as *amiable compositeur*.

534. Arbitral award may be subject to annulment by a common court. Grounds for annulment are listed in Article 1206 §1 and 2 CPC, which include, *inter alia*, public policy clause and *res iudicata*. A Judgment issued as a result of an annulment proceeding may be then subject to cassation proceeding in the Supreme Court (Article 1208 §3 CPC). Any arbitral award (or a settlement) might be declared recognized or enforceable on a request of one of the parties (Article 1213 §1 CPC). Some limited grounds for refusal are listed in Article 1214 §3 CPC, which include, *inter alia*, non-arbitrability and public policy clause. When it comes to a foreign arbitral award (or a settlement) there are additional grounds for refusal listed in Article 1215 §2 CPC including, *inter alia*, annulment of the award. Once an arbitral award is equipped with declaration of enforceability it constitutes in Poland an execution title (1214 §2 CPC), based on which the creditor may initiate the execution proceeding in accordance with *lex fori processualis*, namely Part III 'Execution Proceeding' CPC.

Selected Bibliography

I. Publications of General Character in Foreign Languages

Ernst, U., *Polen. Gesetz vom 4. Februar 2011: Internationales Privatrecht*, RabelsZ 2012, pp. 639–653.

Twardoch, P.; Zachariasiewicz, M., *Loi du 4 février 2011 – Droit international privé. The Act on Private International Law dated 4 February 2011*, PPPM 2011, t. 8, pp. 108–138.

Krzymuski, M., *Reform des polnischen Internationalen Privatrecht und deutsch-polnische Rechtsbeziehungen im Personen – und Familienrecht*, Teil 1, StAZ 2012, z. 2, pp. 40–44, Teil 2, StAZ 2012, z. 3, pp. 73–80.

László, B., *Hatályba lépett az új lengyel nemzetközi magánjogi törvény*, Magyar Jog 2012, nr 1, pp. 56–61.

Mączyński, A., *Polish Private International Law*, YPIL 2004, vol. 6, pp. 203–220.

Mączyński, A., Pajor, T., *Introduction to the New Polish Act on Private International Law of 4 February 2011*, YPIL 2011, pp. 381–388.

Mączyński, A. in: J. Basedow, G. Rühl, F. Ferrari, P. de Miguel Asensio (eds), *Encyclopedia of Private International Law*, Edward Elgar Publishing, Cheltenham 2017, pp. 2421–2433.

Pajor, T., *La nouvell loi polonaise de droit international privé, Revue critique de droit international privé 2012*, no. 1, pp. 1–5.

Pajor, T., *Introduction to the New Polish Act on Private International Law of 4 February 2011*, YPIL 2011, vol. 13, pp. 381–388.

Pazdan, M., *Das neue polnische Gesetz über das Internationale Privatrecht*, IPRax 2012, nr 1, pp. 77–81.

Pazdan, M., *Recent Codifications of Private International Law. The Polish Experience* in: Rapport polonaise au XVIIIe Congrès international de droit comparé. Washington 25.VII-1.VIII.2010, Łódź 2010, pp. 49–68.

Rajski, J., *The New Polish Private International Law, 1965*, The International and Comparative Law Quarterly 1966, vol. 15, No. 2, pp. 457–469.

Schwierskott-Matheson, E., *Das polnische IPR-Gesetz von 2011. Mitgliedstaatliche Rekodifikation in Zeiten supranationaler Kompetenzwahrnehmung*, RabelsZ 2012, z. 3, pp. 597–638.

Zachariasiewicz, M., *The New Polish Act on Private International Law of 4 February 2011*, YPIL 2011, vol. 13, pp. 641–656.

Zachariasiewicz, M., Wowerka, A., *Das Gesetz vom 4.2.2011 – Das Internationale Privatrecht*, IPRax 2011, z. 6, pp. 609–619, reprint, PPPM 2012, t. 10, pp. 174–204.

Zou, G., *Chinese Translation of Private International Law Act 2011*, PPPM 2012, t. 10, pp. 174–204.

II. Publications of general character in Polish

Balicki, J., *Międzynarodowe prawo prywatne*, Uniwersytet Marii Curie-Skłodowskiej, Lublin 1976.

Pazdan, M. (ed.), *System Prawa Prywatnego. Tom 20 A. Prawo prywatne międzynarodowe*, Wydawnictwo C. H. Beck, Warszawa 2014.

Pazdan, M. (ed.), *System Prawa Prywatnego. Tom 20 B. Prawo prywatne międzynarodowe*, Wydawnictwo C. H. Beck, Warszawa 2015.

Pazdan, M. (ed.), *System Prawa Prywatnego. Tom 20 C. Prawo prywatne międzynarodowe*, Wydawnictwo C. H. Beck, Warszawa 2015.

Pazdan, M. (ed.), *Prawo prywatne międzynarodowe. Komentarz*, Wydawnictwo C. H. Beck, Warszawa 2018.

Pazdan, M., *Prawo prywatne międzynarodowe*, Wolters Kluwer, Warszawa 2017.

Pazdan, M., *Prawo prywatne międzynarodowe*, LexisNexis, Warszawa 2012.

Poczobut, J. (ed.), *Prawo prywatne międzynarodowe. Komentarz*, Wolters Kluwer, Warszawa 2017.

Przybyłowski, K., *Prawo prywatne międzynarodowe. Część ogólna*, Księgarnia Gubrynowicza i syna, Lwów 1935.

Walaszek, B., Sośniak, M., *Międzynarodowe prawo prywatne. Część ogólna*, Uniwersytet Jagielloński, Kraków 1965.

Walaszek, B., Sośniak, M., *Międzynarodowe prawo prywatne. Część szczególna*, Uniwersytet Jagielloński, Kraków 1965.

Zoll, F., *Międzynarodowe prawo prywatne w zarysie*, Księgarnia Powszechna, Kraków 1947.

III. Publications on specific issues in Polish and foreign languages

Bělohlávek, A., *Law Applicable to International Carriage: EU Law and International Treaties*, Czech Yearbook of International Law 2015, pp. 27–60.

Bobrzyńska, O., Mostowik, P., *Zwykły pobyt dziecka jako postawa jurysdykcji krajowej oraz łącznik kolizyjny*, Zeszyty Naukowe Uniwersytetu Szczecińskiego. Acta Iuris Stetinensis 2014, no 2, pp. 509–550.

Bonomi, A., Wautelet, P., *Le droit européen des successions commentaire du Règlement (UE) no 650/2012 du 4 juillet 2012*, Bruylant: Bruxelles 2016.

Cichomska, M., *Metody ustalania treści prawa obcego a Europejska Sieć Sądownicza*, Polski Proces Cywilny 2012, vol. 2, pp. 292–311.

Cieszewski, J., *Zakazy i ograniczenia małżeństw z cudzoziemcami a klauzula porządku publicznego*, Państwo i Prawo 1984, z. 3, pp. 90–101.

Czarnecki, M., Bagińska, L., *Prawo wekslowe i czekowe. Komentarz*, Wydawnictwo C. H. Beck, Warszawa 2018.

Czepelak, M., *Autonomia woli w prawie prywatnym międzynarodowym Unii Europejskiej*, Poltext, Warszawa 2015.

Czepelak, M., in: M. Stec (ed.), *Prawo instrumentów finansowych*, Wydawnictwo C. H. Beck, Warszawa 2016, pp. 115–230.

Czepelak, M., *Międzynarodowe prawo zobowiązań Unii Europejskiej*, LexisNexis, Warszawa 2012.

Czepelak, M., *Zasada najściślejszego związku jako reguła kierunkowa prawa prywatnego międzynarodowego*, PPPM 2016, vol. 18, pp. 81–97.

Czubik, P., *Rzecz o praktyce sądów krajowych badających prawo obce zgodnie z art. 1143 kpc*, NPN 2010, nr 3, pp. 5–19.

Czubik, P., *Czy polskiemu notariuszowi jest potrzebny status inicjującego postępowanie celem ustalenia treści prawa obcego?*, NPN 2014, nr 4, pp. 23–30.

Dajczak, W., Szwarc, A., Wiliński, P. (eds), *Handbook of Polish Law*, Wydawnictwo Szkolne PWN, Warszawa 2011.

Dyrda, Ł., *Konwencyjne prawo jednolite a normy kolizyjne*, KPP 2013, nr 2, pp. 483–512.

Ereciński, T., *Kodeks postępowania cywilnego. Komentarz. Tom VI. Międzynarodowe postępowanie cywilne. Sąd polubowny (arbitrażowy)*, Wolters Kluwer, Warszawa 2017.

Figura-Góralczyk, E., *Nieuczciwa konkurencja w prawie prywatnym międzynarodowym*, Wolters Kluwer, Warszawa 2017.

Frankowski, S., *Introduction to Polish Law*, Kluwer Law International, The Hague 2005.

Gajda, J., *Klauzula porządku publicznego w prawie o aktach stanu cywilnego z 29 września 1986 r. oraz z 28 listopada 2014 r.*, Administracja: teoria, dydaktyka, praktyka 2015, nr 4, pp. 5–46.

Gocek, M., *Podstawowe zagadnienia zastosowania klauzuli porządku publicznego w orzecznictwie Sądu Najwyższego*, Rejent 2005, nr 6, pp. 56–73.

Jagielska, M., *Ewolucja ochrony konsumenta w prawie kolizyjnym Unii Europejskiej w zakresie zobowiązań umownych*, Wydawnictwo C. H. Beck, Warszawa 2010.

Jaremba, U., *National Judges as EU Law Judges: The Polish Civil Law System*, Brill, Nijhoff 2014.

Juryk, A., *The Protection of Adults in Private International Law*, Silesian Journal of Legal Studies 2016, vol. 8, pp. 27–43.

Juryk, A., *Alimenty w prawie prywatnym międzynarodowym,* Lexis Nexis, Warszawa 2015.

Kamarad, E., *Zawarcie małżeństwa jako zagadnienie prawa rodzinnego, prawa prywatnego międzynarodowego i prawa konsularnego*, Wydawnictwo Uniwersytetu Jagiellońskiego, Kraków 2019.

Kamarad, E., *Matrimonium per procura – uwagi na tle prawa materialnego i prawa kolizyjnego*, PWPM 2013, vol. XI, pp. 31–42.

Kamarad, E., *Prawo właściwe dla czynności prawnych mortis causa – uwagi de lege lata i de lege ferenda*, PPPM 2011, vol. 9, pp. 55–91.

Kamarad, E., *Zastosowanie klauzuli porządku publicznego w sprawach dotyczących zawarcia małżeństwa – wybrane zagadnienia*, PWPM 2012, vol. 10, pp. 106–118.

Karasek, I., *Kolizyjnoprawna problematyka nieposesoryjnych zabezpieczeń rzeczowych ustanowionych pod rządem praw obcych*, Transformacje Prawa Prywatnego 2006, vol. 2, pp. 17–40.

Kłoda, M., *Zagadnienia międzyczasowe nowego prawa prywatnego międzynarodowego*, KPP 2011, no 2, pp. 507–560.

Kozieł, G., *Dopuszczalność i zasady przeniesienia siedziby statutowej polskiej spółki handlowej do innego państwa członkowskiego Unii Europejskiej. Glosa do wyroku TS z dnia 25 października 2017 r., C-106/16*, EPS 2018, nr 2, pp. 25–32.

Kropka, M., *Kolizyjnoprawna regulacja umowy ubezpieczenia według rozporządzenia Rzym I*, PPPM 2011, t. 9, pp. 129–148.

Krzymuski, M., *Wybór prawa właściwego dla pozaumownej odpowiedzialności cywilnej wynikającej z wypadków drogowych*, in: M. Krzymuski, M. Margoński (eds), Znad granicy ponad granicami. Księga dedykowana prof. Dieterowi Martiny, Warszawa 2014, pp. 133–151.

Kurowski, W., *Prawo właściwe dla przelewu wierzytelności. Glosa do wyroku Sądu Najwyższego z dnia 19 grudnia 2003 r. (III CK 80/02)*, PPPM 2007, pp. 145–152.

Machnikowski, P., Balcarczyk, J., Drela, M., *Contract Law in Poland*, Wolters Kluwer, Alphen aan der Rijn 2014.

Machnikowski, P., *Międzynarodowe prawo wekslowe i czekowe*, Studia Prawa Prywatnego 2013, nr 3, pp. 17–29.

Magnus, U., Mankowski, P., *European Commentaries on Private International Law. Commentary. Volume II. Rome I Regulation*, OttoSchmidt: Köln 2017.

Magnus, U., Mankowski, P., *European Commentaries on Private International Law. Volume III. Commentary. Rome II Regulation*, Otto Schmidt, Köln 2019.

Mataczyński, M., *Przepisy wymuszające swoje zastosowanie – wybrane zagadnienia*, PPPM 2016, t. 18 pp. 59–80.

Mataczyński, M., *Seat of the company in private international law. Selected issues*, Wydawnictwo naukowe UAM, Poznań 2018.

Mączyński, A., *Wskazanie kilku praw przez normę kolizyjną prawa prywatnego międzynarodowego* in: A. Mączyński, M. Pazdan, A. Szpunar (eds), Rozprawy z polskiego i europejskiego prawa prywatnego. Księga pamiątkowa ofiarowana Profesorowi Józefowi Skąpskiemu, Wydawnictwo i Drukarnia 'Secesja', Kraków 1994.

Mączyński, A., *Zamieszkanie jako podstawa łącznika normy kolizyjnej in: A. Mączyński, Rozprawy i studia z prawa prywatnego międzynarodowego*, Wolters Kluwer, Warszawa 2017, pp. 184–202. First published in Zeszyty Naukowe Uniwersytetu Jagiellońskiego. Prace prawnicze 1978, pp. 41–62.

Mączyński, A., *Ustawowe odesłania do umów międzynarodowych i rozporządzeń unijnych dotyczących prawa prywatnego międzynarodowego* in: A. Mączyński, Rozprawy i studia z prawa prywatnego międzynarodowego, Wolters Kluwer, Warszawa 2017, pp. 169–183. First published in J. Gołaczyński, P. Machnikowski (eds), Współczesne problemy prawa prywatnego. Księga pamiątkowa ku czci Profesora Edwarda Gniewka, Warszawa 2010, pp. 373–384.

Mączyński, A., *Stosowanie norm kolizyjnych obcego prawa prywatnego międzynarodowego*, Wolters Kluwer, Warszawa 2017, pp. 223–231. First published in A. Matlak (ed.), Spory o własność intelektualną. Księga jubileuszowa dedykowana Profesorom Januszowi Barcie i Ryszardowi Markiewiczowi, Warszawa 2013, pp. 571–595.

Mączyński, A., *Dziedziczenie testamentowe w prawie prywatnym międzynarodowym. Ustawowe i konwencyjne unormowanie problematyki formy*, Zeszyty Naukowe Uniwersytetu Jagiellońskiego. Prace prawnicze 1976, vol. 75.

Mączyński, A., *Rozwód w prawie prywatnym międzynarodowym*, Wydawnictwo Prawnicze, Warszawa 1983.

Mączyński, A., *Działanie klauzuli porządku publicznego w sprawach dotyczących zawarcia małżeństwa z cudzoziemcami* in: E. Łętowska (ed.), *Proces i prawo. Rozprawy prawnicze, Zakład Narodowy im.* Ossolińskich, Wrocław 1989, pp. 157–167.

Mączyński, A., *Kolizyjna problematyka nazwiska* in: J. Gudowski, K. Weitz (eds), *Aurea praxis, aurea teoria.* Księga pamiątkowa ku czci Profesora Tadeusza Erecińskiego, t.2, Warszawa 2011.

Mikša, K., *Nazwisko w prawie prywatnym międzynarodowym*, Technika IT, Gliwice 2015, p. 149.

Mostowik, P., *Bezpodstawne wzbogacenie w prawie prywatnym międzynarodowym*, LexisNexis, Warszawa 2006.

Mostowik, P., *Kwestie kompetencji Unii Europejskiej oraz warunków pomocniczości i proporcjonalności prawodawstwa unijnego na tle projektów rozporządzeń o jurysdykcji, prawie właściwym i skuteczności zagranicznych orzeczeń w majątkowych sprawach małżeńskich i partnerskich*, Zeszyty Prawnicze 2011, nr 3(31), pp. 9–41.

Mostowik, P., *Władza rodzicielska i opieka nad dzieckiem w prawie prywatnym międzynarodowym*, Wydawnictwo JAK, Kraków 2015.

Mostowik, P., *Kwestia przystąpienia przez Polskę do rozporządzenia unijnego Rzym III*, EPS 2016, nr 10, pp. 36–43.

Mostowik, P., *Problem obywatelstwa dziecka prawdopodobnie pochodzącego od obywatela polskiego niebędącego mężem surrogate mother. Uwagi aprobujące wyroki NSA z 6 maja 2015 r. (II OSK 2372/13 i II OSK 2419/13)*, PWPM 2018, vol. XVI, pp. 55–75.

Mostowik, P., *O postępowaniu w razie nieustalenia łączników kolizyjnych lub treści prawa obcego* in: M. Pecyna, J. Pisuliński (eds), *Rozprawy cywilistyczne: księga pamiątkowa dedykowana profesorowi Edwardowi Drozdowi*, LexisNexis, Warszawa 2013, pp. 709–725.

Nowak, F., *Kilka uwag na temat wskazania prawa właściwego dla imienia i nazwiska osoby fizycznej w ustawie z dnia 4 lutego 2011 r. – Prawo prywatne międzynarodowe*, Metryka 2015, nr 1, pp. 79–100.

Oplustil, K., *Łącznik siedziby spółki w nowym Prawie Prywatnym międzynarodowym – uwagi na tle prawa europejskiego*, KPP 2011, z. 3, pp. 635–680.

von Overbeck, A., *Divers aspects de l'unification du droit international privé, spécialement en matière de successions*, Recueil des Cours de l'Académie de droit international de La Haye 1961, pp. 593–622.

Pacuła, K., *Przepisy wymuszające swoje zastosowanie jako instrument ochrony 'strony słabszej' umowy ubezpieczenia*, PPPM 2014, t. 15, pp. 31–48.

Pajor, T., *Odpowiedzialność deliktowa w prawie prywatnym międzynarodowym*, Państwowe Wydawnictwo Naukowe, Warszawa 1989.

Pamboukis, C., *EU Succession Regulation No 650/2012. A Commentary*, C. H. Beck, München 2017.

Pazdan, M., *Stosowanie obcych norm kolizyjnych*, PPPM 2016, t.18, pp. 19–30.

Pazdan, M., *Nazwisko w prawie prywatnym międzynarodowym* in: P. Machnikowski, J. Gołaczyński (eds), Współczesne problemy prawa prywatnego. Księga pamiątkowa ku czci Profesora Edwarda Gniewka, Warszawa 2010.

Pazdan, J., *Zawarcie małżeństwa przez pełnomocnika w prawie prywatnym międzynarodowym* in: L. Ogiegło, W. Popiołek, M. Szpunar (eds), *Rozprawy prawnicze. Księga pamiątkowa Profesora Maksymiliana Pazdana*, Zakamycze, Kraków 2005, pp. 263–268.

Pazdan, M., *Cudzoziemiec klientem polskiego notariusza*, Rejent 2001, nr 7–8, pp. 172–189.

Pazdan, M., *Czynności notarialne w międzynarodowym prawie spadkowym*, Rejent 1998, nr 4, pp. 99–115.

Pazdan, M., *Notariat a prawo prywatne międzynarodowe (uwagi ogólne)*, Rejent 1995, nr 9, pp. 197–209.

Pazdan, M., *Dziedziczenie ustawowe w prawie prywatnym międzynarodowym. Metody regulacji właściwości prawa*, Prace Naukowe Uniwersytetu Śląskiego w Katowicach 1973, nr 45.

Pazdan, M., *Zdolność do czynności prawnych osób fizycznych w polskim prawie prywatnym międzynarodowym*, Zeszyty Naukowe Uniwersytetu Jagiellońskiego, Kraków 1967.

Pietrzykowski, K., *Zawarcie małżeństwa i przesłanki jego ważności w prawie prywatnym międzynarodowym*, Warszawa 1985.

Pilich, M., *Związki quasi-małżeńskie w polskim prawie prywatnym międzynarodowym*, PiP 2011, z. 2, pp. 84–94.

Pilich, M., *Zasada obywatelstwa w prawie prywatnym międzynarodowym*, Wolters Kluwer Polska, Warszawa 2015.

Pilich, M., *Law Applicable to Insurance Contracts in the Light of the Rome I Regulation*, Studia Iuridica 2012, nr 54, pp. 197–220.

Pilich, M., *Klauzula porządku publicznego w postępowaniu o uznanie i wykonanie zagranicznego orzeczenia arbitrażowego*, KPP 2003, z. 1, pp. 157–187.

Pilich, M., *Mater semper certa est? Kilka uwag o skutkach zagranicznego macierzyństwa zastępczego z perspektywy stosowania klauzuli porządku publicznego*, PWPM 2018, vol. XVI, pp. 7–37.

Poczobut, J., *Właściwość prawa dla umowy leasingu – zagadnienia węzłowe*, Rejent 2001, nr 7–8, pp. 216–244.

Popiołek, W., *Separacja w prawie prywatnym międzynarodowym* in: M. Pazdan (ed.), Valeat aequitas, Wydawnictwo Uniwersytetu Śląskiego, Katowice 2000, pp. 351–361.

Przybyłowski, K., *Z problematyki stosowania obcych norm kolizyjnych*, Państwowe Wydawnictwo Naukowe, Kraków 1959.

Rodziewicz, P., *Stwierdzenie treści oraz zastosowanie prawa obcego przez notariusza wykonującego zawód w Rzeczypospolitej Polskiej*, PPPM 2015, t. 17, pp. 125–160.

Rodziewicz, P., *Stwierdzenie treści oraz zastosowanie prawa obcego w sądowym postępowaniu cywilnym*, Wydawnictwo C. H. Beck, Warszawa 2015.

Sapota, A., *Wybór prawa w międzynarodowym prawie rodzinnym*, Wydawnictwo C. H. Beck, Warszawa 2016.

Sikorski, R., *O prawie właściwym dla licencji praw autorskich*, PPPM 2009, t. 4, pp. 117–133.

Skąpski, J., *Autonomia woli w prawie prywatnym międzynarodowym w zakresie zobowiązań z umów*, Zeszyty Naukowe Uniwersytetu Jagiellońskiego, Kraków 1964.

Skrzydło-Tefelska, E., *Uznanie dziecka w prawie prywatnym międzynarodowym*, Zakład Narodowy im. Ossolińskich, Wrocław 1990.

Sokołowski, M., *Stosowanie rozporządzenia nr 2016/1103 przez polskie sądy – nowe majątkowe prawo małżeńskie Unii Europejskiej a sytuacja obywateli polskich*, EPS 2017, nr 11, pp. 4–12.

Sokołowski, M., *Intercyza europejska jako metoda kształtowania małżeńskich ustrojów majątkowych*, Wydawnictwo C. H. Beck, Warszawa 2018.

Sośniak, M., *Klauzula porządku publicznego w prawie międzynarodowym prywatnym*, Państwowe Wydawnictwo Naukowe, Warszawa 1961.

Sośniak, M., Walaszek, B., Wierzbowski, E. (eds), *Międzynarodowe prawo rodzinne*, Wydawnictwo PAN, Wrocław-Warszawa-Kraków 1969.

Sznajder-Peroń, K., *Zagadnienia związane z pojmowaniem i stosowaniem prawa właściwego*, Studia Prawa Prywatnego 2012, z. 2, pp. 3–30.

Tereszkiewicz, P., Wysocka-Bar, A., *Legacy by Vindication Under the EU Succession Regulation No. 650/2012 Following the Kubicka Judgment of the ECJ*, European Review of Private Law 2019, vol. 4, pp. 875–894.

Trammer, H., *Z rozważań nad strukturą normy kolizyjnej prawa prywatnego międzynarodowego*, Studia Cywilistyczne 1964, pp. 399–405.

Weitz, K., *Wyłączenie fikcyjnych doręczeń krajowych w stosunkach między państwami członkowskimi? Glosa do wyroku Trybunału Sprawiedliwości Unii Europejskiej (ETS) z dnia 19 grudnia 2012 r., C-325/11 w sprawie Krystyna Alder i Ewald Alder przeciwko Sabina Orłowska i Czesław Orłowski*, Polski Proces Cywilny 2013, vol. 2, pp. 265–278.

Wojewoda, M., *Poland: Proof and Information About Foreign Law – Theory and Reality* in: Y. Nishitani, Treatment of Foreign Law – Dynamics Towards Convergence?, Springer: Cham 2017, pp. 289–308.

Wojewoda, M., *Rozszczepienie statutu kontraktowego w Konwencji rzymskiej o prawie właściwym dla zobowiązań umownych*, PPPM 2008, pp. 63–76.

Wojewoda, M., *Uznanie rozstrzygnięć organów państw obcych a przesłanki transkrypcji zagranicznych aktów stanu cywilnego*, Studia Prawno-Ekonomiczne 2018, t. CIX, pp. 159–172.

Wojewoda, M., *Problematyka kolizyjnoprawna w praktyce urzędów stanu cywilnego oraz w ustawie – Prawo o aktach stanu cywilnego z 2014 roku*, PPPM 2015, t. 17, pp. 25–67.

Wojewoda, M., *Transkrypcja aktu stanu cywilnego sporządzonego za granicą*, KPP 2009, nr 4, pp. 1089–1124.

Wolski, D., *Prawo właściwe dla umowy mieszanej w oparciu o postanowienia rozporządzenia rzymskiego pierwszego oraz wcześniej obowiązujących regulacji*, PWPM 2010, vol. 8, pp. 113–137.

Wowerka, A., *Prawo właściwe dla transakcji faktoringowych*, PPPM 2009, t. 4, pp. 135–158.

Wowerka, A., *Umowa faktoringu w świetle konwencji ottawskiej o faktoringu międzynarodowym*, PPPM 2009, t. 5, pp. 57–85.

Wypych, P., *Prawo właściwe dla nabycia i zmiany nazwiska* in: P. Kasprzyk (ed.) *Prawo rodzinne w Polsce i Europie*. Zagadnienia wybrane, Lublin 2005, p. 570.

Wysocka, A., *How can a valid professio iuris be made under the EU Succession Regulation?,* 'Nederland Internationaal Privaatrecht' 2012, vol. 4, pp. 569–575.

Wysocka-Bar, A., *Enhanced cooperation in property matters and non-participating Member States*, ERA Forum 2019, vol. 20, pp. 187–200.

Wysocka-Bar, A., *EU Succession Regulation: Choice of applicable law and protection of family members* w: K. Boele-Woelki, *The Future of Family Property in Europe,* Intersentia: Antwerp 2011, pp. 383–405.

Wysocka-Bar, A., *Nabycia polskiego obywatelstwa a urodzenie przez matkę zastępczą – uwagi na tle wyroków Naczelnego Sądu Administracyjnego z 6 maja 2015 r., sygnatura akt: II OSK 2372/13 oraz II OSK 2419/13*, PWPM 2018, vol. XVI, pp. 38–54.

Wysocka-Bar, A., *Prawo właściwe dla dziedziczenia w polskim prawie prywatnym międzynarodowym z 2011 r.* in: M. Margoński, M. Krzymuski (eds), Znad granicy ponad granicami. Prace z okazji 70 urodzin Profesora Dietera Martiny, Wydawnictwo C. H. Beck Warszawa 2014, pp. 405–422.

Wysocka-Bar, A., *Wybór prawa w międzynarodowym prawie spadkowym*, LexisNexis, Warszawa 2013.

Wysocka-Bar, A., *Jurysdykcja krajowa sądów polskich a kolizyjna jednolitość spadku*, PWPM 2016, t. 14, pp. 90–109.

Wysocka-Bar, A., *Prawo właściwe dla formy rozrządzeń na wypadek śmierci według rozporządzenia spadkowego* w: red. M. Pazdan, J. Górecki, *Nowe europejskie prawo spadkowe*, Wolters-Kluwer, Warszawa 2015, pp. 130–143.

Wysocka-Bar, A., *Prawo właściwe dla dziedziczenia według unijnego rozporządzenia dotyczącego spraw spadkowych*, KPP 2012, z. 4, pp. 899–948.

Wysocka-Bar, A., *Umowy międzynarodowe dotyczące przysposobienia dzieci cz. 1*, Metryka 2018, t. 8, nr 1, pp. 69–76.

Wysocka-Bar, A., *Umowy międzynarodowe dotyczące przysposobienia dzieci cz. 2*, Metryka 2018, t. 8, nr 2, pp. 65–75.

Zachariasiewicz, M. A., *Nowa ustawa o prawie prywatnym międzynarodowym a małżeństwa i związki osób tej samej płci*, PPPM 2012, t. 11, pp. 71–113.

Zachariasiewicz, M., *Klauzula porządku publicznego jako podstawa odmowy uznania lub wykonania orzeczenia sądu polubownego w polskim prawie arbitrażowym na tle prawnoporównawczym*, PPPM 2010, t. 6, pp. 61–114.

Zachariasiewicz, M., *Klauzula porządku publicznego jako instrument ochrony materialnoprawnych interesów i wartości fori*, Wydawnictwo C. H. Beck Warszawa 2018.

Zachariasiewicz, M., *Transkrypcja aktów urodzenia dzieci par jednopłciowych*, Studia Prawno-Ekonomiczne 2019, t. CXI, pp. 143–170.
Załucki, M., *Prawo właściwe dla umów licencyjnych znaku towarowego (cz. I)*, Prawo i Podatki Unii Europejskiej w Praktyce 2007, nr 12, pp. 26–32.
Załucki, M., *Prawo właściwe dla umów licencyjnych znaku towarowego (cz. II)*, Prawo i Podatki Unii Europejskiej w Praktyce 2008, nr 1, pp. 22–26.
Zawada, K., *Klauzula porządku publicznego w prawie prywatnym międzynarodowym (na tle orzecznictwa Sądu Najwyższego w sprawach z zakresu prawa rodzinnego i spadkowego)*, Nowe Prawo 1979, Nr 4, pp. 71–84.
Zawada, K., *Klauzula porządku publicznego w międzynarodowym postępowaniu cywilnym (na tle orzecznictwa Sądu Najwyższego w sprawach z zakresu prawa rodzinnego i spadkowego)*, Nowe Prawo 1979, nr 5, pp. 73–79.

Selected Bibliography

Table of Cases

I. Polish Courts

Judgments of Polish courts are presented in the following way: form of the decision issued (Polish *wyrok* – judgment, *postanowienie* – decision, *uchwała* – resolution), name of the court (Polish *Sąd Najwyższy* – Supreme Court), date of the issuance and case signature (e.g., I CSK 45/18). By the case signature a decision may be found in paid databases or in public, free databases. For decisions of the Supreme Court *see* the data based on its website: www.sn.pl and for decisions of lower instances' courts: https://orzeczenia.ms.gov.pl/. Decisions are published in Polish language only.

Resolution of the Supreme Administrative Court of 2 December 2019, II OPS 1/19.
Judgment of Supreme Administrative Court of 29 August 2018, II OSK 2129/16.
Judgment of the Supreme Court of 6 April 2017, III CSK 174/16.
Decision of Supreme Court of 9 April 2015, II CKS 550/14.
Judgment of Supreme Administrative Court of 17 December 2014 r., II OSK 1298/13.
Judgment of Supreme Administrative Court of 6 May 2015, II OSK 2372/13 and II OSK 2419/13.
Judgment of Supreme Court of 23 May 2013, II CKS 250/12.
Decision of Supreme Court of 14 February 2013, II CSK 294/12.
Judgment of Supreme Court of 29 November 2012, II CSK 96/12.
Judgment of Supreme Court of 15 March 2012, I CSK 286/11.
Decision of Supreme Court of 15 April 2011, III CSK 223/10.
Judgment of Supreme Court of 11 March 2011, II CSK 435/10.
Decision of Court of Appeal in Katowice of 20 August 2009, I ACa 410/09.
Judgment of Supreme Court of 9 May 2007, II CSK 60/07.
Decision of Supreme Court of 26 January 2006, II CSK 124/05.
Judgment of Supreme Court of 11 August 2005, V CK 86/05.
Judgment of Supreme Court of 11 August 2004, II CK 489/03.
Judgment of Supreme Court of 19 December 2003, III CK 155/02.
Decision of Supreme Court of 26 February 2003, II CK 13/03.
Judgment of Supreme Court of 22 March 2002, I CKN 1137/99.
Resolution of Supreme Court of 22 September 1995, III CZP 118/95.
Resolution of Supreme Court of 30 March 1992, III CZP 17/92.
Judgment of Supreme Court of 31 March 1988, I KR 50/88.

Resolution of Supreme Court 20 January 1983, III CZP 37/82.
Resolution of Supreme Court of 22 June 1972, III CZP 34/72.

II. Court of Justice of the European Union

CJEU judgments are published online in all EU languages at https://curia.europa.eu/.

Case C-80/19 *E. E.*, Judgment of the Court (First Chamber) of 16 July 2020.

Case C-393/18 *UD v. XB*, Judgment of the Court (First Chamber) of 17 October 2018.

Case C-54/16 *Vinyls Italia*, Judgment of the Court (Fifth Chamber) of 8 June 2017.

Case C-111/17 *OL v. PQ*, Judgment of the Court (Fifth Chamber) of 8 June 2017.

Case C-20/17 *Oberle*, Judgment of the Court (Second Chamber) of 21 June 2018.

Case C-218/16 *Kubicka*, Judgment of the Court (Second Chamber) of 12 October 2017.

Case C-558/16 *Mahnkopf*, Judgment of 1 March 2018.

Case C-106/16 *POLBUD*, Judgment of the Court of 25 October 2017.

Case C-350/14 *Lazar*, Judgment of the Court (Fourth Chamber) of 10 December 2015.

Case C-325/11 *Alder*, Judgment of the Court (First Chamber) of 19 December 2012.

Case C-412/10 *Homawoo*, Judgment of the Court (First Chamber) of 17 November 2011.

Case C-585/08 *Pammer and Hotel Alpenhof*, Judgment of the Court (Grand Chamber) of 7 December 2010.

Case C-497/10 *Mercredi*, Judgment of the Court (First Chamber) of 22 December 2010.

Case C-523/07 *A.*, Judgment of the Court (Third Chamber) of 2 April 2009.

Case C-208/00 *Überseering BV v Nordic Construction Company Baumanagement GmbH (NCC)*, Judgment of the Court of 5 November 2002.

Case 161/84 *Pronuptia de Paris GmbH v Pronuptia de Paris Irmgard Schillgallis*, Judgment of the Court of 28 January 1986.

Table of Statutory Instruments

Legal acts are promulgated in Poland in the official journal, which is called *Dziennik Ustaw* (Dz. U.). *Dziennik Ustaw* is accessible online at https://isap.sejm.gov.pl/. Each legal act promulgated before 2012 may be located by the year, number (*nr*) and position (*poz.*) in *Dziennik Ustaw* and starting from 2012 by the year and position in *Dziennik Ustaw*. Sometimes consolidates versions of legal acts, which were subject to numerous amendments, are published in *Dziennik Ustaw*. In such case a reference to consolidated version is made. Legal acts are promulgated in Polish. No official translations into English are provided in systematic way. Translations of some legal acts might be found on the websites of different national authorities.

Constitution of 2 April 1997 of the Republic of Poland (*Konstytucja Rzeczpospolitej Polskiej*), Dz. U. 1997 nr 78 poz. 483.
Act of 24 March 1920 on the acquisition of real estate by foreigners (*Ustawa o nabywaniu nieruchomości przez cudzoziemców*), Dz. U. 2017 poz. 2278.
Act of 2 August 1926 on the Law Applicable to International Private Relations (*Ustawa o prawie właściwem dla stosunków prywatnych międzynarodowych*), Dz. U. 1926 nr 101 poz. 581.
Act of 2 August 1926 on the Law Applicable to Internal Private Relations (*Ustawa z dnia 2 sierpnia 1926 r. o prawie właściwem dla stosunków prywatnych wewnętrznych*), Dz. U. 1926 nr 101 poz. 580.
Act of 28 April 1936 – Bill of Exchange Law (*Prawo wekslowe*), Dz. U. 1936 nr 37 poz. 282.
Act of 28 April 1936 – Cheque Law (*Prawo czekowe*), Dz. U. 1936 nr 37 poz. 283.
Act of 25 February 1964 – Family and Guardianship Code (*Kodeks rodzinny i opiekuńczy*), Dz. U. 1964 nr 9 poz. 59.
Act of 23 April 1964 – Civil Code (*Kodeks cywilny*), Dz. U. 1964 nr 16 poz. 93.
Act of 17 November 1964 – Civil Procedure Code (*Kodeks postępowania cywilnego*), Dz. U. 1964 nr 43 poz. 296.
Act of 12 November 1965 – Private International Law (*Prawo prywatne międzynarodowe*), Dz. U. 1965 nr 46 poz. 290.
Act of 17 May 1989 on guarantees of freedom of conscience and religion (*Ustawa o gwarancjach wolności sumienia i wyznania*), Dz. U. 1989 nr 29 poz. 155.
Act of 14 February 1991 – Notary law (*Prawo o notariacie*), Dz. U. 1991 Nr 22 poz. 91.
Act of 27 July 2001 on the System of Common Courts (*Prawo o ustroju sądów powszechych*), Dz. U. 2001 Nr 98 poz. 1070.

Table of Statutory Instruments

Act of 18 September 2001 – Maritime Code (*Kodeks morski*), Dz. U. 2018 poz. 2175.

Act of 3 July 2002 – Aviation Law (*Prawo lotnicze*), Dz. U. 2019 poz. 1580.

Act of 28 February 2003 – Bankruptcy Law (*Prawo upadłościowe*), Dz. U. 2003 nr 60 poz. 535.

Act of 23 July 2003 on the protection and care of monuments (*Ustawa o ochronie zabytków i opiece nad zabytkami*), Dz. U. 2020 poz. 282.

Act of 17 December 2004 on the law of assistance in proceedings in civil cases conducted in the Member States of the European Union and on the law of assistance for the purpose of amicable settlement of a dispute prior to the initiation of such proceedings (*Ustawa o prawie pomocy w postępowaniu w sprawach cywilnych prowadzonym w państwach członkowskich Unii Europejskiej oraz o prawie pomocy w celu ugodowego załatwienia sporu przed wszczęciem takiego postępowania*), Dz. U. 2005 nr 10 poz. 67.

Act of 28 July 2005 on judicial costs in civil cases (*Ustawa o kosztach sądowych w sprawach cywilnych*), Dz. U. 2020 poz. 755.

Act of 4 February 2011 – Private International Law (*Prawo prywatne międzynarodowe*), Dz. U. 2011 nr 80 poz. 432. There is no official English translation. Unofficial English translation by M. Zachariasiewicz is available in YPIL, vol. 13 (2011), pp. 641–656. YPIL 2011 is available online at the website of Swiss Institute of Comparative Law: https://www.isdc.ch/en/publications/yearbook.

Act of 28 November 2014 – Law on civil status records (*Prawo o aktach stanu cywilnego*), Dz. U. 2014 poz. 1741.

Act of 26 June 2015 on the treatment of infertility (*Ustawa o leczeniu niepłodności*), Dz. U. 2015 poz. 1087.

Act of 25 May 2017 on the restitution of national cultural property (*Ustawa o restytucji narodowych dóbr kultury*), Dz. U. 2017 poz. 1086.

EC/EU Instruments

EU law is promulgated in Official Journal of the EU published online in all EU languages at https://eur-lex.europa.eu/.

Principal EC/EU Regulations in the PIL Field

Brussels Convention of 27 September 1968 on jurisdiction and the enforcement of judgments in civil and commercial matters, OJ L 299, 31.12.1972, pp. 32–42 (not applied anymore).

Rome Convention 80/934/EEC on the law applicable to contractual obligations opened for signature in Rome on 19 June 1980, OJ L 266, 9.10.1980, pp. 1–19 (not applied in Poland anymore).

Lugano Convention of 16 September 1988 on jurisdiction and the enforcement of judgments in civil and commercial matters, OJ L 319, 25.11.1988, pp. 9–48 (not applied anymore).

Council Regulation (EC) No 1346/2000 of 29 May 2000 on insolvency proceedings, OJ L 160, 30.6.2000, pp. 1–18.

Council Decision of 28 May 2001 establishing a European Judicial Network in civil and commercial matters, OJ L 174, 27.6.2001, pp. 25–31.

Council Regulation (EC) No 1206/2001 of 28 May 2001 on cooperation between the courts of the Member States in the taking of evidence in civil or commercial matters, OJ L 174, 27.6.2001, pp. 1–24.

Council Directive 2002/8/EC of 27 January 2003 to improve access to justice in cross-border disputes by establishing minimum common rules relating to legal aid for such disputes, OJ L 26, 31.1.2003, pp. 41–47.

Council Regulation (EC) No 2201/2003 of 27 November 2003 concerning jurisdiction and the recognition and enforcement of judgments in matrimonial matters and the matters of parental responsibility (Brussels II bis), repealing Regulation (EC) No 1347/2000, OJ L 338, 23.12.2003, pp. 1–29.

Regulation (EC) No 805/2004 of the European Parliament and of the Council of 21 April 2004 creating a European Enforcement Order for uncontested claims, OJ L 143, 30.4.2004, pp. 15–39.

Regulation (EC) No 1896/2006 of the European Parliament and of the Council of 12 December 2006 creating a European order for payment procedure, OJ L 399, 30.12.2006, pp. 1–32.

Regulation (EC) No 861/2007 of the European Parliament and of the Council of 11 July 2007 establishing a European Small Claims Procedure, OJ L 199, 31.7.2007, pp. 1–22.

Regulation (EC) No 1393/2007 of the European Parliament and of the Council of 13 November 2007 on the service in the Member States of judicial and extrajudicial documents in civil or commercial matters (service of documents), and repealing Council Regulation (EC) No 1348/2000, OJ L 324, 10.12.2007, pp. 79–120.

Regulation (EC) No 864/2007 of the European Parliament and of the Council of 11 July 2007 on the law applicable to non-contractual obligations (Rome II), OJ L 199, 31.7.2007, pp. 40–49.

Lugano II Convention of 30 October 2007 on jurisdiction and the recognition and enforcement of judgments in civil and commercial matters, OJ L 339, 21.12.2007, pp. 3–41.

Regulation (EC) No 593/2008 of the European Parliament and of the Council of 17 June 2008 on the law applicable to contractual obligations (Rome I), OJ L 177, 4.7.2008, pp. 6–16.

Council Regulation (EC) No 4/2009 of 18 December 2008 on jurisdiction, applicable law, recognition and enforcement of decisions and cooperation in matters relating to maintenance obligations, OJ L 7, 10.1.2009, pp. 1–79.

Hague Protocol on the Law Applicable to Maintenance Obligations. The text of the Protocol is an annex to 2009/941/EC: Council Decision of 30 November 2009 on the conclusion by the European Community of the Hague Protocol of 23 November 2007 on the Law Applicable to Maintenance Obligations, OJ L 331, 16.12.2009, pp. 17–23.

Council Regulation (EU) No 1259/2010 of 20 December 2010 implementing enhanced cooperation in the area of the law applicable to divorce and legal separation, OJ L 343, 29.12.2010, pp. 10–16 (not applied in Poland).

Table of Statutory Instruments

Regulation (EU) No 650/2012 of the European Parliament and of the Council of 4 July 2012 on jurisdiction, applicable law, recognition and enforcement of decisions and acceptance and enforcement of authentic instruments in matters of succession and on the creation of a European Certificate of Succession, OJ 2012 L 201, pp. 107–134.

Regulation (EU) No 1215/2012 of the European Parliament and of the Council of 12 December 2012 on jurisdiction and the recognition and enforcement of judgments in civil and commercial matters (Brussels I bis), OJ L 351, 20.12.2012, pp. 1–32.

Regulation (EU) No 606/2013 of the European Parliament and of the Council of 12 June 2013 on mutual recognition of protection measures in civil matters, OJ L 181, 29.6.2013, pp. 4–12.

Directive 2014/60/EU of the European Parliament and of the Council of 15 May 2014 on the return of cultural objects unlawfully removed from the territory of a Member State and amending Regulation (EU) No 1024/2012 (Recast), OJ L 159, 28.5.2014, pp. 1–10.

Regulation (EU) No 655/2014 of the European Parliament and of the Council of 15 May 2014 establishing a European Account Preservation Order procedure to facilitate cross-border debt recovery in civil and commercial matters, OJ L 189, 27.6.2014, pp. 59–92.

Council Regulation (EU) 2016/1103 of 24 June 2016 implementing enhanced cooperation in the area of jurisdiction, applicable law and the recognition and enforcement of decisions in matters of matrimonial property regimes, OJ L 183, 8.7.2016, pp. 1–29 (not applied in Poland).

Council Regulation (EU) 2016/1104 of 24 June 2016 implementing enhanced cooperation in the area of jurisdiction, applicable law and the recognition and enforcement of decisions in matters of the property consequences of registered partnerships, OJ L 183, 8.7.2016, pp. 30–56; OJ L 199, 31.7.2007, pp. 40–49 (not applied in Poland).

Other EC/EU Instruments

First Council Directive 73/239/EEC of 24 July 1973 on the coordination of laws, regulations and administrative provisions relating to the taking-up and pursuit of the business of direct insurance other than life assurance, OJ L 228, 16.8.1973, pp. 3–19.

Council Directive 93/13/EEC of 5 April 1993 on unfair terms in consumer contracts, OJ L 95, 21.4.1993, pp. 29–34.

Directive 96/71/EC of the European Parliament and of the Council of 16 December 1996 concerning the posting of workers in the framework of the provision of services, OJ L 18, 21.1.1997, pp. 1–6.

Directive 97/7/EC of the European Parliament and of the Council of 20 May 1997 on the protection of consumers in respect of distance, OJ L 144, 4.6.1997, pp. 19–27. No longer in force, repealed by Directive 2011/83/EU of the European Parliament and of the Council of 25 October 2011 on consumer rights, amending

Council Directive 93/13/EEC and Directive 1999/44/EC of the European Parliament and of the Council and repealing Council Directive 85/577/EEC and Directive 97/7/EC of the European Parliament and of the Council Text with EEA relevance, OJ L 304, 22.11.2011, pp. 64–88.

Directive 1999/44/EC of the European Parliament and of the Council of 25 May 1999 on certain aspects of the sale of consumer goods and associated guarantees, OJ L 171, 7.7.1999, pp. 12–16.

Council Decision 2001/539/EC of 5 April 2001 on the conclusion by the European Community of the Convention for the Unification of Certain Rules for International Carriage by Air (the Montreal Convention), OJ L 194, 18.7.2001, p. 38.

Directive 2002/65/EC of the European Parliament and of the Council of 23 September 2002 concerning the distance marketing of consumer financial services and amending Council Directive 90/619/EEC and Directives 97/7/EC and 98/27/EC, OJ L 271, 9.10.2002, pp. 16–24.

Directive 2008/122/EC of the European Parliament and of the Council of 14 January 2009 on the protection of consumers in respect of certain aspects of timeshare, long-term holiday product, resale and exchange contracts, OJ L 33, 3.2.2009, pp. 10–30.

Directive 2008/48/EC of the European Parliament and of the Council of 23 April 2008 on credit agreements for consumers and repealing Council Directive 87/102/EEC, OJ L 133, 22.5.2008, pp. 66–92.

Council Regulation (EC) No 116/2009 of 18 December 2008 on the export of cultural goods, OJ L 39, 10.2.2009, pp. 1–7.

Table of International Treaties

International agreements are promulgated in Poland in the official journal, which is called *Dziennik Ustaw* (Dz. U.). It is accessible online at https://isap.sejm.gov.pl. Each legal act promulgated before 2012 may be located by the year, number (*nr*) and position (*poz.*) in *Dziennik Ustaw* and starting from 2012 by the year and position in *Dziennik Ustaw*. Legal acts are promulgated in Polish. No official translations into English are provided in systematic way. Translations of some legal acts might be found on the websites of different national authorities. International agreements, which are approved by EU in the name of EU Member States, including Poland, are promulgated in Official Journal of the EU published online in all EU languages at https://eur-lex.europa.eu/.

I. Multilateral agreements

(in the chronological order by the date of adoption)

Hague Convention of 12 June 1902 on Guardianship (*Convention du 12 juin 1902 pour régler la tutelle des mineurs*), Dz. U. 1929 nr 80 poz. 596.

Hague Convention of 17 July 1905 on Deprivation of Civil Rights (*Convention du 17 juillet 1905 concernant l'interdiction et les mesures de protection analogues*), Dz. U. 1929 nr 80 poz. 598.

Hague Convention on Certain Questions relating to the Conflict of Nationality Laws and Protocol Relating to the Case of Statelessness, signed at The Hague on 12 April 1930, Dz. U. 1937 nr 47 poz. 361.

Convention providing a Uniform Law for Bills of Exchange and Promissory Notes signed in Geneva on 7 June 1930, Dz. U. 1937 nr 26 poz. 175.

Convention for the Settlement of Certain Conflicts of Laws in connection with Cheques signed in Geneva on 19 March 1931, Dz. U. 1937 nr 26 poz. 181.

Convention for the Protection of Human Rights and Fundamental Freedoms (The European Convention on Human Rights) opened for signature in Rome on 4 November 1950, Dz. U. 1993 nr 61 poz. 284.

Hague Convention of 14 May 1954 for the Protection of Cultural Property in the Event of Armed Conflict, Dz. U. z 1957 r. nr 46 poz. 212.

Convention on the Contract for the International Carriage of Goods by Road (CMR), done at Geneva on 19 May 1956, Dz. U. 1962 nr 49 poz. 238.

Convention on the Recovery Abroad of Maintenance concluded on 20 June 1956, Dz. U. 1961 nr 17 poz. 87.

Table of International Treaties

United Nations Convention on the Recognition and Enforcement of Foreign Arbitral Awards singed in New York on 10 June 1958, Dz. U. z 1962 r. nr 9 poz. 41 and 42.

European Convention on International Commercial Arbitration done at Geneva on 21 April 1961, Dz. U. 1964 nr 40 poz. 270 and 271.

Hague Convention of 5 October 1961 on the Conflicts of Laws Relating to the Form of Testamentary Dispositions, Dz. U. 1969 nr 34 poz. 284.

Convention on Consent to Marriage, Minimum Age for Marriage and Registration of Marriages opened for signature and ratification on 7 November 1962, Dz. U. 1965 nr 9 poz. 53.

Hague Convention of 15 November 1965 on the Service Abroad of Judicial and Extrajudicial Documents in Civil or Commercial Matters, Dz. U. 2000 nr 87 poz. 968.

European Convention on the Adoption of Children signed in Strasbourg on 24 April 1967 r., ETS No.058, Dz. U. 1999 nr 99 poz. 1157.

Paris Convention for the protection of industrial property as revised at Stockholm on 14 July 1967, Dz. U. z 1975 r. nr 9 poz. 51.

European Convention on Information on Foreign Law signed in London on 7 June 1968, ETS No.062, Dz. U. 1994 r. nr 64 poz. 272.

Hague Convention of 18 March 1970 on the Taking of Evidence Abroad in Civil or Commercial Matters, Dz. U. 2000 nr 50 poz. 582.

Convention of 14 November 1970 on the Means of Prohibiting and Preventing the Illicit Import, Export and Transfer of Ownership of Cultural Property, Dz. U. z 1974 r. nr 20 poz. 106.

Paris Act of 24 July 1971 concerning Berne Convention for the protection of literary and artistic works, Dz. U. z 1990 r. nr 82 poz. 474.

Universal Copyright Convention as revised at Paris on 24 July 1971, Dz. U. z 1978 r. nr 8 poz. 28.

Hague Convention on the Law Applicable to Traffic Accidents signed at The Hague on 4 May 1971, Dz. U. 2003 nr 63 poz. 585.

Hague Convention of 2 October 1973 on the Recognition and Enforcement of Decisions Relating to Maintenance Obligations, Dz. U. 2000 nr 2 poz. 13.

Hague Convention of 2 October 1973 on the Law Applicable to Maintenance Obligations, Dz. U. 2000 nr 39 poz. 444.

Additional Protocol to the European Convention on Information on Foreign Law signed in Strasbourg on 15 March 1978, ETS No.097, Dz. U. 1994 r. nr 64 poz. 274.

Vienna Convention of 11 April 1980 on Contracts for the International Sale of Goods, Dz. U. 1997 nr 45 poz. 286.

Hague Convention of 25 October 1980 on the Civil Aspects of International Child Abduction, Dz. U. 1995 nr 108 poz. 528.

Hague Convention of 29 May 1993 on Protection of Children and Co-operation in Respect of Intercountry Adoption, Dz. U. 2000 nr 39 poz. 448.

Hague Convention of 19 October 1996 on Jurisdiction, Applicable Law, Recognition, Enforcement and Co-operation in Respect of Parental Responsibility and Measures for the Protection of Children, Dz. U. 2010 nr 172 poz. 1158.

Concordat between the Holy See and the Republic of Poland, signed in Warsaw on 28 July 1993, Dz. U. 1998 nr 51 poz. 318.

Convention for the Unification of Certain Rules for International Carriage by Air (the Montreal Convention), OJ L 194, 18.7.2001, pp. 39–49.

Hague Convention of 30 June 2005 on Choice of Court Agreements, OJ L 133, 29.5.2009, pp. 1–13.

Lugano II Convention of 30 October 2007 on jurisdiction and the recognition and enforcement of judgments in civil and commercial matters, OJ L 339, 21.12.2007, pp. 3–41.

Convention of 23 November 2007 on the International Recovery of Child Support and Other Forms of Family Maintenance, OJ L 192, 22.7.2011, pp. 39–50.

II. Bilateral Agreements

(in the alphabetical order)

Austria: Umowa między Polską Rzecząpospolitą Ludową a Republiką Austrii o wzajemnych stosunkach w sprawach z zakresu prawa cywilnego oraz o dokumentach, podpisana w Wiedniu dnia 11 grudnia 1963 r., Dz. U. z 1974 r. nr 6 poz. 33.

Algeria: Umowa między Polską Rzecząpospolitą Ludową a Algierską Republiką Ludowo-Demokratyczną dotycząca obrotu prawnego w sprawach cywilnych i karnych, podpisana w Algierze dnia 9 listopada 1976 r., Dz. U. 1982 r. nr 10 poz. 73.

Belarus: Umowa między Rzecząpospolitą Polską a Republiką Białoruś o pomocy prawnej i stosunkach prawnych w sprawach cywilnych, rodzinnych, pracowniczych i karnych, sporządzona w Mińsku dnia 26 października 1994 r., Dz. U. 1995 r. nr 128 poz. 619.

Belgium: Umowa między Polską Rzecząpospolitą Ludową a Królestwem Belgii o informacji prawnej podpisana w Brukseli dnia 17 grudnia 1986 r., Dz. U. 1990 r. nr 46 poz. 267.

Bosnia and Herzegovina: Umowa między Polską Rzecząpospolitą Ludową a Federacyjną Ludową Republiką Jugosławii o obrocie prawnym w sprawach cywilnych i karnych, podpisana w Warszawie dnia 6 lutego 1960 r., Dz. U. 1963 r. nr 27 poz. 162. *See also*: Porozumienie między Rządem Rzeczypospolitej Polskiej a Radą Ministrów Bośni i Hercegowiny o sukcesji prawnej Bośni i Hercegowiny w stosunku do umów zawartych między Rzecząpospolitą Polską a Socjalistyczną Federacyjną Republiką Jugosławii, zawarte w Sarajewie dnia 22 grudnia 2006 r. M.P. 2008 r. nr 52 poz. 462.

Bulgaria: Umowa między Polską Rzecząpospolitą Ludową a Ludową Republiką Bułgarii o pomocy prawnej i stosunkach prawnych w sprawach cywilnych, rodzinnych i karnych, podpisana w Warszawie dnia 4 grudnia 1961 r., Dz. U. 1963 r. nr 17 poz. 88.

Cuba: Umowa między Polską Rzecząpospolitą Ludową a Republiką Kuby o pomocy prawnej w sprawach cywilnych, rodzinnych i karnych podpisana w Hawanie dnia 18 listopada 1982 r., Dz. U. 1984 r. nr 47 poz. 247.

China: Umowa między Polską Rzecząpospolitą Ludową a Chińską Republiką Ludową o pomocy prawnej w sprawach cywilnych i karnych, podpisana w Warszawie dnia 5 czerwca 1987 r., Dz. U. 1988 r. nr 9 poz. 65.

Croatia: Umowa między Polską Rzecząpospolitą Ludową a Federacyjną Ludową Republiką Jugosławii o obrocie prawnym w sprawach cywilnych i karnych, podpisana w Warszawie dnia 6 lutego 1960 r., Dz. U. 1963 r. nr 27 poz. 162.

Czech Republic: Umowa między Polską Rzecząpospolitą Ludową a Czechosłowacką Republiką Socjalistyczną o pomocy prawnej i stosunkach prawnych w sprawach cywilnych, rodzinnych, pracowniczych i karnych, podpisana w Warszawie dnia 21 grudnia 1987 r., Dz. U. 1989 r. nr 39 poz. 210.

Cyprus: Umowa między Rzecząpospolitą Polską a Republiką Cypru o współpracy prawnej w sprawach cywilnych i karnych, sporządzona w Nikozji dnia 14 listopada 1996 r., Dz. U. 1999 r. nr 39 poz. 383.

Egypt: Umowa między Rzecząpospolitą Polską a Arabską Republiką Egiptu o pomocy prawnej w sprawach cywilnych i handlowych, sporządzona w Kairze dnia 17 maja 1992 r., Dz. U. 1994 r. nr 34 poz. 126.

Estonia: Umowa między Rzecząpospolitą Polską a Republiką Estońską o pomocy prawnej i stosunkach prawnych w sprawach cywilnych, pracowniczych i karnych, sporządzona w Tallinie dnia 27 listopada 1998 r. Dz. U. 2000 r. nr 5 poz. 49.

Finland: Umowa między Polską Rzecząpospolitą Ludową a Republiką Finlandii o ochronie prawnej i pomocy prawnej w sprawach cywilnych, rodzinnych i karnych, podpisana w Helsinkach dnia 27 maja 1980 r., Dz. U. 1981 r. nr 27 poz. 140. This agreement was denounced by Poland as of 2021. *See* Wypowiedzenie przez Rzeczpospolitą Polską Umowy między Polską Rzecząpospolitą Ludową a Republiką Finlandii o ochronie prawnej i pomocy prawnej w sprawach cywilnych, rodzinnych i karnych, podpisanej w Helsinkach dnia 27 maja 1980 r., Dz. U. 2019 r. poz. 2016.

France: Umowa między Polską Rzecząpospolitą Ludową a Republiką Francuską o prawie właściwym, jurysdykcji i wykonywaniu orzeczeń w zakresie prawa osobowego i rodzinnego, sporządzona w Warszawie dnia 5 kwietnia 1967 r., Dz. U. 1969 r. nr 4 poz. 22.

Greece: Umowa Polską Rzecząpospolitą Ludową a Republiką Grecką o pomocy prawnej w sprawach cywilnych i karnych, podpisana w Atenach dnia 24 października 1979 r., Dz. U. 1982 r. nr 4 poz. 24.

Hungary: Umowa między Polską Rzecząpospolitą Ludową a Węgierską Republiką Ludową o obrocie prawnym w sprawach cywilnych, rodzinnych i karnych, podpisana w Budapeszcie dnia 6 marca 1959 r., Dz. U. 1960 r. nr 8 poz. 54.

Italy: Umowa między Polską Rzecząpospolitą Ludową a Republiką Włoską o pomocy sądowej oraz o uznawaniu i wykonywaniu wyroków w sprawach cywilnych, podpisana w Warszawie dnia 28 kwietnia 1989 r., Dz. U. 1992 r. nr 23 poz. 97.

Iraq: Umowa między Polską Rzecząpospolitą Ludową a Republiką Iraku o pomocy prawnej i sądowej w sprawach cywilnych i karnych, sporządzona w Bagdadzie dnia 29 października 1988 r., Dz. U. 1989 r. nr 70 poz. 418.

Latvia: Umowa między Rzecząpospolitą Polską a Republiką Łotewską o pomocy prawnej i stosunkach prawnych w sprawach cywilnych, rodzinnych, pracowniczych i karnych, sporządzona w Rydze dnia 23 lutego 1994 r., Dz. U. 1995 r. nr 110 poz. 534.

Libya: Umowa między Polską Rzecząpospolitą Ludową a Libijską Arabską Dżamahiriją Ludowo-Socjalistyczną o pomocy prawnej w sprawach cywilnych, handlowych, rodzinnych i karnych, podpisana w Trypolisie dnia 2 grudnia 1985 r., Dz. U. 1987 r. nr 13 poz. 80.

Lithuania: Umowa między Rzecząpospolitą Polską a Republiką Litewską o pomocy prawnej i stosunkach prawnych w sprawach cywilnych, rodzinnych, pracowniczych i karnych, sporządzono w Warszawie dnia 26 stycznia 1993 r., Dz. U. 1994 r. nr 35 poz. 130.

Mongolia: Umowa między Rzecząpospolitą Polską a Mongolią o pomocy prawnej i stosunkach prawnych w sprawach cywilnych, rodzinnych, pracowniczych i karnych, sporządzona w Warszawie dnia 19 października 1998 r., Dz. U. 2003 r. nr 43 poz. 370.

Montenegro: Umowa między Polską Rzecząpospolitą Ludową a Federacyjną Ludową Republiką Jugosławii o obrocie prawnym w sprawach cywilnych i karnych, podpisana w Warszawie dnia 6 lutego 1960 r., Dz. U. 1963 r. nr 27 poz. 162. *See also*: Porozumienie między Rzecząpospolitą Polską a Czarnogórą o uregulowaniu dwustronnych stosunków traktatowych, zawarte w Podgoricy dnia 23 kwietnia 2009 r. M.P. 2011 r. nr 74 poz. 739.

North Korea: Umowa między Polską Rzecząpospolitą Ludową a Koreańską Republiką Ludowo-Demokratyczną o pomocy prawnej w sprawach cywilnych, rodzinnych i karnych, podpisana w Phenianie dnia 28 września 1986 r., Dz. U. 1987 r. nr 24 poz. 135.

North Macedonia: Umowa między Polską Rzecząpospolitą Ludową a FederacyjnąLudową Republiką Jugosławii o obrocie prawnym w sprawach cywilnych i karnych, podpisana w Warszawie dnia 6 lutego 1960 r., Dz. U. 1963 r. nr 27 poz. 162. *See also* Porozumienie między Rzecząpospolitą Polską a Republiką Macedonii o uregulowaniu dwustronnych stosunków traktatowych, podpisane w Warszawie dnia 9 maja 2007 r. Dz. U. 2009 r. nr 27 poz. 163.

Romania: Umowa między Rzecząpospolitą Polską a Rumunią o pomocy prawnej i stosunkach prawnych w sprawach cywilnych, sporządzona w Bukareszcie dnia 15 maja 1999 r., Dz. U. 2002 r. nr 83 poz. 752.

Russia: Umowa między Rzecząpospolitą Polską a Federacją Rosyjską o pomocy prawnej i stosunkach prawnych w sprawach cywilnych i karnych, sporządzona w Warszawie dnia 16 września 1996 r., Dz. U. 2002 r. nr 83 poz. 750.

Serbia: Umowa między Polską Rzecząpospolitą Ludową a Federacyjną Ludową Republiką Jugosławii o obrocie prawnym w sprawach cywilnych i karnych, podpisana w Warszawie dnia 6 lutego 1960 r., Dz. U. 1963 r. nr 27 poz. 162.

Slovakia: Umowa między Polską Rzecząpospolitą Ludową a Czechosłowacką Republiką Socjalistyczną o pomocy prawnej i stosunkach prawnych w sprawach cywilnych, rodzinnych, pracowniczych i karnych, podpisana w Warszawie dnia 21 grudnia 1987 r., Dz. U. 1989 r. nr 39 poz. 210.

Slovenia: Umowa między Polską Rzecząpospolitą Ludową a Federacyjną Ludową Republiką Jugosławii o obrocie prawnym w sprawach cywilnych i karnych, podpisana w Warszawie dnia 6 lutego 1960 r., Dz. U. 1963 r. nr 27 poz. 162.

Syria: Umowa między Polską Rzecząpospolitą Ludową i Arabską Republiką Syryjską o pomocy prawnej w sprawach cywilnych i karnych, podpisana w Damaszku dnia 16 lutego 1985 r., Dz. U. 1986 r. nr 37 poz. 181.

Turkey: Umowa między Polską Rzecząpospolitą Ludową a Republiką Turecką o pomocy prawnej w sprawach cywilnych i handlowych, podpisana w Warszawie dnia 12 kwietnia 1988 r., Dz. U. 1992 r. nr 3 poz. 13.

United Kingdom: Konwencja między Polską a Wielką Brytanią i Północną Irlandiąw przedmiocie postępowania w sprawach cywilnych i handlowych, podpisana w Warszawie dnia 26 sierpnia 1931 r., Dz. U. z 1932 r. nr 55 poz. 533. This agreement covers also some Member States of the Commonwealth.

Ukraine: Umowa między Rzecząpospolitą Polską a Ukrainą o pomocy prawnej i stosunkach prawnych w sprawach cywilnych i karnych sporządzona w Kijowie dnia 24 maja 1993 r. Dz. U. 1994 r. nr 96. poz. 465.

Vietnam: Umowa między Rzecząpospolitą Polską a Socjalistyczną Republiką Wietnamu o pomocy prawnej i stosunkach prawnych w sprawach cywilnych, rodzinnych i karnych, sporządzona w Warszawie dnia 22 marca 1993 r., Dz. U. 1995 r. nr 55 poz. 289.

Index

The numbers here refer to paragraph numbers.

Index

www.ingramcontent.com/pod-product-compliance
Ingram Content Group UK Ltd.
Pitfield, Milton Keynes, MK11 3LW, UK
UKHW020143290926
15471UKWH00004B/670

9 789403 530208